"*The Joy of Freedom* is the only book I've ever read by someone who tells how he learned to love freedom, and he does it with fascinating stories and facts. This book is an exciting, 'you-are-there' page-turner."

—STEVE CHAPMAN,
Chicago Tribune

"A dazzling intellectual memoir, a high-level lesson in market economics, a terrific read."

—DAN SELIGMAN
Forbes magazine

"*The Joy of Freedom* is a quasi-autobiographical clarion call for a free society. It is passionate and eloquent, yet at the same time, thoughtful, informed, and profound. A splendid statement of the moral case for a free society, at the same time it is an informed and comprehensive survey of its practical virtues and of the harm done by widespread government intervention."

—MILTON FRIEDMAN
*Senior Research Fellow, Hoover Institution,
and Nobel Laureate*

"An engaging tale of Henderson's odyssey to the wonders of freedom."

—JOHN STOSSEL
ABC News

"Economics, like politics, has its 'great communicators.' David Henderson is one of them. A superb lesson from one of the more masterly of our economics teachers."

—AMITY SHLAES
Financial Times

"If you think, as I did, that economics is a tedious and finally impenetrable subject, this is the book for you. It is a can't-put-it-down read that engages you in story and events even as it educates. Here economic principles are not dry theories; they are events in Henderson's life. And we come to root for him as he struggles to see through one economic commonplace after another. I congratulate him on a fine achievement."

—SHELBY STEELE
author of *A Dream Deferred:*
The Second Betrayal of Black Freedom in America

"This charming book is part memoir and part history, supported by a good bit of economics and a touch of political philosophy and all decorated with some mighty telling anecdotes."

—SUSAN LEE
Wall Street Journal

"David Henderson provides a delightful personal narrative of a libertarian's lifelong journey through the maze of modern government policy. He demonstrates how straightforward economic reasoning can expose the multitude of fallacies that are used to justify government's role in the economy—in matters as diverse as modern environmental policy and the military draft. This is a must read for non-economists and particularly for those who obtain most of their information from *The New York Times, National Public Radio,* or *CBS Evening News.*"

—BOB CRANDALL
Brookings Institution

THE JOY OF FREEDOM
AN ECONOMIST'S ODYSSEY

ISBN 0-13-062112-9

90000

9 780130 621122

FINANCIAL TIMES

Prentice Hall

In an increasingly competitive world, it is quality
of thinking that gives an edge—an idea that opens new
doors, a technique that solves a problem, or an insight
that simply helps make sense of it all.

We work with leading authors in the various arenas
of business and finance to bring cutting-edge thinking
and best learning practice to a global market.

It is our goal to create world-class print publications
and electronic products that give readers
knowledge and understanding which can then be
applied, whether studying or at work.

To find out more about our business
products, you can visit us at www.ft-ph.com

Pearson
Education

FINANCIAL TIMES PRENTICE HALL BOOKS

For more information, please go to www.ft-ph.com

Deirdre Breakenridge
Cyberbranding: Brand Building in the Digital Economy

Jonathan Cagan and Craig M. Vogel
Creating Breakthrough Products: Innovation from Product Planning to Program Approval

Sherry Cooper
Ride the Wave: Taking Control in a Turbulent Financial Age

James W. Cortada
21st Century Business: Managing and Working in the New Digital Economy

James W. Cortada
Making the Information Society: Experience, Consequences, and Possibilities

Aswath Damodaran
The Dark Side of Valuation: Valuing Old Tech, New Tech, and New Economy Companies

David Gladstone and Laura Gladstone
Venture Capital Handbook: An Entrepreneur's Guide to Raising Venture Capital, Revised and Updated

David R. Henderson
Joy of Freedom: An Economist's Odyssey

Dale Neef
E-procurement: From Strategy to Implementation

John R. Nofsinger
Investment Madness: How Psychology Affects Your Investing... And What to Do About It

THE JOY OF FREEDOM
AN ECONOMIST'S ODYSSEY

DAVID R. HENDERSON

AN IMPRINT OF PEARSON EDUCATION
LONDON • NEW YORK • SAN FRANCISCO • TORONTO • SYDNEY
TOKYO • SINGAPORE • HONG KONG • CAPE TOWN • MADRID •
PARIS • MILAN • MUNICH • AMSTERDAM

Library of Congress Cataloging-in-Publication Data
Henderson, David R.
    The joy of freedom: an economist's odyssey/David Henderson.
        p.cm.—(Financial Times Prentice Hall books)
    Includes bibliographical references and index.
    ISBN 0-13-062112-9
    1.Free enterprise. 2. Self interest. I. Title. II. Series

    HB95.H463 2002
    320.51'2—dc21   2001133027

Editorial/Production Supervision: Kerry Reardon
Production Coordinator: Anne R. Garcia
Acquisitions Editor: Tim Moore
Marketing Manager: Te Leszczynski
Manufacturing Buyer: Maura Zaldivar
Manufacturing Manager: Alexis R. Heydt-Long
Cover Design Director: Jerry Votta
Cover Design: Anthony Gemmellaro
Interior Design: Gail Cocker-Bogusz
Author Photo: Kendra Floyd, Sooter's
Editorial Assistant: Allyson Kloss

© 2002 Prentice Hall PTR
Prentice-Hall, Inc.
Upper Saddle River, NJ 07458

Prentice Hall books are widely used by corporations and government agencies for training, marketing, and resale.

The publisher offers discounts on this book when ordered in bulk quantities.
For more information, contact: Corporate Sales Department, Phone: 800-382-3419;
Fax: 201-236-7141; E-mail: corpsales@prenhall.com; or write: Prentice Hall P T R,
Corp. Sales Dept., One Lake Street, Upper Saddle River, NJ 07458.

Parts of Chapter 15 were originally published in a slightly altered form in David R. Henderson, "The Perverse Economics of Health Care and How We Can Fix It," 1994 and revised with permission from Hoover Institution Press.

Sections of this book are based on material previously published by the author in Red Herring.

Printed in the United States of America

10 9   8   7   6   5   4   3   2   1

ISBN 0-13-062112-9

Pearson Education LTD
Pearson Education Australia PTY, Limited
Pearson Education Singapore, Pte. Ltd.
Pearson Education North Asia Ltd.
Pearson Education Canada, Ltd.
Pearson Educaçion de Mexico, S.A. de C.V.
Pearson Education Japan
Pearson Education Malaysia Pte. Ltd.
Pearson Education, Upper Saddle River, New Jersey

To the unknown civilization that is growing in the world

CONTENTS

PREFACE

When I was about 12 years old, my father took my brother, Paul, and me on a tour of the legislative building in Winnipeg, Manitoba. Although on the outside it looked impressive, on the inside it was just a bunch of boring offices. Or so I thought. But then my dad took us to a special roped-off area, a large circular room with a big star in the middle of its marble floor.

This room, he explained, is a replica of something that existed in England centuries ago called the Court of Star Chamber. Back then, he said, the king would single out his political enemies and make them stand alone in the middle of the room while the king's allies circled around and made accusations at the person in the middle. The accused had no legal right to have a lawyer or anyone else to help defend him, and, after the trial was over, would often be hauled away and imprisoned or put to death. This replica was put in the legislative building, my dad explained, as a reminder that people have rights that no government may trample. What a neat idea, I thought to myself, that there are limits on what government can do to people. That is my earliest memory of knowing clearly, in my mind and in my heart, that freedom was important and right.

Little did I know then that, just a few years later, I would discover the philosophy of freedom that is behind the idea of limiting government's power over us. This book is the story of that discovery, not just of freedom, but of the joy of freedom, of the power of freedom to create well-being for the billions of people on the planet. It is also the story of my own and others' attempts, sometimes successful, to expand people's freedom. This story is told through a series of shorter stories, my own and those of others.

Many of my own stories are about my attempts to understand the world through experience, conversation, and reading. In Chapter 5, you'll read about the manager of a large business with whom my school-teacher father argued with, and of how I discovered that private property rights could protect us from his wrath. In Chapter 8, I describe the incredible bounty created by free markets and how this bounty has affected my life and the lives of those around me. Chapter 1 recounts a debate I had as a teenager with a former vice-president of the United States. Early in my education as an economist, I got to be an intern with President Nixon's Council of Economic Advisers. In Chapter 12, I tell of that experience and others that led me to believe that most government most of the time wreaks incredible destruction on people's lives and is completely unaccountable for it.

I also tell stories from later in my life, after I had become a policy economist, of interactions with Nobel laureates Friedrich Hayek, Milton Friedman, and George Stigler, with former treasury secretary Lawrence Summers, and with Ralph Nader, to name a few. In Chapter 6, for example, I tell of a hearing at which I testified in favor of a Reagan administration proposal to let hundreds of women knit ski caps in their home for profit after the Department of Labor had tried to shut them down. Chapter 2 recounts an interview I conducted with Ralph Nader, in which Nader, who made his reputation as a critic of unsafe cars, defended federal laws that kill thousands of people a year. And in Chapter 16, I relate my experiences and those of others that have convinced me that government schooling is a failure. My stories about others tend to focus on people who had a clear insight while young or who carried out courageous acts in the battle for freedom. In Chapter 10, I tell of my economist friend, Francois Melese, who, as a teenage volunteer, saw incredible poverty in Nicaragua in the early 1970s and gradually figured out what caused it and how it could be ended. In

Chapter 4, I introduce Walter Oi, who, as a young blind economist in the 1960s, and with no personal stake in the issue, did some seminal work showing that military conscription is inefficient and should be abolished.

I also tell important stories from history that put well-known events in a completely new perspective. Many people have heard of the Detroit race riot in 1964, but few know how that riot started. Chapter 7 tells how, and it will surprise you. Chapter 7 also points out an important fact about the famous bus in which Rosa Parks refused to sit.

These are just a sliver of the stories that are told in greater detail in this book. But I want to end with one that is not told elsewhere in this book. One of the most famous and exciting pieces of music ever is the fourth movement of Beethoven's Ninth Symphony, which uses as its text the poem "Ode to Joy," by German poet Friedrich von Schiller. Schiller had originally written the poem as an ode to freedom, and wherever the word "freude" (joy) appears in the known version, Schiller had first written "freiheit" (freedom). To satisfy the Prussian censor, though, Schiller replaced "freedom" with "joy," probably in full knowledge that his readers would know what he really meant. Then, on Christmas Eve 1989, just a few weeks after the Berlin Wall came down, Leonard Bernstein celebrated the Berliners' freedom by conducting Beethoven's symphony in Berlin, having the chorus use the original "freiheit" instead of "freude." Appropriate, don't you think?

David R. Henderson

ACKNOWLEDGMENTS

First, I thank my loving wife Rena, not only for her moral support throughout the six years this book took, but also for her awesome editing job. Next, I thank the late Roy Childs, who encouraged me when I first conceived this book in the early 1990s, and my friend and mentor Clancy Smith, whose contribution is noted in Chapter 1.

Economist Russell Roberts went way beyond what he was paid for when he was hired as the technical editor; I accepted over 90 percent of his suggestions and loved working with him on the phone. Development editor Russ Hall made some key corrections and, more important, his enthusiastic response confirmed my belief that this book would be enjoyed by people with political beliefs very different from my own. Carol J. Lallier, the copy editor hired by Prentice Hall, did a quick, high-quality turnaround, and I appreciated her statement that, "if David Henderson were running for President, I'd definitely vote for him." Marshall Fritz made helpful comments on Chapter 16.

Many people taught me a lot about the ideas in this book, whether in classrooms, in conversations, or in writing. They include Harold Demsetz, Armen Alchian, Milton Friedman, the late George Stigler, the late Ayn Rand, James Buchanan, Gordon Tullock, E.G. West, Alan Reynolds, Michael Prime, Perry Taylor, David Friedman, the late Friedrich Hayek, the late Ludwig von Mises, the late Henry Hazlitt, the late Murray Rothbard, the late Yale Brozen, the late Merton Miller, Joan

Kennedy Taylor, and Paul Samuelson. I apologize to those teachers whose names I may have overlooked.

Many editors have given me space to develop my ideas in their magazines and newspapers, including Jason Pontin of the *Red Herring;* Dan Seligman and Rob Norton of *Fortune;* David Frum, James Taranto, Max Boot, Mary O'Grady, and Erich Eichman of the *Wall Street Journal;* and Marty Zupan, Virginia Postrel, and Nick Gillespie of *Reason.*

For financial support I thank the John M. Olin Foundation, the American Enterprise Institute, and the Hoover Institution.

The former chairman of my department, Reuben Harris, and the provost of the Naval Postgraduate School, Dick Elster, were willing to let me take leave without pay so that I could find time to work on the book.

My friends have been a good, discerning audience for many of the ideas in this book. I want particularly to single out my friends Tom Nagle and Greg De Young. Also, my students at the Naval Postgraduate School were an appreciative and generous audience for some of the ideas.

I have appreciated the enthusiasm and professionalism of my publisher, Tim Moore, a vice president at Prentice Hall, and have enjoyed working with production editor Kerry Reardon and Anne Garcia of Prentice Hall. Finally, my agent, Henning Gutmann, has done, and, I'm sure, will continue to do, a great job.

Finally, I want to thank my daughter, Karen, for her joyous laugh.

THE JOY
OF FREEDOM

For the last two centuries, economics has been called "the dismal science." The person who coined the phrase was British anticapitalist author Thomas Carlyle. You'll probably never guess why he called it that. I'd always thought it was because he was thinking of Thomas Robert Malthus, the economist who claimed, incorrectly, that population would grow exponentially while agricultural output would grow only arithmetically, resulting in mass starvation. Wrong. Economics is a dismal science, wrote Carlyle, because the free-market economists of his time, who dominated economics in the nineteenth century, strongly opposed slavery.[1]

For me, economics has always been the joyous science. It says that a good deal of freedom is necessary for prosperity, which means that not only can you have freedom, but also that you get prosperity as a bonus. First came my belief in freedom.

1

JUNE 1968, WINNIPEG, MANITOBA, CANADA

I'm sitting waiting for an appointment at the University of Manitoba with a midlevel official of the Canadian government. At age 17, I have just quit after only two weeks of working at an easy, somewhat fun, fairly well-paying job in one of Canada's beautiful national parks. Had I kept the job, the earnings for that summer combined with my savings would have paid for my second year of college. Those around me, including my mother, have questioned my judgment. My boss's boss has asked me to come and explain my action. Although my decision doesn't depend on his understanding why I quit, I have agreed to meet with him.

When I entered his office, the official asked me why I quit. I explained.

In my job, we went around tagging trees and noting the growth of trees under different conditions. Because I have always liked to understand how what I'm doing is useful, I had asked my immediate boss how our research results would be used. He explained that for various reasons of climate, they wouldn't be useful for growing trees in Canada. "Where will they be useful?" I asked. He answered that actually they would be most useful to the Soviets. I paused and thought hard before asking the next question. "How do we justify taxing Canadians to subsidize the Soviets?" I asked. He didn't have an answer. That evening, back at our cabin in Riding Mountain National Park, I kept rolling this over and over in my mind. I just didn't feel good about. And it wasn't just my feeling. It was also my thinking. It just didn't seem right to tax Canadians to help the Soviets.

The next day, I had a new question to think about: What if the results of our research were used to help Canadians? Would taxes to pay for the research be justified even then? They would be more justified, I thought, but would they be justified enough? They would help some Canadians at the expense of those who paid taxes and had no choice in the matter. This seemed wrong. Then I started thinking about the books I had been reading by Ayn Rand, the philosopher/ novelist advocate of freedom, for the last few months. I suddenly realized in a very concrete way what she had been saying. Taxing some people to help others, she had written, violated the rights of those who were taxed. I concluded that taxing innocent Canadians for this project, whoever benefited, was wrong. The next thought was immediate. I must leave; I can no longer participate in this. I sat with the thought all that day, wanting to find a flaw. After all, this was a good job and I had lobbied hard to get it. We lived well, ate well, didn't work very hard, did somewhat interesting work, and were paid well. I badly wanted to talk myself out of quitting. But I kept coming back to how my job was being paid for. The money to pay me was coming from some anonymous taxpayer who had no say. I couldn't get away from it; I had a moral certainty and a quiet strength that told me I needed to quit. That evening I gave my boss notice that I would leave at the end of the week.

I told all this to my boss's boss in Winnipeg. He was a decent man who didn't undercut or ridicule me. Instead, he tried to persuade me of the value of scientific research. I reminded him that I was questioning not the value of his project but the means—using taxpayers' funds to pay for it. He pled with me, as eloquently as he could. I gradually realized that instead of my trying to justify my decision, he was trying to justify his. Reading Ayn Rand and arguing her views for the previous few months, mainly with people older than me, had been frustrating because the main objection they had given me, after I had countered all the standard objections, was that life didn't work that way and you couldn't really hold ideals in the face of hard realities. Yet I noticed that I was upholding my ideals in the face of reality, and I suddenly had a feeling of power. It was a very clean power, a power not over others, but over myself.

On the way home, I thought further about what had just happened. My mother had taught me to think things through logically and to stand up for my principles. My father had taught me, by word and deeds, not to steal, not to lie, and not to cheat. Ayn Rand's reasoning seemed like the logical next step. I wasn't doing anything different from what I had been taught to do; it's just that following her thinking was leading me to new conclusions that I had never dreamed of. The main one was that the government simply didn't have the right to push people around the way it was doing. Many adults around me who cared about me—this time including, disappointingly, my mother—were trying to persuade me to moderate my views. But they weren't giving me good reasons to moderate; moderation, for them, seemed a virtue in itself, regardless of context. Still, I had been tempted. Given my upbringing, I probably wouldn't have succumbed to the temptation. But if there was anything calculated to make me realize the power of the philosophy I was espousing, it was the almost-desperate way a 40-year-old adult had tried to persuade a 17-year-old.

AUGUST 1968, WINNIPEG

I'm sitting at my friend Don Redekop's place, reading a recent Newsweek. *An article titled "The Public be Damned" catches my attention. It's about the U.S. Post Office and the author makes the point that "the public be damned" summarizes the Post Office's attitude because it has a legally enforced monopoly over delivery of first-class mail. The reasoning is cogent and passionate, without the Randian rage. The author, an economist, is named Milton Friedman.*

After that first article, I dug through Don's pile of old *Newsweeks,* looking for other articles by Milton Friedman. I found a bunch and read them quickly. When I completed my friend's pile, I dug out more Friedman columns from the college library. I liked everything he wrote, whether I agreed with it or not, and I usually agreed with it. One of my favorites was an article he wrote opposing the military draft, not because he opposed the Vietnam war, but because it was an unjust restriction on young men's freedom. Friedman's writing was calmly reasoned and passionate, all at the same time. It had flashes of outrage, but not the deep anger and sometimes rage that I was already tiring of in Ayn Rand. I had found an intellectual and spiritual soul mate.

SEPTEMBER 1968, WINNIPEG

It's the first day to register for the 1968–69 academic year at the University of Winnipeg. After completing my forms, I head over to the orientation tables. I see one table behind which is a big banner that says Libertarian Club. That strange word "libertarian" catches my attention because, in a discussion the previous month, a sociology professor called me a libertarian.

"A what?" I asked, thinking of librarian and libertine at the same time.

"A libertarian," she said, "you know, that group that ran the student newspaper last year—Dennis Owens, Clancy Smith, those guys."

"No," I replied, "I didn't know, but I'm sure going to look them up."

"Damn," she said.

Standing by the table was a guy who looked about 21 or so whom I recognized from a philosophy class I had taken. Spread out on the table were about 40 books, some by authors whose names I recognized, including Milton Friedman and another economist named Ludwig von Mises, and some by authors whom I had never heard of: Friedrich Hayek, Joseph Schumpeter, and others. Then my eye caught a book that looked very familiar: *The Fountainhead*, the first novel I had read by Ayn Rand. "Have you read this?" I asked the man. "Over and over," he replied. We introduced ourselves; he was Clancy Smith, one of the people the sociology professor had told me about.

Later that week, Clancy called to invite me to meet with his group on Saturday evening at 8:30 p.m. For me the meeting was late, since my usual bedtime was about 11:00 p.m. So Saturday night at about 8:00 p.m., Don, who was also getting interested in libertarianism, and I walked to the meeting. I was a little nervous, but also excited. At the meeting were about five or six guys, all 2 to 4 years older than us. That evening was one of the most exciting of my life.

First, they talked about politics, but in a way that I had never heard anyone, young or old, talk. They knew so much, both about current events and about history. They talked about the Democratic convention in Chicago the previous month, William F. Buckley, Jr.'s run-in with Gore Vidal when both were commentators for one of the networks (I had heard of neither), and Buckley's thoughts about Catholicism and the Pope and how that compared to those of some nineteenth-century British guy named Lord Acton. Their talk was matter-of-fact, yet focused and sometimes passionate. I was used to people who talked politics quickly turning to personal attack and rage. I had never heard anything like this. Two of them—Clancy and Michael Prime—talked about the trip that they had taken the previous month to visit Milton Friedman at his summer home in Vermont, and how welcoming and warm Milton and his wife Rose had been. They also spoke of visiting Leonard Peikoff, an associate of Ayn Rand, in New York. Peikoff had asked each of them in turn if they had any disagreements with Rand's philosophy of Objectivism. They stated that they had just a few and, in fact, had come to discuss them. Peikoff then asserted that they had misrepresented themselves in their letter and that the meeting was over. After that, Clancy referred to him as Professor Pissoff.

Besides knowing so much, they spoke clearly and were open-minded. They were partisans, but honest partisans. In their discussion of the conflict between Buckley and Vidal, for example, they were on Buckley's side, but not uncritically so. They seemed to think they had the right, and the ability, to evaluate what people 30 and 40 years older than they were thinking and doing. I had always thought I had that right too. But what I often didn't have was the information to evaluate people's ideas, which is what they seemed to have in abundance. I was used to having a big role in conversations. Yet, even though everything they discussed was interesting to me, I said almost nothing all evening and stuck to asking questions because I wanted to know more. They were always able to answer me. This was totally new territory for me.

After about two hours of listening to conversation in which hockey, football, or other sports hadn't been mentioned even once, I was firmly convinced that these guys were gay. (At age 17, I carried a few stereotypes.) They were totally into ideas, and I had never met any other males like them. Then we got talking about women. They seemed to have a real appreciation of women too. They talked about women they found attractive, but even there it was different from what I had heard before in my life; it wasn't crass, but was more the talk of connoisseurs admiring paintings. They also talked about what women said and thought, not just what they looked like. I liked that.

Then, at about midnight, which was well after my bedtime, someone announced that he was hungry. Okay, I thought, here's where I get left behind. They probably have expensive tastes in food and I won't be able to afford to eat where they want to go to eat. Wrong. We all piled into Clancy's father's big Oldsmobile and drove to Lockport, a town north of Winnipeg, where they knew of a great hotdog stand open till the wee hours.

I got home at about 2:30 a.m. I lay in bed, unable to sleep, thinking about what had just happened. I had found some friends. The next day, I rode my bicycle over to visit Don, who had accompanied me the night before, and the first thing I said was, "Do you think it was real?" Don's grin showed that he had been thinking the same thing. I felt as if I had enlisted in a grand moral crusade that would also be a lot of fun.

In the final two years of my three-year degree (the standard length of a college degree program in Canada), I got two college educations. For approximately the first half of the day, I faithfully attended classes for my math major and physics minor and did the homework for those classes. As soon as I finished, I would spend the rest of the day getting my two main rewards. One was the chance to read a book or article on economics, politics, history, or philosophy that Clancy or one of the other libertarians had recommended. I, who had never been a regular reader, was reading about a book a week. The second reward was even more fun: the chance to be together with Clancy and the other libertarians. If I didn't see Clancy around in the library, I would usually find him in the cafeteria, arguing with a liberal or socialist or, occasionally, a conservative. I learned a lot just from being around him.

First, I learned that the philosophy of libertarianism didn't begin with Ayn Rand. It had a rich tradition dating back hundreds of years. The Magna Carta, signed in 1215, for example, was a major restriction on the powers of the king. And although it mainly restricted what the king could do to the lords and not to the serfs, the respect for people's rights slowly trickled down so that in the seventeenth century, there were further limits in Britain on what governments could do to the common man. And of course there was the American revolution in 1776, which was, at its core, about freedom from government. I learned also about some of the key thinkers in this tradition: the British philosophers John Locke and David Hume, Scottish economist Adam Smith, and the United States' Thomas Jefferson and James Madison. These people really had thought through the meaning and value of freedom, and I started to realize that they were way more than just old boring guys in history books.

Second, I learned a lot from watching Clancy discuss and debate. Clancy never debated for the sole purpose of winning. He always sought to understand the other person's side before trying to make himself understood. I had the bad habit of trying to beat the other person in an argument without first making sure what he or she was saying. Clancy's style was different. He noticed subtle distinctions in the way people said things, and he probed the subtleties with a series of questions. To Clancy, each person was an individual whose views differed, if only slightly, from everyone else's. It was very important for him to find out exactly what the person was saying before arguing with that person. So, for example, a socialist would say that the problem with capitalism is that the rich get richer and the poor get poorer. Clancy would ask, "Do you really mean that the poor get poorer, or do you mean that they're getting richer but that the gap between rich and poor is growing?" You could tell by the person's response to Clancy's question that typically the person hadn't even made that distinction, but Clancy credited him with having done so and gave him time to think about what he was saying. He wasn't setting traps; he was just trying to understand exactly what people were saying.

I got something else from Clancy, too, that I had never had before: uncompromising moral support in the face of hostility from some of the more powerful adults around us. One incident still stands out. In 1969, a year after losing the presidential election to Richard Nixon, former vice-president Hubert

Humphrey came to speak to a large audience at our university. During the question-and-answer period, Clancy got up to one of the microphones on the floor and quoted from a story in the *Denver Post* a year earlier. Humphrey, a strong defender of the military draft, had been asked during the presidential campaign whether he thought a young man should be able to be exempt from the draft on grounds of conscientious objection if he objected to a specific war rather than to war in general. The *Post* had quoted Humphrey's answer that to permit an individual to decide which war is moral and which is not would "give a man God-like powers."[2] Clancy asked Humphrey if he had said that. Humphrey answered that he didn't remember saying it but that, because it did reflect his views, he would take responsibility for it.

Clancy then said, "If giving an individual the right to decide for himself is to give him a god-like power, then what kind of power are we giving the government when it has the power to decide for millions of young men?"

I don't remember Humphrey's specific response but I remember that he addressed Clancy as "young man" once or twice and talked about rights implying responsibility. He didn't answer Clancy's question.

After the speech ended, Clancy and I went up to the stage where Humphrey was standing with the university president. I looked up at Humphrey, who was about 6 feet tall. Because he was on the stage, his shoes were at about the same level as my head, and I had to look way up.

HENDERSON: Do you believe in the U.S. Constitution?

HUMPHREY: Yes.

HENDERSON: Do you believe in the Thirteenth Amendment to the Constitution, which forbids involuntary servitude?

HUMPHREY: Yes.

HENDERSON: Then how do you reconcile your belief in the Thirteenth Amendment with your belief in the draft?

HUMPHREY: They are reconciled.

HENDERSON: How?

HUMPHREY: We have the Thirteenth Amendment and we have the draft.

I was momentarily stunned. It seemed that in this guy's mind, principles and concepts were infinitely elastic or, even worse, that words meant literally nothing to him. I continued.

HENDERSON: Do you agree that the draft is involuntary servitude?
HUMPHREY: Taxes are involuntary.

I was getting somewhere. I said, "Then you do agree that the draft is involuntary servitud?"

But my progress was stopped. Before Humphrey got to answer, the university president stepped in and said, "The Vice President is our guest here, and I expect students at this campus to treat our guests courteously."

An intense shame came over me instantly. I didn't even think about whether I had been discourteous to Humphrey. A powerful adult towering over me had said that I had been rude, and so my mind clicked off and I reverted to the mentality of a 4-year-old. I looked at Humphrey and said, as I had been trained to do from an early age when accused of being rude, "I'm sorry."

Clancy, who had been following the whole incident, stepped in and said very forcefully, "David, don't apologize. You've done nothing wrong."

I realized instantly that Clancy was right. I had been pushy, but I hadn't come close to being rude or disrespectful. "You're right," I said to Clancy, awed and excited that someone supported me when a powerful person had attacked me. I looked back up at the university president and then at Humphrey and said, "I take it back. I don't apologize."

Two years ago, I recounted this story to Clancy, who is in advanced stages of multiple sclerosis. I wanted to make sure he knew how important his support for me had been.

I had thought, after first meeting Clancy and the other libertarians, that I was joining a cause. And it turned out I was. The cause was freedom. That cause would lead me to leave Canada to earn a Ph.D. in economics at the University of California in Los Angeles. It would lead me to testify against draft registration before the Senate Armed Services Committee in 1979. It would lead me to represent Libertarian presidential candidate Ed Clark on a panel at the American Economics Association's annual meetings, along with President Carter's chief economic adviser, Charles Schulze, and candidate Ronald Reagan's adviser, Alan Greenspan.

The cause of freedom would lead me to testify against federal laws that prevented innocent women in Vermont from knitting for pay in their homes. It would lead me to join the Reagan administration as a senior economist with the Council of Economic Advisers, to become the economics editor for *National Review*, and to make the case for freedom in dozens of articles in *Fortune* and the *Wall Street Journal*. It would lead me to appear on CNN as a result of an article I wrote in the *Wall Street Journal*, pointing out that we didn't need to go to war for oil. It would lead me to put together the first, and still the only, encyclopedia of economics, *The Fortune Encyclopedia of Economics*, and to teach economics to federal judges. It would lead me to many other actions, all chosen to help defend freedom. It would also lead me to spend thousands of hours reading, thinking, and writing about the many ways freedom makes our lives richer.

One result of all this reading, thinking, and writing is this book. This book is about freedom, about how well freedom works and how government, by crushing freedom, messes up our lives. It's based on my own experiences and the experiences of others, famous and otherwise.

ENDNOTES

1. For more on this, see David M. Levy and Sandra J. Peart, "The Secret History of the Dismal Science: Economics, Religion, and Race in the 19th Century," *Contributors' Forum,* January 22, 2001, *www.econlib.org.*

2. *The Denver Post,* September 10, 1967.

2

HOOKED ON ECONOMICS

O nce I had the basic idea down—that people should be free—I saw all kinds of implications. Should the government impose heavy taxes on the earnings of working people to give those revenues to older retired people? No. Thus was the issue of so-called social security resolved. Should the government interfere with contracts between employers and employees? No. Thus was the issue of compulsory unionism resolved. Should the government prevent people from starting their own taxicab businesses? No. That resolved the issue of government licensing. Should the government be able to prevent people from smoking cigarettes—whether containing marijuana or nicotine—or require them to wear helmets while driving motorcycles? No. Should the government have the power to force people, under threat of prison, to join the military?

13

Again, no. These conclusions, at least, were what the principle of freedom implied.

But I still had no idea how *practical* these ideas were. I was 17 and I had no basis in experience or in the modest amount I had read for judging how workable a free society was. I noticed something interesting about the discussions and arguments I was starting to have with professors, fellow students, and people generally: I would start by advocating freedom, and within two rounds of the debate, their problems with freedom came down to whether it would work. The person opposing freedom thought, for example, that in a free market, a few firms in each industry would have monopolistic strangleholds over the buyers of their products. Or, they thought, if working people weren't heavily taxed, they would spend all their money and be destitute at retirement. Or without the government limiting the number of taxicabs, fly-by-night operators would rip off innocent, unknowing consumers. These were the views of the vast majority of opponents of freedom that I talked to. All hinged on economics.

So I started reading economics. I read books and articles by Henry Hazlitt, Ludwig von Mises, Milton Friedman, and Murray Rothbard. They reasoned out, in their writing, how a free economy would work and why government regulation usually failed to achieve its stated ends. It sometimes achieved the opposite of what it was supposed to, and occasionally achieved the undesirable ends that the special interests pushing for the government regulation really wanted. Among the many things I learned, four stand out.

The first came from a short article, "I, Pencil," written in 1958 by a man named Leonard Read. In the article, the pencil, given a voice, says that no one, no single person, knows how to make it. If one person tried to do the whole thing himself, he would fail. Instead, the pencil is made by literally thousands of people, each doing a tiny part, in an incredibly complex international division of labor. The graphite for the lead comes from Ceylon (now Sri Lanka). The rubber for the eraser comes from Dutch East Indies (now Indonesia). The wood comes from Oregon. And so on. That all sounds basic. But the insight that really grabbed me was the pencil's statement that none of the thousands of people involved in making it cares as much about the pencil as the child who buys it and uses it. All of the people involved in making the pencil care only because it is a way of making money and providing for them and their families. Yet that "derivative caring" causes them to focus on producing a high-quality, low-cost pencil. Even today, after 30 years of understanding basic economics and after about 20 years of teaching it and using "I, Pencil" as a reading, I pinch myself at the wonder of the market. When I'm driving and my thoughts idly turn to whether I can trust the brakes in my car, I remember that they work so well because an engineer in Tokyo, or Detroit, or somewhere cared so much about whether my brakes worked, not because he cared about me per se, but because he cared about himself and his family. When I get afraid of going blind, or getting cancer, or developing Alzheimer's' disease in my sixties or seventies, I remember "I, Pencil" and realize that somewhere right now, and in fact in more than one somewhere, researchers are trying to figure out how to prevent my getting that disease, others are trying to figure out how to cure it if I get it, and others are trying to figure out how to allay the symptoms if they can't cure my disease. They don't know who I am, don't care who I am, and don't need to in order to do their job well. The knowledge that they are led by their own desires to produce things that are crucial to my life gives me a lot of comfort.

A second thing I learned from this early reading, which both Henry Hazlitt and Ludwig von Mises pointed out, is that when people want government to fund something, say art, agriculture, or education, they are really saying that they want the government to take money from people who have chosen not to buy a product or service in order to fund those items that they have chosen not to buy. Once I saw it this way, it made sense not to have government fund normal everyday goods—it was a denial of people's right to choose.

A third thing I learned is that tariffs hurt not only the country whose goods are subject to the tariff but also the country whose citizens now have to pay a higher price for the good. One author I came across was prolific nineteenth-century French journalist Fredric Bastiat, who in one memorable phrase called tariffs "negative railroads." His point was that a railroad between two countries makes goods cheaper to ship and raises living standards. Imposing tariffs raises the cost of shipping goods and thus acts like the elimination of a railroad. That tariffs hurt the country imposing them still comes as a surprise even to sophisticated reporters. Most of the positive coverage of free-trade agreements is devoted to the great gains to our exporters and not to the gains to our consumers of newly cheap imports.

The fourth thing I learned, which both von Mises and Rothbard pointed out, is that when government intervenes to solve an apparent problem, its intervention usually leads to more problems, which often leads the government to intervene further, which causes more problems and more intervention, and so on. The example I'm most familiar with, because it led me to become an energy economist in the late 1970s, is price controls on oil and gasoline. When President Nixon imposed price controls on oil in 1971, they didn't cause much difficulty at first. But when the Organization of Petroleum Exporting Countries (OPEC) raised the world price from about $3 a barrel to about $11 over a few months, and when Nixon's price controllers wouldn't let refiners pass on the whole price increase in the price of gasoline, there was a massive shortage of gasoline. Rather than remove the price controls, Nixon had government officials start allocating the gasoline by various arbitrary criteria, a process that continued when President Ford replaced Nixon and when President Carter replaced Ford.

Then President Carter noticed that, surprise, surprise, some of the people who got the gasoline and other petroleum products were acting like "energy pigs," a term that some government officials used. They operated power boats, bought big cars, and heated buildings in winter and cooled them in summer. In other words, they were getting gasoline and oil at an artificially low price and were acting as if they were getting gasoline and oil at an artificially low price. What nerve! So Carter, again rather than ending the controls that had caused the problem in the first place, added to them by putting limits on how much you could heat a building in winter or cool it in summer. He, along with Congress, also tightened the so-called CAFE (Corporate Average Fuel Economy) standards on cars and trucks. These standards required automakers to achieve a certain average fuel economy for their whole year's sales of cars and a different level for their whole year's sales of trucks. While I was the senior economist for energy with President Reagan's Council of Economic Advisers in 1983 and 1984, I pushed, unsuccessfully, to get rid of the CAFE law. In a 1985 article,[1] I pointed out that CAFE was the reason stationwagons were disappearing from the market and that they would be replaced with trucks, which had to meet a lower standard. A few years later, along came the sport utility vehicle (SUV), which is classified as a truck.

The CAFE laws led to another problem. One of the main ways automakers responded to the legal requirement to increase fuel economy was to make cars smaller and lighter. That made them less safe. Two economists, Robert Crandall of the Brookings Institution and John Graham of Harvard University's John F. Kennedy School, found that, adjusting for the downsizing of cars that would have occurred anyway, the CAFE laws would cause an extra 2,200 to 3,900 deaths over the life of a 1989-model-year car.[2] Seeing this evidence, Harvard's Lawrence Summers, the chief economic adviser to 1988 Democratic presidential candidate Michael Dukakis, called for the "immediate" repeal of CAFE. Ironically, Ralph Nader, who first made his reputation as an advocate of car safety, and Clarence Ditlow, who heads the Nader-founded Center for Auto Safety, were strong advocates of CAFE laws and have continued to push for more stringent CAFE laws.

While writing an article[3] on Nader and CAFE for *Barron's* in the late 1980s, I interviewed a long-time friend, Sam Kazman, a lawyer with the Competitive Enterprise Institute, who brought a suit, on safety grounds, against the federal government's CAFE law. Said Kazman,

> This is the first time that the Center for Auto Safety
> has knowingly chosen between more safety and
> more government. They chose more government.

I then interviewed Ditlow. He admitted immediately that CAFE makes cars smaller. I asked him whether, during a collision, he would rather be in a big car or a small car.

DITLOW: I would take the small car with an air bag over a large car.

HENDERSON: Over a large car with an air bag?

DITLOW: You simply will not get me to say that there's been any impact of CAFE on safety.

That last statement of Ditlow's *was* an admission.

I ALSO DID A 90-MINUTE INTERVIEW WITH RALPH NADER.[4] HERE ARE THE MOST INTERESTING SEGMENTS.

NADER: [upon hearing that my *Barron's* article was commissioned by editor Robert Bleiberg who, Nader claimed, had treated him unfairly 10 times before] If you were in my position, would you try for number eleven?

HENDERSON: Yes.

NADER: Why? Because of your high journalistic integrity?

HENDERSON: That too, but I'm putting myself in your position. If you were asking to interview me, David Henderson, I would say yes because I have nothing to hide.

. . .

HENDERSON: What about someone who wants to drive a big souped-up car and to risk endangering himself? Why shouldn't he be able to?

NADER: Once when I gave a talk at a college, a student stood up and said that people have the right to buy a car without an air bag. I asked him if they have the right to buy a car without doors. Realizing that he had to be philosophically consistent, even though he probably felt implausible, he said yes.

HENDERSON: But Henry Ford put doors on cars as standard equipment long before the government required it.

NADER: But big cars pollute more and harm more people.

HENDERSON: So make people pay a tax that reflects this harm, but let them still drive that big car if they're willing to pay the tax.

NADER: What if someone got a real kick out of hitting people? Would you let him do it as long as he paid a tax?

HENDERSON: But that's exactly what we do. We call the tax a fine or a prison sentence.

. . .

HENDERSON: What is your argument for not letting workers choose risky jobs?

NADER: The market for safety doesn't work because many data on job hazards—benzene, et cetera—escape the workers' information sensory systems.

HENDERSON: Workers are ignorant of the risks?

NADER: Yes.

HENDERSON: If workers weren't ignorant, would you let them choose?

NADER: What do you mean by "choose"? Workers are coerced by their circumstances into "choosing" between starvation and taking risky jobs.

HENDERSON: No, they aren't. No one's coercing them. We can both admit that some workers face two unpleasant choices, but you want to remove from them the one that's least unpleasant. How would that make them better off?

NADER: I want to give them more choices.

HENDERSON: Great. But meanwhile, before these other choices exist, you want to take away their best option.

NADER: I want to assure them of a safe job.

. . .

HENDERSON: Can you think of an example where you ever opposed a regulation?

NADER: A safety regulation?

HENDERSON: Yes.

NADER: Sure. [3-second pause.] Just because I can't think of many doesn't mean that much, because it's not as if there are a lot of people out there advocating them. But one regulation I opposed was the requirement for lap belts in rear seats. I wanted them combined with shoulder belts. Also, I oppose regulations requiring people to buckle up.

ME: Why?

NADER: I want the air bag.

Again, rather than advocate ending the CAFE laws that caused the problem, some of its proponents want to tighten the standard on trucks, making SUVs less economically feasible. They would rather have small cars running into small cars than small cars running into heavy trucks. Safety studies show, though, that we're better off with heavy vehicles running into heavy vehicles.

After reading books and articles on economic freedom for about a year, I started thinking that not only was freedom highly desirable morally, but also that it was incredibly practical. I was hooked on economics.

One day I was arguing the merits of economic freedom with my favorite math professor, a British socialist named Robert Coates. He said, "Well, I admit that I can't answer your economic arguments, but if you're so confident that you're right, why don't you go over to the economics department and take a course there? I bet you they have good criticisms of your ideas."

That shut me up. *"He's right,"* I thought. *"All I've been doing is reading economists who strongly believe in the free market. Why not take a course from one of the interventionist economics professors and see what they have to say?"* So the next year (in Canadian universities, most courses were year-long rather than semester-long), my last year of college, I signed up for an introductory economics course based on a textbook written by Paul Samuelson and Anthony Scott. (Scott, a Canadian economist at the University of British Columbia, supplied the sections dealing with Canadian institutions.)

The course was a profound disappointment. Neither the book nor the classes in which we tediously worked our way through the book addressed the issues that had come up in most of my discussions and debates with people. Did, for example, free economies tend to degenerate into monopolies? The issue wasn't directly addressed. Instead, the focus was on weird things like "perfect competition" in which every company produces exactly the same product as every other company in the industry, no company spends a cent on advertising because every buyer is assumed to be perfectly informed already, and all companies charge the same price to the penny. This didn't seem perfect to me at all. It just seemed boring. I later learned that this was the standard way economics was taught. It still is.

I distinctly remember one exception. Samuelson had a section discussing how futures markets worked—and he explained it beautifully. I had never thought about the issue, but Samuelson showed that when people think a drought is coming, the futures market works, without any government planning, to give people an incentive to store goods now for when they become more scarce later. In 1990, 21 years later, when I wanted to commission an article on futures markets for my book *The Fortune Encyclopedia of Economics,* I called Samuelson, told him that story, and asked him to write the article. He declined, but nicely. But other than some nice pithy quotes on various economic issues, Samuelson's text and the class using it was, for me, a bust.

If you had asked me at the time whether I wanted to become an economist, I would have said, "No way." The things they wrote and talked about were, with few exceptions, completely uninteresting to me and completely removed from my concerns and those of other people I knew. And I needed to figure out what to do for a living. Within a few months, I would graduate. I was about to receive some money from a modest life insurance policy that my brother, sister, and I had received after my mother's death, so I didn't need to figure it out immediately. But I wanted a plan. I had always been fascinated by airplanes and so I planned a career in the aviation industry. But a couple of days after my third flying lesson, something happened that gave me a new direction. That something was a visit from a professor I hadn't previously heard of, a University of Chicago economist named Harold Demsetz.

Our libertarian club at the University of Winnipeg spent its whole annual budget that year on getting Demsetz to give three speeches over a two-day period. He had been recommended to us by an American organization named the Intercollegiate Studies Institute, which had offered to chip in a few hundred bucks because our modest annual budget didn't quite cover his costs.

Demsetz's speeches were eye-opening. He explained how rent controls and minimum wage laws increase the amount of discrimination against black people and other disfavored groups. So, for example, if rent control keeps rents below their free-market level, a white landlord with even slight racist tendencies, facing a line of people wanting the apartment, will be inclined to choose the white tenant. *Rent control,* he said, *makes the cost of discriminating effectively zero.* Then Demsetz reported data on the percentage of ads in the *Chicago Tribune* classifieds during World War II that carried the word "restricted" (i.e., no blacks allowed) or that tied in the sale of furniture with the lease (a way, he noted, around the rent controls). As the war proceeded and the controlled rents got further below free-market rents, said Demsetz, the percent of such ads rose until by 1945, over 90 percent of the ads contained either one or both mentions.

I also liked Demsetz's style. In the back and forth between him and members of the audience who disagreed, he was pushy and combative, but fair. Throughout, he seemed calmly certain. After a speech Demsetz gave on how property rights can solve the problem of pollution, for example, a professor in the audience quoted socialist author Michael Harrington's line that in every exchange there is a winner and a loser. I'd gotten used to such ain't-it-awful lines, and had never even thought to analyze them. But Demsetz shot back: "That's not true. In every exchange both sides are winners, or else they wouldn't exchange."

Demsetz did something else I had never seen: He cited evidence for almost everything he said. A member of the audience would say, for example, that without airline regulation, airlines would gouge passengers, and Demsetz would cite a study, usually from a journal I had never heard of called the *Journal of Law and Economics,* that showed that in the unregulated intrastate California market, airline fares for a given distance were 30 percent *lower.*

In the downtimes after his speeches, he was equally impressive. I had a reservoir of questions I had been wondering about—tough problems posed to me by critics of economic freedom that I had been unable to answer, neither to their satisfaction nor to my own. One I remember is whether governments should keep their hands off "electric utilities" and other so-called "natural monopolies." His answer was yes, and he referred me to one of his own articles, "Why Regulate Utilities?" in that now-legendary *Journal of Law and Economics*.

Suddenly, my interest in economics was revived. Here was a guy who was actually making a good living at it, with probably the best economics faculty in the world, and he was doing and saying things I found interesting, rather than what I had seen in class. It opened a whole new world for me. Then Demsetz added a bonus. When we said good-bye to him at the airport, he told me that I should consider coming to Chicago and getting a Ph.D.

Then he gave me one last tip. Get all the back issues of the *Journal of Law and Economics*, he said, and read them. The next morning, I called up the flying school and cancelled my lessons. I was "rehooked" on economics.

I had taped Demsetz's speeches—I still have the tapes— and every few weeks after he left, I would replay the tapes. I found myself imitating his debating style and even his Chicago accent.

Then, after graduating in May, I went down to the University of Chicago, visited Demsetz, who took me for lunch with his colleagues, visited Milton Friedman, and bought all the past issues of the *Journal of Law and Economics*. When I brought the approximately 20 volumes back in my old beat-up black cardboard suitcase, the suitcase broke after coming down the baggage carousel at the Winnipeg airport. The Canadian Customs officer asked me to open the bag. I said I'd rather not because I wasn't sure I would get it together again. Wrong answer. He insisted—and we both regretted it. When I opened the bag, out popped a bunch of journals amidst an assortment of underwear. Then he gave me a big spool of pink ribbon to tie the irretrievably broken suitcase back together.

What a sight I must have looked—hauling a heavy old suitcase, spun round and round with pink ribbon, to the nearest bus.

That summer, my brother, who had been in a long-term depression made worse by my mother's death from cancer seven months earlier, committed suicide. I had been close to my brother—he and I had been living together—and so, after the deaths of two people I had been close to, I decided that I needed to be around my friends. I put on hold my plans to do an advanced undergraduate year of economics at the University of Western Ontario and moved in with one friend—Ron Robinson, who now does a radio show on Canada's government-run network, the CBC. Throughout that year, I spent about four hours each morning reading through interesting articles in the *JLE,* as I started to call the *Journal of Law and Economics*, and following up footnotes that led me to other journal articles and books. That's how, for example, I discovered the work of James Buchanan and Gordon Tullock, who applied the economic way of thinking to understanding the incentives that motivate politicians and bureaucrats.

In fact, one of the most important principles I learned that year, although I don't recall anyone saying it or writing it so succinctly, is the following: *incentives matter*. In other words, you can understand and predict a lot of human behavior by paying attention to the incentives that various humans face. If, for example, large profits can be made by discovering a cure for cancer, many people will try very hard to discover a cure for cancer. If, on the other hand, the government announced that no one would be able to price an anti-cancer drug above the production cost, the quest for a cancer cure would slow dramatically. Or, to take a more subtle instance of the principle, my teenage daughter recently completed a mandatory class in driver education, a class that cost my wife and me over $200 and my daughter 30 hours of her time. Yet she, who is very bright, learned very little. The students didn't sit at driver simulation machines and they didn't even look at board diagrams of driving lanes. Instead, they spent a huge percent of the time watching anti-drug and anti-alcohol videos. The course was almost a total waste. But I should have predicted it. The key is that it was mandatory. That meant that even though we were paying and our daughter was taking it, we weren't the customers. The customer was the state government, which had made it mandatory.

But the government wasn't attending these classes or paying for them. So the government didn't have an easy means of making sure that the courses contained good content. And, let's face it, even if some state government employee had been able to monitor quality, that person would not necessarily have insisted on any changes because that state employee would not necessarily have anything at stake—he or she wouldn't be paying for the course or taking the course. Thus, it's a classic setup for a useless course. In fact, this was a mini-case of socialism. One of the main reasons socialism failed was that when no one owned anything, no one had much incentive to take care of anything. Why fill the car you drive with gas if you can't ensure that you will get to drive it tomorrow? Why take care of the cow on the collective farm when you don't personally benefit? And when producers were producing to fill a quota rather than to satisfy customer demand, the quota setters, not the consumers, were the customers.

The principle that incentives matter comes up again and again in the writing of economists. Virtually all economists know and understand it, but few state it as a principle and few consistently apply it. You will often hear economists, for example, point to some problem that exists in the free market, and then advocate a government regulation or spending program to solve the problem. But the analysis typically stops there. The economists typically don't explain why they think a government worker with a budget and/or regulatory authority will do the right thing. They fail, in short, to take account of the fact that incentives matter. The principle that incentives matter is so powerful that at the start of many economics courses I teach, I list this as one of what I call The Ten Pillars of Economic Wisdom.

THE TEN PILLARS OF ECONOMIC WISDOM

1. TANSTAAFL: There ain't no such thing as a free lunch.
2. Incentives matter.
3. Economic thinking is thinking on the margin.
4. The only way to create wealth is to move it from a lower valued to a higher valued use. Corollary: Both sides gain from exchange.
5. Information is valuable and costly.
6. Every action has unintended consequences.
7. The value of a good or a service is subjective.
8. Costs are a bad, not a good.
9. The only way to increase a nation's real income is to increase its real output.
10. Competition is a hardy weed, not a delicate flower.

Throughout that year, I became more convinced that free markets are powerful at creating good and that governments generally cause destruction in people's lives. But it was a nuanced belief; I was also learning of pitfalls in the case for free markets. I was becoming increasingly curious about why a substantial number of economists did not believe strongly in economic freedom. I looked forward to attending the University of Western Ontario the next fall so that I could try my arguments on the professors there and see how they responded.

I got to UWO in the fall of 1971, having chosen it because I wanted to do a year of advanced undergraduate and some graduate courses, and because it was reputed to have the best undergraduate economics program in Canada. That year, besides learning a lot of solid economic reasoning from some very good economists, I learned two main lessons about the debate between economic freedom and government intervention.

The first lesson I learned was that the rules for the debate between freedom and government intervention varied from one economic subdiscipline to another. Take international trade. My professor, J. Clark Leith, appeared to be a complete free trader, as were the other trade economists in a school that was thought of as having the strongest international trade group in Canada, a country known for producing economists who are strong in trade. In a large part of the course, Leith considered the various arguments that had been made for tariffs rather than free trade. In each case, he would lay out the argument clearly and then show the problems: Imposing tariffs would cause other countries' governments to retaliate with tariffs of their own; in rare circumstances, tariffs could benefit a country, but the information a government needed to set tariffs at the "right" level was information it was unlikely to have; governments with the power to set tariffs would abuse it because the government officials involved didn't have the right incentives. These were not just Leith's views but were—and are—the dominant views of international trade economists around the world. An international trade economist who advocates tariffs or import quotas is about as rare as a whooping crane.

But when I went to my class on welfare economics, I learned that the rules are different. The professor, Charles Plourde, spent lecture after lecture carefully going through the literature on "market failure." He taught us that the free market is efficient if a number of very stringent conditions hold. But if these conditions don't hold, he said, then all bets are off. One possible cause of such market failure was "externalities." The classic example and, I later learned, the one most commonly taught, was of apples and bees. Apples provide nectar, which bees use to make honey. If unable to charge the beekeepers for the use of their apples, the orchard owners, in deciding how many apples to grow, will not take account of the gains to beekeepers. Therefore, they will produce too few apples. The positive effect of apple growing on honey production is called a positive externality. A few years later, two articles were published in the *Journal of Law and Economics*, laying out the details of *actual* contracts between orchard owners and beekeepers.[5] It turns out that owners of bee colonies are paid to have their bees pollinate crops, and the payment varies directly with their productivity. The apple-bee externality argument, in short, was made up rather than based on anything in the real world. I'd guess that of the few million students who have been given the apple-bees story as an example of an externality, fewer than 5 percent know the truth.

Another case of market failure was "public goods." One of the standard arguments there, which I had already accepted, was that a government that provides national defense must tax people to pay for it because of the "free-rider" problem: If the government or any other organization that provided defense tried to charge for it, the provider wouldn't easily be able to withhold defense from nonpayers, giving everyone an incentive to free-ride, and thus causing defense not to be provided in the first place. That is a tough problem, and I still don't have a good resolution. Interestingly, though, the example given was not defense, but lighthouses. Economists argued that because a lighthouse owner couldn't charge passing ships for the benefit they got, lighthouses would be underprovided. A few years later, though, an article by Ronald Coase, who was later to win the Nobel prize in economics, revealed something quite different.[6] He pointed out that the increase in the number of lighthouses in Britain a few centuries earlier was due to more privately owned lighthouses, whose owners were able to charge ships that came into nearby ports. So economists' favorite example of a public good with a free-rider problem was actually a poor example. Interestingly, many economists still use the lighthouse example, and *Economics of the Public Sector*, a textbook by noted economist Joseph Stiglitz, published in 1988, 14 years after Coase's article, had on its cover a lighthouse.

Plourde's assigned reading included an article, "The Anatomy of Market Failure," by former JFK advisor Francis Bator, which took the public goods rationale for intervention further. Even a radio signal is a public good, wrote Bator, because one person's tuning in doesn't prevent others from doing so. How about allowing the radio station to scramble its signal and charge people for descramblers to exclude nonpayers? Bator objected that excluding nonpayers is economically inefficient, since the cost of servicing each additional person is zero.

Bator's analysis was not a foot in the door for government intervention—it removed the door completely. Plourde's explicit bottom line was that government intervention could be justified in virtually every area of people's economic lives.

One day, though, Plourde started discussing the effects of actual, rather than hypothetical, government intervention. He showed that oil import quotas raised the price of domestic oil, that agricultural price supports caused farmers to overproduce crops that the government then lets rot, and that airline regulation prevented airlines from competing on price. These regulations and government programs were pernicious, he said, and ought to be abolished. It was the first and only time in the semester that I sensed real passion in the guy. As he attacked program after program, my like-minded classmate, Harry Watson, and I could barely suppress a cheer. We egged him on, asking about this intervention and that, and in each case his answer was that the government should get the hell out. By the end of the hour, I was exhilarated. Whatever this guy's views about the theoretical case for government intervention, he seemed to oppose almost all that existed.

But that was the problem and—I later learned—the problem was not specific to my particular professor. Economists often made theoretical cases for government intervention and yet tended to oppose most that exist. Unlike in the study of tariffs, none of the practical results made them question their theories. *What seemed to be missing was any realistic view about how government actually works.* When economists study private businesses, they tend to assume that the businesses are trying to maximize profits, and they get a lot of mileage out of that self-interest assumption. But when they study governments, they tend to throw out the self-interest assumption and instead assume that politicians and bureaucrats are trying to maximize some version of the public good. In fact, government is typically a tool for the politically strong to use against the politically weak.

The second major lesson I learned that year was that economists often advocated government intervention out of despair or fear. You could often get them to admit, especially in one-on-one discussions, that a particular government intervention was not a good idea, but then they would refuse to attack it, saying, "We've got to do something," or "If I advocate getting rid of government intervention, I'll sound too much like Milton Friedman."

The following year I went to UCLA, to which Demsetz had moved from Chicago and joined the Ph.D. program there. Most of my professors were very pro-free-market. I loved that, but I also wondered at times whether there were some really sophisticated cases for regulation in the literature that I hadn't learned about at the University of Western Ontario and that our professors weren't telling us about. But I got a number of chances to find out.

The first was when I was an intern with the Council of Economic Advisers in Washington, D.C., for the summer of 1973. My immediate boss, a senior economist named Robert Tollison, left for his next academic job about three weeks after I arrived. During those three weeks, he brought me into all the projects he was working on, with the plan of asking council chairman Herb Stein if I could be an acting senior economist in his place until his replacement showed up at the end of the summer. Herb agreed. As a result, I got to be the Council's sole representative at meetings with high officials from other government agencies. At a meeting on transportation deregulation, chaired by the undersecretary of the Department of Transportation, we discussed the form that deregulation of railroads should take. The Department of Justice's chief antitrust economist, George Hay, usually an ally of deregulation, wanted to require railroads to grant other railroads right-of-way over their tracks. I was against this. My most basic reason was that it was their property and that forcing them to allow others to use it was a fundamental violation of their property rights. But I didn't make this point because, after only six weeks in Washington, I had already learned that moral arguments in favor of people's rights didn't get very far. I did see a very practical objection to Hay's position, though, based solely on economics, and I stated it: "If you require railroads to let other railroads use their tracks, then you reduce the railroads' incentive to take care of their track." Making this argument after being steeped in the work of my UCLA professors Harold Demsetz and Armen Alchian came naturally to me, but I also made it because I would finally get a chance to see what a more mainstream economist, and quite a good economist, would say. I waited for Hay's answer. He had none.

I've noticed over the years how common it is even for professional economists to attack other economists' motives rather than their arguments. One of the most memorable such incidents happened in the fall of 1973, when I was in my second year of graduate work at UCLA. I was invited to be on a panel at the meetings of the Ripon Society in Washington to discuss a paper by University of Michigan economist William Shepherd. Shepherd was known for wanting to break up industrial firms into smaller industries to make the industries, he thought, more competitive. We had studied and talked about this at UCLA, and my UCLA professors, especially Demsetz, were quite critical of the idea. I found problems with Shepherd's data and with his arguments and laid them out in my presentation. Again, I thought, I'll get to see "the other side's" arguments that I'm not hearing at UCLA. Two aspects of Shepherd's response still stand out. First, he didn't respond to any of my specific criticisms of his paper. Second, he made nasty comments about my character and patronizing comments about my lack of economic knowledge. That was all.

Another such incident happened in the summer of 1983, when I was a senior economist with President Reagan's Council of Economic Advisers. My boss, Martin Feldstein, had just rehired me for a second year. Two of my colleagues at the time were Larry Summers (who went on to become secretary of the U.S. Treasury under President Clinton) and Stephen McNees (who was on leave from the Boston Federal Reserve Bank). Larry, Steve, and I were invited to a roundtable luncheon at the Heritage Foundation to discuss tax policy. At the lunch, economist Bruce Bartlett and others advocated moving toward a flat-rate, or proportional, income tax. Larry didn't say much at the meeting, but his facial expressions suggested that he didn't like much of what he heard. Larry, Steve, and I shared a cab back to the White House. Larry didn't argue with anything Bartlett had said. But he wasn't silent. As we drove up to the south gate of the White House, Larry said angrily, "Bartlett's just advocating lower tax rates on rich people because he's trying to protect the class he came from."

Lawyers have a saying: When the facts are against you, argue the law; when the law is against you, argue the facts; and when both are against you, pound the table and shout. Similarly, when I see smart economists who, rather than handle my arguments, attack my character or the character of those who agree with me, I suspect that they don't have any further argument to make.

ENDNOTES

1. David R. Henderson, "The Economics of Fuel Economy Standards," *Regulation,* January/February 1985.

2. Robert W. Crandall and John D. Graham, "The Effect of Fuel Economy Standards on Automobile Safety," *Journal of Law and Economics,* Vol. XXXII (April 1989), pp. 97–118.

3. David R. Henderson, "Less Good Than Harm: On Balance, That's What Ralph Nader Has Wrought," *Barron's,* July 31, 1989, p. 9. For Ralph Nader's and Clarence Ditlow's letter in response, and my response to them, see "Safety and Economy: An Exchange," *Barron's,* August 21, 1989.

4. Conducted by telephone in July 1989.

5. Steven N. S. Cheung, "The Fable of the Bees: An Economic Investigation," *Journal of Law and Economics,* Vol. XVI (1), April 1973, pp. 11–33; David B. Johnson, "Meade, Bees, and Externalities," *Journal of Law and Economics,* Vol. XVI (1), April 1973, pp. 35–52.

6. R. H. Coase, "The Lighthouse in Economics," *Journal of Law and Economics,* Vol. XVII (2), October 1974, pp. 357–376.

WE WON, BUT...

CHAPTER 3

SEPTEMBER 1978, HONG KONG

I am in the audience at the biannual meeting of the Mont Pelerin Society, an organization of people who believe in personal liberty. At age 27, I am at these meetings for my first time. The lead speaker that first morning, a world-famous economist, gets up to give the opening speech. People have come from around the world to see and hear him. He is the first strongly pro-free market and antisocialist economist to have won the Nobel prize, the most prestigious prize that an economist can win. In a series of articles in the late 1930s and early 1940s, he drove the final intellectual nail in the coffin of socialism. He pointed out that the information required for a government to plan an economy rationally is far too vast for a small number of even the most brilliant minds to use effectively and that the information required is generated only by a free market. In one of his most famous books, The Road to Serfdom, *written at the height of World War II and still a classic, he pointed out the strong totalitarian similarities among socialism, communism, fascism, and Nazism. After World War II, the four-power-occupation authorities in Germany, representing the governments of France, Britain, the United States, and the Soviet Union, had, at the behest of the Soviet Union, banned* The Road to Serfdom.[1] *The author's name: Friedrich Hayek.*

Hayek started the Mont Pelerin Society in 1947 when he was one of only a few intellectuals who opposed socialism and favored economic freedom. People with his views were so few that he felt an international group was needed to give each other moral support and comfort for one week every two years. At the first meeting, only a handful of people attended. But what a handful! The 36 attendees included Milton Friedman and George Stigler, then relatively unknown economists in their mid-thirties, who themselves went on to win the Nobel prize; Walter Eucken, a German economist who, along with Ludwig Erhard, had ripped away the Nazi-imposed and Allied-enforced regulations that were stifling the German economy; Ludwig von Mises, an Austrian economist who was the first to lay out analytically why socialist economic planning could not work; Maurice Allais, a French economist who was later to win the Nobel prize; and Michael Polanyi, Karl Popper, and Lionel Robbins, all from Britain, all of whom were later to become Sir or Lord.

The Mont Pelerin Society, named after the place in Switzerland where the group first met, expanded a good bit after 1947. In the 1960s, Hayek had retired to Freiberg, Germany, profoundly depressed about both the state of the world and the apparent lack of acceptance of his free-market ideas and his criticisms of socialism. But the recognition that came with his Nobel prize revived him. In 1978, at the Mont Pelerin Society's meeting in Hong Kong, Friedrich Hayek was in his glory and brimming with optimism.

Hayek told us that socialism was on the ropes and that we must try to arrange a grand debate, the topic of which should be "resolved that coercion as a means of organizing the economy has failed." He envisioned having the debate in Paris and inviting the leading socialists and the leading advocates of freedom.

I stood and asked the first question. I like your idea, I said to Hayek, but do you really think that socialists are going to consent to wording the debate question that way? Many of them don't believe that they're advocating coercion. Why not make it a more neutral question like, "Has socialism failed?" He took it under advisement. Many of the next questioners were skeptical of the whole idea. Not that they thought socialism worked. But they thought the debate would never happen because socialists would simply not admit that it's debatable. George Stigler, the president of the Mont Pelerin Society that year and the person who invited me to the meetings, came up to me at the break.

In his banquet speech the night before, Stigler had said that ideas and debates don't matter; no one, Stigler had insisted, changes his or her mind on the basis of ideas. Stigler thought, mistakenly, that he had found a kindred spirit in me. "Hayek has always been an actionist," said Stigler dismissively, using his unusual term for proselytizer.

JUNE 12, 1987, BRANDENBERG GATE, BERLIN

On the western side of Brandenberg Gate stands U.S. President Ronald Reagan. Reagan, the eternal optimist, senses that Gorbachev, the General Secretary of the Communist Party and leader of the Soviet Union, differs from his predecessors. The Brandenberg Gate is famous, or, more exactly, infamous. It is one of the gates in the Berlin Wall that you pass through if you leave East Berlin to go to West Berlin. There's one little problem: If you're East German you can't do so without permission. Since August 1961, East Berliners have been unable to get permission, and most of those who have tried to leave illegally have been shot at. For the last three decades, the leaders of the Soviet Union have made clear to the leaders of East Germany that they want the border closed.

Reagan says,

> General Secretary Gorbachev, if you seek peace, if you seek prosperity for the Soviet Union and Eastern Europe, if you seek liberalization: Come here to this gate! Mr. Gorbachev, open this gate! Mr. Gorbachev, tear down this wall![2]

A year later, West German Chancellor Helmut Kohl says that the Berlin Wall will not come down in his lifetime.[3]

JANUARY 23, 1989, NEW YORK

The New Yorker publishes an article by noted socialist economist Robert Heilbroner. Nothing new about that. Heilbroner, the famous author of The Worldly Philosophers, *a book that hundreds of thousands of undergraduate economics students have read, often writes for* The New Yorker. *Except that this article is different. Here's how this long-time advocate of socialism begins: "Less than seventy-five years after it officially began, the contest between capitalism and socialism is over: Capitalism has won."*

Heilbroner pointed to the Soviet Union, China, and Eastern Europe as giving "the clearest possible proof that capitalism organizes the material affairs of humankind more satisfactorily than socialism." In the early 1960s, the Soviet Union achieved a dubious first: It became the first industrially developed country in history to suffer a prolonged peacetime fall in its population's life expectancy. Stories of tragic, life-destroying waste in the Soviet economy were widespread, and some would have been funny had innocent lives not been at stake. Government-set prices that were too low caused serious shortages, which meant that the average Soviet citizen had to line up for basic necessities for hours a day.[4] One joke about shortages that made the rounds in 1988 was the following:

CUSTOMER IN MEAT STORE: Miss, can you slice 100 grams of ham for me?

SALESWOMAN: Certainly, citizen, if you bring me the ham.[5]

Because no one person or company could own grain produced by the Soviet Union's vast collective farms, no one had an incentive to take care of it, which is why a huge percent of it rotted every year. The fact that factories were judged by rough physical quotas rather than by their ability to satisfy customers—their customers were the state—had predictably bad results. If, to take a real case, a nail factory's output was measured by number, factories produced large numbers of small pin-like nails. If output was measured by weight, the nail factories shifted to fewer, very heavy nails. Government-set prices that were too high caused huge surpluses of shoes and other things that people didn't particularly want, surpluses that sometimes ended up in landfills.[6] Wasteful use of metals in producing drilling equipment and pipelines often meant that the cost of drilling and shipping oil from the Soviet Union's vast oil reserves exceeded its value at its final destination;[7] instead of adding value, much Soviet production was devoted to subtracting value. In December 1984, months before becoming the new Soviet leader, Mikhail Gorbachev had concluded that it was "impossible to live that way."[8] Gorbachev was correct. Upon becoming Soviet leader, Gorbachev took halting, often contradictory steps toward allowing more economic freedom for the Soviet Union's residents. The disaster of socialism that Ludwig von Mises had predicted as early as 1920[9] and that Hayek elaborated on in the 1930s and 1940s[10] was happening. In a later article, Heilbroner gave explicit credit to von Mises and Hayek for being over 40 years ahead of their time with their clear-eyed assessment of the chaos of economic life under socialism.[11] Although the grand debate in Paris that Hayek had so ardently wanted in 1978 was never held, it didn't need to be. The evidence was popping out left and right, literally. Heilbroner, one of socialism's leading proponents, had written that socialism "has far surpassed capitalism in both economic malfunction and moral cruelty."[12] The belief in socialism was crumbling. Also about to crumble was one of socialism's most hated symbols, a symbol that reminded people that socialism, at its roots, was about the government's naked use of force against innocent men, women, and children.

NOVEMBER 9, 1989, EAST BERLIN

Gunter Schabowski, the head of the Communist Party of Berlin, is about to go on television for a live press conference. Egon Krenz, Party secretary and leader of East Berlin, hands him a draft of a new regulation from the Interior Ministry. The draft describes new procedures for obtaining visas to visit the West. Minutes later, in reply to an Italian journalist, he seems to say that East Germans can go to the West with no restrictions, starting right now. Immediately, thousands of East Germans head to the Wall, some of them dressed in their pajamas. For three hours the crowd swells in front of the hated Wall. They refuse to move, and they chant, "Open the gate! Open the gate!" The guards, unsure what to do, decide to open the gates. Hundreds of thousands of East Berliners swarm through into the welcoming arms of their West German brothers and sisters. The invincible Wall has fallen— without a shot being fired.

A few days later, I was lying on the floor, looking at the latest *Newsweek* with my 4-year-old daughter Karen. I showed her the famous picture from about 25 years earlier of the armed East German guard who himself successfully escaped from East Germany. Karen asked me why I was so excited about the Berlin Wall falling. I reached for words that a 4-year old could understand.

I said, "These men were told to kill anyone who tried to get from East Berlin to West Berlin. And some other men had suddenly decided that they were no longer going to shoot people; they were going to let them leave. This meant that these people who before were trapped where they lived now were not trapped. They could get out and go places they'd always wanted to go."

"Like Disneyland?" said Karen.

"That's right," I answered. "Not only can they go where they want, but also they can buy things they have always wanted to buy."

And my daughter, grinning, said, "Like candy?"

"Yes," I said, "like candy." I later learned that that weekend, the candy stores in West Berlin actually were sold out.

My daughter had understood the essence of totalitarian socialism.

In just 12 years, the gleam in Friedrich Hayek's eye had become a reality. And although the debate he wished for had never happened, socialist economist Heilbroner wrote, in September 1990, that after having dismissed von Mises' arguments against socialism in the 1930s, "it turns out, of course, that von Mises was right."[13]

Since then, there have been major gains in economic freedom around the world. In 1922, Vladimir Illyich Lenin, the leader of the Communists in Russia, had said that the government should control the "commanding heights," the most important sectors, of the economy. A few years later, the Soviets, under Lenin's successor, Joseph Stalin, proceeded to take over the commanding heights by murdering millions of Ukranian farmers, called *kulaks,* and taking over their land. From the late 1920s until the 1980s, virtually all productive assets in the Soviet Union were owned and operated by the government. All factories, all power plants, all trucks, trains, and airplanes, all stores, and all apartments were government owned. The only privately owned means of production were small farm plots, which was fortunate because these plots were highly productive, producing, on only 3 percent of the sown acreage,[14] over 25 percent of the Soviet Union's meat and about 50 percent of its potatoes.[15] Yet by 1996, most assets in Russia (which had lost its colonies) were privately owned. Seventy percent of Russia's Gross Domestic Product is now privately produced.

In China in 1978, peasants facing a severe drought needed to break through the parched land of the farms they were working. There was one main problem: The farms were collectivized and the peasants were simply unwilling to exert hard effort to improve what wasn't theirs. The peasants pleaded for the return of the household responsibility system, which allowed a family to keep some of the benefits of its labor. In desperation, communist dictator Deng Xiaoping granted their wish. Henceforth, peasants had to deliver a certain quota to the government; production above that quota was theirs to keep and sell. In essence, the government had implemented a system of de facto property rights. Moreover, the output above the quota was tax free, which created a powerful incentive for the farmers to produce beyond the quota. The result was that between 1978 and 1990, the share of agricultural output sold in open markets rose from 8 percent to 80 percent, and in the six years after 1978, real income in farm households rose by 60 percent. Deng also allowed more freedom to companies located in Special Economic Zones along China's coast, which have since grown much faster than the rest of China. "I have two choices," said Deng. "I can distribute poverty or I can distribute wealth."[16]

There has also been a shift away from government power and toward economic freedom in the formerly communist European countries such as Poland, Hungary, and the two parts of what was Czechoslovakia, in India, in the rest of Asia, in Latin America, and in Britain. In short, economic freedom has increased dramatically in parts of the world that, in total, contain over half of the world's population.

How did it all happen? There were two main causes. First, people, including government planners, noticed how badly government ran things. "Between the fall of the Berlin Wall in 1989 and the collapse of the Soviet Union in 1991," recalled a high-level government planner in India, "I felt as though I were awakening from a thirty-five year dream. Everything I had believed about economic systems and tried to implement was wrong."[17] The head of the Chinese Communist Party's propaganda department was shocked when he visited Japan and noticed that half of Japan's households owned cars and over 95 percent owned TVs, refrigerators, and washing machines. In his report of his trip to Japan, this official wrote, "One Sunday we went out to a busy street. Of all the women we saw, no two wore the same style of clothes." He added, "The female workers accompanying us also changed clothes every day."[18]

Second, ideas really did matter. The fact that the von Mises, the Hayeks, and the Friedmans of the world had been slugging it out for decades had made a difference. One of the leading reformers who helped Russia get rid of socialism was economist Yegor Gaidar. As a young boy, Gaidar had lived in Cuba during Castro's revolution, and his family often had Che Guevara, the famous Cuban communist revolutionary, as a guest. He began to doubt communism when the Soviet Union's military invaded Czechoslovakia in 1968. Then he started reading more in the 1970s and 1980s about free markets. Asked who were the main influences on his economic thinking, Gaidar responded, "Of course, Hayek."[19]

The world seems to be going the right way. Countries around the world are becoming freer, and that freedom is generating wealth for masses of people such as the world has never seen.

Yet despite the proven economic success of freedom, much of the world, including the United States, is hanging on to freedom's opposite, government control. The government does not allow us complete freedom to save for our own retirement, but instead takes a substantial bite of our income in payroll taxes through our working years and gives us a lousy rate of return on those taxes during our retirement years. If you are an employer who wants to provide insurance coverage for your employees, various state and federal laws force you to include various benefits, whether or not your employees want them, and these requirements may cause you not to provide the coverage. If you are trying to get on the lower rung of the economic ladder by selling goods out of a street cart or turning your car into a taxi, you must first get government permission, and often the government won't give you permission. If you persist in spite of the government, you could go to jail. If you are unhappy with the education your child is getting in tax-financed schools and you decide to take your child out of that school, you don't get a refund of the taxes you pay towards government schools. Moreover, if you put your child in a private school, that school may be regulated by the government. Those who sell items whose use carries certain risks—items ranging from cigarettes and firearms to ladders and airplanes—

are often sued when the users are harmed by their product. Users of those products pay more for them because the risk of a lawsuit drives up the product's price.

The list of government rules and regulations goes on and on. The Federal Register, which contains just the new and proposed regulations of the federal government, has grown from 53,376 pages in 1988, before the Wall fell, to 68,571 pages in 1998. Governments at all levels in the United States take about 30 percent of the average person's income and regulate in various degrees how we can spend much of the other 70 percent. The nastiest government leaders of the twentieth century—Stalin, Mao, and Hitler—murdered tens of millions of people and oppressed hundreds of millions of others. Fortunately, the U.S. and other governments of industrialized countries are much tamer. Yet the small and medium intrusions committed by these tamer governments add up. Governments in the United States and other industrialized countries chip away at our freedom in literally thousands of ways.

As recently as 25 years ago, when you got into an argument with someone about some choice that person had made, a common, debate-ending and debate-winning comeback from the person making the allegedly unwise choice was, "It's a free country." You don't hear that expression much any more. Instead, government is thought of more and more as the parent or as Big Brother, the term George Orwell made famous in *1984*, his grim novel depicting a totalitarian state. A recent vice president of the United States, Albert Gore, apparently aware of the unease that many Americans still have about being regulated, stated that the federal government "should never be the baby sitter, the parents." That sounded good. Gore, however, was not rejecting the idea of government power over people's lives. Instead, he was making fine distinctions about what role in the "family" the government properly plays. The government, he said, should be "more like grandparents in the sense that grandparents perform a nurturing role and are aware of what parenting was like but no longer exercise that kind of authority."[20] But the government is not our parent, our big brother, our baby sitter, or our grandparent. Government, as George Washington said, is force. So if you want to stick with the vice president's model, think of the government as grandparents with guns who have never met you and don't care much about you.

The fall of the Berlin wall and the utter collapse of the vicious antihuman communist regimes around the world *was* a great victory. But the victory is incomplete. People should be much freer than any government in the world is letting them be.

ENDNOTES

1. Daniel Yergin and Joseph Stanlislaw, *The Commanding Heights,* New York: Simon and Schuster, 1998, p. 143.

2. Quoted in Dinesh D'Souza, *Ronald Reagan: How an Ordinary Man Became an Extraordinary Leader,* New York: Free Press, 1997, p. 194.

3. Daniel Yergin and Joseph Stanlislaw, *The Commanding Heights,* New York: Simon and Schuster, 1998, p. 126.

4. Hedrick Smith, *The Russians,* 1977.

5. Scott Shane, *Dismantling Utopia: How Information Ended the Soviet Union,* Chicago: Ivan R. Dee, 1994, p. 75.

6. Scott Shane, *Dismantling Utopia: How Information Ended the Soviet Union,* Chicago: Ivan R. Dee, 1994, pp. 77–78.

7. Marshall I. Goldman, "Perestroika," in David R. Henderson, ed., *The Fortune Encyclopedia of Economics,* New York: Warner Books, 1993, p. 163.

8. Goldman, "Perestroika," p. 747.

9. Ludwig von Mises, "Economic Calculation in the Socialist Commonwealth," 1920, reprinted in Friedrich Hayek, ed., *Collectivist Economic Planning: Critical Studies on the Possibilities of Socialism,* 1935.

10. Friedrich A. Hayek, "Socialist Economic Calculation: The Present State of the Debate," in Friedrich Hayek, *Individualism and Economic Order,* 1942. Reprint. 1972.

11. Robert Heilbroner, "After Communism," *The New Yorker,* September 10, 1990.

12. Robert Heilbroner, "Socialism," in David R. Henderson, ed., *The Fortune Encyclopedia of Economics,* New York: Warner Books, 1993, p. 161.

13. Heilbroner, "After Communism," p. 91.

14. Eugene Lyons, *Workers' Paradise Lost,* New York: Funk & Wagnalls, 1967, p. 200.

15. Yergin and Stanislaw, *Commanding Heights,* p. 272.

16. Yergin and Stanislaw, *Commanding Heights,* p. 196.

17. Quoted in Yergin and Stanislaw, *Commanding Heights,* p. 138.

18. Quoted in Yergin and Stanislaw, *Commanding Heights,* p. 200.

19. Yergin and Stanislaw, *Commanding Heights,* p. 277.

20. Associated Press, June 12, 1997.

YOU BELONG TO YOU

There will be no license, no free space, in which the individual belongs to himself. This is Socialism—not such trifles as the private possession of the means of production. Of what importance is that if I range men firmly within a discipline they cannot escape? Let them own land or factories as much as they please. The decisive factor is that the State, through the party, is supreme over them regardless whether they are owners or workers. All that, you see, is unessential. Our Socialism goes far deeper....Why need we trouble to socialize banks and factories? We socialize human beings.

—ADOLPH HITLER TO HERMANN RAUSCHNING[1]

What is the thinking of the people who advocate the draft? Whatever their differences, they have one thing in common: They believe that you are a national resource. Well, I am here to tell you that you belong to you. That you are not a piece of clay to be molded by others, that nobody has the right to take you against your will, no matter who they are, how many votes they have, or what they intend to use you for.

—DAVID R. HENDERSON, ANTIDRAFT SPEECH GIVEN AT CARNEGIE-MELLON UNIVERSITY, MAY 1979

In civilized societies, the vast majority of people think that slavery is wrong. I share that belief. But *why* is slavery wrong? Was pre-Civil War slavery wrong because the slaves were forced to pick cotton? Hardly. Not all were forced to pick cotton or even to harvest other crops; some were forced to do other tasks around the plantation. Not all slaves worked on plantations. Indeed, one famous slave, Simon Gray, actually became captain of a Natchez flatboat, and managed and paid a crew that included white men. Gray also conducted other business for his company, business that required that he travel freely, handle large sums of money, and even carry a gun. Yet Gray was still a slave.[2] So, the particular tasks the slaves were forced to do are not what made slavery morally odious.

Perhaps, then, slavery was wrong because of how badly the slaves were treated. Certainly that was one very vicious aspect of slavery. But the bad treatment of slaves was not the fundamental problem with slavery, as is illustrated by the following joke, told about an escaped slave from Kentucky who was brought before an Indiana justice of the peace:

JUDGE: Were you unhappy there?

SLAVE: Oh no. I had a good life there.

JUDGE: Were you mistreated?

SLAVE: No. Old Massa and me was the greatest friends. Fished and hunted together.

JUDGE: Did you have good food and housing?

SLAVE: Sure enough. Ham and 'taters. Molasses. My little cabin had roses over the door.

JUDGE: I don't understand. Why did you run away?

SLAVE: Well your Honor, the situation is still open down there if you'd like to apply for it.[3]

The essence of slavery, and what makes it morally repugnant, is that the very bodies of slaves are treated as if they are owned by others. In a famous speech that Frederick Douglass gave at an abolitionist meeting in New England, shortly after escaping from slavery, Douglass told his audience that he had stolen this body that was standing before them. The point of his bitter irony was that if slavery is justified, then the body that he occupied was owned by the man whose plantation he escaped and that, by escaping, Douglass had committed theft. It wasn't theft. Douglass was just reclaiming what was rightfully his. Which means that the essence of slavery, and its essential evil, was that it was based on the idea that one person can own another.

What if, instead of a particular person owning a slave, the government had claimed to own slaves? That is what Hitler meant when he said, "We socialize human beings." Does government ownership of slaves make slavery morally acceptable? No. So that excludes the idea that other people can own you and the idea that the government—which is also other people—can own you. Whom does that leave? Here's a hint: Look in the mirror. The only person who can own you is you. You own yourself.

Your right to yourself, sometimes called self-ownership, is something that British philosopher John Locke asserted over 300 years ago. The founding fathers of the United States were strongly influenced by Locke's thinking, although they had a huge lapse when they allowed slavery. Nowadays, your right to yourself might seem uncontroversial in the United States. It's not. Here is what Robert Heilbroner, the socialist economist mentioned in Chapter 3, wrote as recently as 1980:

> Indeed, the creation of socialism as a new mode of production can properly be compared to the moral equivalent of war—war against the old order, in this case—and will need to amass and apply the power commensurate with the requirements of a massive war. This need not entail the exercise of command in an arbitrary or dictatorial fashion, but certainly it requires the curtailment of the central economic freedom of bourgeois society, namely the right of individuals to own, and therefore to withhold if they wish, the means of production, *including their own labor*. [Italics added][4]

In other words, fully implemented socialism would require the introduction of mass slavery, with the government as slave owner. Although Heilbroner stopped short of advocating slavery, he treated it as if it were a completely respectable idea worth considering.

Mass slavery of whites and blacks was never implemented in a widespread fashion in the United States, but we did come within a whisker of having it in the United States. The year was 1945 and the United States was months away from winding up World War II. President Franklin D. Roosevelt proposed a new law giving the federal government the power to prevent workers from quitting their jobs and to prevent people from taking new jobs without the government's permission. (See sidebar for details.) Because those who violated the law could have been thrown in prison for up to one year, the bill became known as "work-or-jail" bill.[5] Under Roosevelt's bill, one official in the government, the Director of War Mobilization, would have had the power to enslave people. Roosevelt's officials claimed that the law was needed to maintain industrial production for the war. That apparently was good enough for the U.S. House of Representatives, which on March 27 voted 167 to 160 for the bill.[6] Three important things happened just days before the April 3 Senate vote. First, Paul McNutt, the Roosevelt administration's War Manpower Commissioner, admitted that the manpower situation, far from being critical, was "in excellent shape."[7] The Army and Navy, which wanted the work-or-jail bill, had successfully threatened the War Manpower Commission into withholding its January report showing "the best manpower situation since the war began."[8] Second, the War Production Board's monthly report showed that February production was the highest ever,[9] giving the lie to the backers' claim of a crisis in war production. Finally, just three days before the Senate vote, the Director of War Mobilization and Reconversion let slip that "the need for manpower legislation continues...not only for war production but also for the production of essential civilian goods; and later to facilitate reconversion."[10] Translation: The Roosevelt administration had planned the bill all along to be not just a wartime measure, but a measure to impose long-term slavery on a substantial portion of the workforce. On April 3, 1945, the U.S. Senate voted 46 to 29 to kill the bill.[11] So Americans' freedom to choose their jobs, to choose what to do with their own property in their bodies, was saved by a mere 17 votes. Had just nine senators switched their votes, a limited form of slavery would have existed in America. It can't happen here? It almost did.

THE LAW THAT NEARLY ENSLAVED
AMERICAN WORKERS

Here is the language of the key provision of the so-called "work-or-jail" bill, which passed the House of Representatives but was voted down in the U.S. Senate, 46 to 29.[12]

Sec. 5 (a) To the extent deemed by the Director [of War Mobilization] to be necessary and appropriate to carry out the purposes and means declared in section 2 of this act and also for the purpose of keeping activities and places of employment essential to the war effort in productive operation, the Director is authorized, by regulation—

(1) to prescribe employment ceilings in designated areas, activities, or places of employment, fixing the maximum number of workers by age, sex, or occupational qualifications, who may be there employed, and prohibiting the employment of workers beyond such maximum numbers;

(2) to prohibit or regulate the hiring, rehiring, solicitation or recruitment of new workers by employers and the acceptance of employment by workers; and

(3) to prohibit the individuals employed in designated areas, activities, plants, facilities and farms, which the Director deems are essential to the war effort, from voluntarily discontinuing such employment unless, in the case of any individual so employed, the Director determines that it is no longer necessary to the interest of the war effort for him to remain in such employment or that he has a justifiable reason for leaving such employment.

(b) Whoever wilfully violates the provisions of any regulation made under subsection (a) shall be guilty of a misdemeanor and, upon conviction thereof, shall be punished by imprisonment for not more than twelve months or by a fine not to exceed $10,000, or both.

THE DRAFT

Actually, it did happen here in World War II, in World War I, and for all but one year between 1945 and 1973. During the four major wars that the United States fought during this century, the U.S. government imposed conscription. The government told people unlucky enough to be young and male that they had to register with the government's Selective Service system. Of these, millions were drafted and sent to war, hundreds of thousands of them never to return. A young man who refused to register for the draft or to be inducted into the military could be thrown in prison for up to five years. So the government's power to deny people's ownership of themselves has been a reality for young male Americans for much of the twentieth century.

Of course, the government justifies conscription by claiming that without it not enough people will volunteer. The reality is that people volunteer in large numbers when they believe in the cause they are joining—384,000 men joined the military in the three months following Pearl Harbor, for example, presumably to "get back at the Japanese." In fact, at the start of World War I, Woodrow Wilson's government actually used the high number of volunteers as an excuse for imposing conscription. His government said that it needed conscription to discourage certain people from enlisting because these people were needed in civilian life, and to replace them with those who were less willing to join. And early in World War II, the government prevented people from joining voluntarily.

Some unelected governments have been more blunt in admitting their true motives for wanting a draft. When Napoleon Bonaparte, the founder of the modern system of conscription, was told that a planned operation would cost too many men, he replied, "That is nothing. The women produce more of them than I can use." Fortunately, in the United States today, young men are not drafted. Since July 1, 1973, not one single person has been forced to join the U.S. military. In renewing that important respect for people's private property in themselves, the U.S. government leapt ahead of many other governments—in France, Russia, and Spain, to take just three.

I said earlier that my desire to work for freedom was what led me to become an economist. One of the things that impressed me early on about economists was that so many of those I came across in my reading were against the draft, on both economic and philosophical grounds. Not only that, but they were also the leading intellectuals against it in the 1960s. Economist John Kenneth Galbraith opposed the draft in the 1960s, stating that "the draft survives principally as a device by which we use compulsion to get young men to serve at less than the market rate of pay."[13] Milton Friedman made a principled case against the draft at a conference held at the University of Chicago in 1966, when the draft seemed clearly ensconced in U.S. society and few people, even in the growing anti-Vietnam War movement, opposed the draft on principle. Friedman once stated that the draft was the only issue on which he had ever personally lobbied Congressmen. And in eliminating the draft from American life, economists had a huge role. In fact, it's possible that we would still have the draft today if not for the heroic efforts of many of these economists, none of them of draft age.

One economist particularly worth noting is Martin Anderson, who is now my colleague at the Hoover Institution and who joined Richard Nixon's campaign for president in 1967. Anderson wrote the antidraft speech that Nixon gave on CBS radio during the 1968 election. As an adviser to President Nixon, Anderson helped choose the members of Nixon's commission on the all-volunteer force, the so-called Gates Commission. Four other economists who were instrumental in ending the draft were the aforementioned Milton Friedman, W. Allen Wallis (later undersecretary of state for economic affairs under President Reagan), and Alan Greenspan, who were on the commission, and William Meckling, the executive director of the commission. They all saw the draft as an unfair implicit tax on young men that forced them out of other pursuits that they would prefer. If, for example, a young man could earn $20,000 in the private sector and was drafted for pay and benefits worth $8,000, the "draft tax" was $12,000. They pointed out that the draft tax on many young men was well in excess of 50 percent. They believed that to the extent the whole society gains from defense, the whole society should pay for it with explicit taxes rather than just implicit taxes on an unlucky few. In his recent coauthored book, *Two Lucky People,* Friedman writes that 5 of the 15 commissioners—including himself, Greenspan, and Wallis—were against the draft to begin with.

Five members were undecided, and 5 were pro-draft. Yet when the commission's report came out less than a year later and became a paperback book, all 15 members favored ending the draft.

How did this happen? One main reason was that the economists on the commission were so persuasive. One incident stands out, which Becky Meckling, Bill Meckling's widow, recalled in an interview a few months after he died. (I got to know Bill and Becky well in the late 1970s, when Bill was the dean of the business school at the University of Rochester and I was an assistant professor there.) Becky told me that one day Bill came home from the commission's hearings particularly happy about what had happened that day. What had him beaming, she said, was an interchange between Milton Friedman and one of the witnesses, General William Westmoreland, who had been the commander of the troops in Vietnam and was at the time Chief of Staff of the U.S. Army. I had heard Bill tell this story a few times, and the day stood out in Milton Friedman's mind too. Friedman reports the dialogue in his memoirs, *Lucky People*, coauthored with his wife, Rose. In his testimony, Westmoreland stated that he didn't want to command an army of mercenaries. Friedman asked, "General, would you rather command an army of slaves?"

WESTMORELAND: I don't like to hear our patriotic draftees referred to as slaves.

FRIEDMAN: I don't like to hear our patriotic volunteers referred to as mercenaries. If they are mercenaries, then I, sir, am a mercenary professor, and you, sir, are a mercenary general; we are served by mercenary physicians, we use a mercenary lawyer, and we get our meat from a mercenary butcher."

Comments Friedman, "That was the last time that we heard from the general about mercenaries."[14]

Another person who did a lot of the heavy intellectual lifting by estimating the budgetary cost of eliminating the draft was University of Rochester economist Walter Oi. Oi was, and is, a particularly impressive man, having become completely blind from a degenerative eye disease early in his career, and yet carrying out a very productive career. Walter, who was later one of my colleagues at Rochester, is one of the most principled men I have ever met. Two stories stand out. The first incident was one I heard from Michael Jensen, another Rochester colleague. Walter's first academic job was a short-term appointment at Iowa State University that had the potential to turn into a long-term appointment. At the time, though, his eyesight was deteriorating badly and was almost gone. This was in the early 1960s, when it was still legal to discriminate against handicapped people, although Walter seems never to have regarded himself as handicapped. Some of his colleagues were telling young students that they should major in agricultural business because there was a great future in agriculture. At a faculty meeting, Walter pointed out that agriculture was a declining industry and denounced his colleagues for being less than honest. Now that takes guts. He was out of that job the next academic year.

The other story I remember was a phone call I received from Walter when I was a senior economist with President Reagan's Council of Economic Advisers in the early 1980s. A government commission looking into the World War II imprisonment of all Japanese Americans living on the West Coast had just come out with a report, and its recommendation was that each person imprisoned be compensated with a check for $20,000. Walter wanted me to get him a copy of the report. When I had first met Walter, while interviewing at Rochester, I had followed my curiosity. I have learned that, contrary to what almost all my elders told me when I was growing up, people generally love to talk about themselves, even about sensitive isues, if you ask them with some sensitivity. I had asked Walter if he had been imprisoned as a child during the war. He had been. He reminisced about being taken prisoner by the U.S. government when he was 10 years old and, before being shipped inland, living with his family for the first few days in a horse stall at the Santa Anita race track in Los Angeles. He had some pretty strong feelings about his imprisonment. I told Walter I would get him the report and then asked, "So what do you think of the commission's recommendation?"

"I'm against it," he snapped. He then went on to tell me that yes, the Japanese Americans were treated unjustly but that the best thing to do for Japanese Americans was to move on and not create a new government program.

Three years after the Gates Commission's report came out, the draft was dead. As a result, a whole generation of young men in the United States has been able to grow up, as I did in Canada, with the freedom to prepare for their life after age 18 without having the threat of the draft hanging over them. They have been able to quit college, as Bill Gates did, without losing their draft deferment. This freedom is probably one contributor to the existence of a large entrepreneurial class of people in their twenties.

The economists mentioned above who fought to end the draft are just the most famous ones. A large number of other younger economists did the studies that the Gates Commission drew on in calling for an end to the draft. Other economists that you will probably never hear of have been the strongest opponents of the draft when government officials have advocated reimposing it. Many of them have worked in various military think tanks over the years—the RAND Corporation, the Center for Naval Analyses, and the Institute for Defense Analysis—and in various government agencies such as the Department of Defense and the Congressional Budget Office. What impresses me about literally all of them is their moral certitude in opposing the draft, and that none of them opposed the draft just because they happened to be vulnerable to it themselves or had a son who would be. Hoover's Martin Anderson has no children, and Chris Jehn of the Congressional Budget Office has only a daughter. What impresses me about the incident is that it is the triumph of reason and belief in freedom over a mistaken view of duty. And the role of the economists in this was huge.

Whenever the military has had a little trouble recruiting, advocates of the draft come out from hiding and try to bring it back. Most employers, when they can't get enough employees, ask themselves whether they are paying enough and whether the tasks they want the employees to do are reasonable. Not so with the military. When soldiers are sent to the

Balkans to help impose a quick fix on a centuries-old hatred, for example, it's understandable that American youths who have no quarrel with either side are not excited about enlisting. But rarely do government officials who choose those foreign conquests question the wisdom of their own choices. When they start to push for the draft, the front line of defense against them is still economists.[15]

Some of the politicians who want to reimpose the draft come awfully close to challenging the patriotism of the economists who believe people should be able to choose whether to join the military. Yet what they really show is their own narrow view of patriotism. That point came out in 1979, when I testified against reviving the draft before the Subcommittee on Manpower and Personnel of the U.S. Senate Committee on Armed Services. The following interchange took place between the subcommittee's chairman Senator Sam Nunn, a Democrat from Georgia, and me:

HENDERSON: What I am saying is that the cost of a good quality military is there. There is no avoiding that fact. All you are talking about is whom you make bear the cost. The cost is not any lower when you are paying 30 percent of the budget [in wages]. It is just that you are imposing that cost on these young people. That is what you are advocating. You are not advocating a lower cost military. You are not advocating lower costs of labor. You are just advocating that taxpayers in general not bear the cost and young draftees bear the costs.

SENATOR NUNN: So you don't think anyone has any obligation to the country unless they are paid commensurate with what they want for it? In other words, you reject the premise of any kind of service to the United States of America?

HENDERSON: That is right. I think you have one obligation, and that is to respect other people's rights.

SENATOR NUNN: You have no room for anyone serving the United States of America unless they are adequately paid even in wartime?

HENDERSON: That's right.

SENATOR NUNN: You would have the recruiter come around if were being invaded and ask people how much can we get you for, do we need to raise the ante?

HENDERSON: I think it could be a little more organized than that.

SENATOR NUNN: I don't know. You carry your theory to the logical conclusion, and you have just eliminated the word "patriotism" from the vocabulary.

HENDERSON: No, I haven't. I said pay people whatever it requires to get them. I didn't say that people would not have patriotic motives. In fact, if you believe that people have patriotic motives, why aren't you willing to buy an All-Volunteer Force? If people are so patriotic, they will volunteer at a reasonably low wage. There will be no problem. I am not saying that they are not patriotic. I am saying that the ones who are patriotic will volunteer, and the ones who aren't, won't, and the more patriotic they are, the less you can pay them. That is all right with me.[16]

In Nunn's view, patriotism meant that people should be forced to serve; in my view of patriotism, people choose to serve.

WHOSE BODY IS THIS ANYWAY?

In other important ways, governments in the United States and around the world claim ownership of our bodies. Consider this. If you own your body, don't you have the right to decide what goes on your body? Yet in many U.S. states and Canadian provinces, and in many other countries, if you ride a motorcycle or even a bicycle, you can't make that decision—you must wear a helmet. By making that decision for you, the government is saying, in essence, that it owns you.

Those who want the government to force people to wear helmets argue that helmet laws are required because the taxpayers are stuck with the bill if a motorcycle rider doesn't have insurance or assets to protect him from the consequences of his foolish actions. But I think their argument is insincere. A fair number of motorcycle riders nowadays have ample insurance and assets, and would, if injured, be a burden only on their own resources that they have lined up in advance. Yet I don't see the helmet-law advocates saying that these people should be exempt from having to wear helmets. I strongly suspect that if you scratch a helmet-law advocate, you will find someone who does not believe that you belong to you.

Similarly with laws against various drugs, pharmaceutical or otherwise—if you own your own body and if you have AIDS or some other life-threatening disease, shouldn't you be allowed to take an experimental drug that holds out some hope? So what if the drug company hasn't met the Food and Drug Administration's requirement that the drug be safe and efficacious? By the time the company satisfies the FDA, you may be dead. Yet the drug company is prevented from selling, and you are prevented from buying, that drug. Many of these drugs that the FDA won't allow to be sold in the United States are life-saving drugs available in other countries whose government agencies have approved them, not just poor countries like Mexico but also industrialized countries such as Britain, France, and Japan. Investigative journalist Jonathan Kwitny, formerly a reporter with the *Wall Street Journal,* tells of Jim Corti, a hospital nurse who, in the early 1990s, became a smuggler to get various drugs to his U.S. patients. In Washington, D.C., Corti spoke to an FDA advisory committee, some members of which were doctors who had previously approached him for illegal drugs. Corti said, "Here I am trying to convince you of the value of this compound, and two of you listening to this have already come to me to buy it for your patients." Of the doctors, Kwitny commented, "They offered no signs of reaction."[17]

By deciding what drugs you are allowed to have, the government is substituting its own expertise, such as it is, for the one crucial piece of information on which you are the relative expert: your own thoughts and feelings about risk. The government is saying, in effect, that it knows better than you and that therefore it has the right to say what goes in your body.

David Kessler, while commissioner of the FDA, made a revealing comment in a 1992 article in the prestigious *New England Journal of Medicine*. Wrote Kessler,

> If members of our society were empowered to make their own decisions about the entire range of products for which the FDA has responsibility, however, then the whole rationale for the agency would cease to exist.[18]

I couldn't have said it better.

Similarly, the government will not allow you to take drugs like marijuana, cocaine, LSD, and heroin. The government's stated concern is that you will harm yourself if you take those drugs. No doubt, many of them believe what they say. Nevertheless, the government officials aren't trying to talk you out of something that they think is your decision. They make it very clear, with explicit threats of long prison sentences, that the decision to take those drugs is not yours. They see you as you see a pet, with this difference: When your pet misbehaves you don't lock him up with convicted murderers and pretend that you're doing it for his own good.

No matter what you may learn about those drugs, no matter how valuable you think those drugs would be in your life, your information counts for literally zero. Many Americans who are being treated for cancer and other diseases, for example, are desperately trying to get access to marijuana because it often helps with the nausea they experience from their treatments. Yet in spite of the wishes of a majority of voters in California and in other states, the federal government is taking extreme measures to prevent marijuana from being used for medicinal purposes. The government has threatened to revoke the licenses of doctors who prescribe marijuana. The federal government officials taking these measures are claiming to own your body.

Of course, many government officials don't really mean it when they say that every user of illegal drugs should be thrown in jail. What they really mean is that *you* should be thrown in jail, assuming they don't know you. Jail for their law-breaking kids serves no good purpose. Am I exaggerating? Read the following news story, which appeared in August 1998, and then decide:

The 19-year-old daughter of Gov. George Pataki's running mate was charged with possession of a small amount of marijuana, state police said Tuesday....

Both Pataki and [Sara] Kenney's mother, former Rensselaer County District Attorney Mary Donohue, have admitted to experimenting with marijuana when they were college students.

"What my daughter did was wrong, and she knows that," Donohue said in a statement....We will address this as a family."[19]

Of course, the drug laws *prevent* the rest of us from addressing these matters "as a family." The whole idea of making drugs illegal is to have the government address these matters and replace the family. And whereas the family can't throw someone in jail for using marijuana, the government can and often does.

ENDNOTES

1. From Hermann Rauschning, *The Voice of Destruction,* New York: Putnam's, 1940, pp. 191–193.

2. The story of Simon Gray is taken from Jeffrey Rogers Hummell, *Emancipating Slaves, Enslaving Free Men: A History of the American Civil War,* Peru, Illinois: Open Court, 1996, p. 42.

3. From Jonathan Hughes, *American Economic History,* 3rd ed., New York: HarperCollins, 1990, p. 34. Retold in Jeffrey Rogers Hummell, *Emancipating Slaves, Enslaving Free Men: A History of the American Civil War,* Peru, Illinois: Open Court, 1996, p. 41.

4. Robert L. Heilbroner, *Marxism: For and Against,* New York: W.W. Norton, 1980, p. 157.

5. Allen Drury, *A Senate Journal, 1943–1945,* New York: McGraw-Hill, 1963, p. 360.

6. Drury, *Senate Journal,* p. 396.

7. Drury, *Senate Journal,* p. 400.

8. Drury, *Senate Journal,* p. 384.

9. Drury, *Senate Journal,* p. 400.

10. Drury, *Senate Journal,* p. 402.

11. Drury, *Senate Journal,* p. 404.

12. This section of the bill is reprinted in Drury, *Senate Journal,* pp. 405–406.

13. Quoted in Richard Gillam, "The Peacetime Draft: Voluntarism to Coercion," *Yale Review,* Vol. 57, #4, June 1968.

14. Milton and Rose Friedman, *Two Lucky People,* Chicago: University of Chicago Press, 1998, p. 380.

15. The honor roll of economists who fought off attempts to reintroduce the draft in the late 1970s and early 1980s includes Paul Hogan and Lee Mairs, both military manpower consultants in Washington; Stanley Horowitz, an economist with the Institute for Defense Analysis in Alexandria, VA; and John Warner, an economics professor at Clemson University.

16. From "Reinstitution of Procedures for Registration under the Military Selective Service Act," Hearing before the Subcommittee on Manpower and Personnel of the Committee on Armed Services, U.S. Senate, 96th Congress, First Session, May 21, 1979, p. 169.

17. Jonathan Kwitny, *Acceptable Risks,* Poseidon, 1992, p. 398.

18. David Kessler, *New England Journal of Medicine,* June 1992.

19. Associated Press, August 25, 1998.

YOUR RIGHT
TO PROPERTY

The poorest man may, in his cottage, bid defiance to all the forces of the Crown. It may be frail; its roof may shake; the wind may blow through it; the storm may enter, the rain may enter, but the King of England may not enter; all his forces dare not cross the threshold of the ruined tenement.

—WILLIAM PENN, FOUNDER OF PENNSYLVANIA, CIRCA 1763[1]

A people adverse to the institution of private property is without the first element of freedom.

—LORD ACTON[2]

My friend and former student Charley Hooper once presented the following situation. You walk by a yard and see someone painting a house. Pointing a gun at him is another man who orders the first man to stop painting. Who is in the right? My guess is that you answered "the man who's painting." That's what I answered. After all, the painter is just peacefully doing his own thing. But, pointed out my friend Charley, what you (probably) and I both failed to find out was whose property the house was. It turns out that the man holding the gun owns the property and is simply trying to get the painter off his property because he doesn't want his house painted. Now that we realize that, we think that the man with the gun is in the right. The reason is that we believe in property rights. We believe that someone who owns something has the right to decide how that something is used. If he wants to decide not to let someone paint his house, that's his right.

Most people understand the right to property better in practice than in theory. This was vividly illustrated by economist Gordon Tullock in a class he taught at the University of Virginia in the late 1960s. An undergraduate student in his class said that there was no such thing as property rights; that was a popular position among students in the late 1960s. So Gordon grabbed the student's wallet. The student asked him to give it back, figuring, presumably, that his simple request would get him his wallet back. But Tullock refused, saying that if there was no such thing as property rights, how could he, the student, own this wallet that he claimed as his. Tullock has the ability to "sell" a position, to make you believe that he really believes in what he just did or said, whether he really does or not. Of course Tullock, a strong believer in property rights, believed that the student's wallet really was the student's, but no way was he going to let the student know that. So Tullock held firm but asked the student why he believed that the wallet was his. The student then told him that he himself had acquired it by peaceful means and hadn't stolen it. Once he laid that out, Tullock gave him back his wallet.

Notice that I said "*back his* wallet." In using the words *back* and *his,* I'm saying that the wallet was owned by the student. And those are the words you probably would have used also. Wouldn't it have been strange had I said that Tullock gave the student Tullock's wallet, or the government's wallet, or the wallet that no one owned? The fact is that the student owned the wallet and the vast majority of people accept that fact. Indeed, when people don't accept the fact of ownership and when they act on that nonacceptance, we have a term for them. We call them thieves.

An incident happened when I was about nine years old that gave me my first real understanding of the power of property rights in protecting people. The incident occurred at Minaki, a summer-resort community in Canada, where my father had half ownership, with his brother, of a modest cottage they had inherited from their father. Because my father was a teacher and my mother raised us three kids full-time, we were probably about the lowest-income people who owned a cottage at Minaki. My father and I were out in our canoe in front of the Minaki Lodge, a large hotel complex where people whom we thought of as really rich stayed. (My father's working definition of "rich," I see in retrospect, tended to be anyone with an income that exceeded ours by over 30 percent.) When we paddled by the Lodge, we recognized the Lodge's manager on the shore, walking his large dog. Our dog, Laddie, was in our canoe, and the large dog started barking at Laddie and going absolutely ape. Then he swam out towards our canoe as if he planned to board it. We worried that Laddie, barking loudly and himself getting increasingly agitated, would jump into the water, try to fight the dog, get hurt, and maybe even drown.

My father yelled angrily at the manager, "Call your dog off." The manager yelled angrily back at my father, and so my father yelled even louder and more angrily, "Call your dog off." This went on for a while, until the manager called his dog off, or the dog, tiring, returned to the shore on his own. I don't remember which.

What I do remember is my incredible fear that the police would come and take my father away. After all, he had yelled angrily at someone who owned (actually managed, not owned, but at that age I didn't make that distinction) a big resort. My father was always complaining about the rich and how they ran everything and there was no room for the little man, and I believed him. So that night, I went to bed afraid that the manager would bring the police to take my father. When I woke up the next morning, nothing had happened. My father went on with his day as if what had happened the previous day was no big deal. And I realized that my father didn't seem at all worried about it. That's when I started to relax and feel secure. Without knowing the term "property rights," I thought that having our own land that people couldn't walk on without permission was really neat. I had just discovered the power of property rights. Whenever I hear someone say that property rights are important only for the rich, I think of that day at Minaki when I learned the truth.

Later in life, when I was in graduate school at UCLA, I learned about the important economic effects of property rights from an economics professor named Armen Alchian, who had made his reputation on that issue. Alchian pointed out that a huge amount of human behavior could be understood if you got straight what the property rights were. In the first class, he gave us two examples of things that didn't work well. One was the student bookstore on campus, where you had to line up for hours to buy books; the other was student parking, which was priced low and oversubscribed. You will feel angry standing in line for books and being unable to get a parking sticker, he said, but what you should notice is that those two examples show that economics works. (Actually, Alchian said, in his impish manner, that you should really feel happy instead of angry, but I'm trying to tell you what I got out of his first lecture—it wasn't happiness.) The student bookstore isn't run well because no one owns it, he pointed out. His point was that no individual or company had a profit motive or a strong incentive to avoid losses. Someone working at the bookstore who figures out a better way of running it doesn't get paid more for doing so, whereas if the store were private property, the owner would have a strong incentive to figure out ways of improving it, because the owner could collect much of the value he or she created. Similarly, Alchian said, the campus employees who decide what price to set on parking have an incentive to set a low price. A high price would earn more revenue for the university, but that revenue would not go in the decision-makers' pockets. However, he pointed out, because the people setting the parking fee are assured of a space, they have an incentive to set a low fee because they will pay that fee. But the low price meant also that we students were not assured of a parking place.

Years later, Tom Hazlett, an economist who also studied under Alchian, used Alchian's insight about the parking fee to explain why Michigan congressman John Dingell, who at the time headed the House Commerce Committee, strongly opposed auctioning off valuable electromagnetic spectrum to broadcasters and other users. Dingell wanted instead to give away the licenses for specific uses and limited periods of time.

Hazlett pointed out that if the government auctioned the spectrum to the highest bidder, the billions of dollars gained would not benefit Dingell. Moreover, the Federal Communications Commission's power to allocate spectrum would drop to zero: When something is allocated to the highest bidder, the bidders, not the auctioneer, determine who gets it. Therefore, Dingell, who had a big oversight role over the FCC, would find his power over allocation dropping to zero also. Without that power, people wouldn't invite him to dinners and hunting parties as frequently, would contribute less to his campaign fund, and would return his calls less quickly, if at all. In short, he would be a less important man in Washington, and probably a less wealthy one.

Interestingly, one of the clearest documented instances in U.S. history of political power moving in to fill the vacuum left when property rights are not well defined occurred with a radio license granted by the FCC. There was once a congressman who used his political power over the FCC to create a fortune for himself. The cornerstone of that fortune was a license from the FCC to operate a radio station. In 1943, he and his wife had a net worth of approximately zero. But by 1964, when he was elected President of the United States, their net worth was at least $14 million, and the radio station's value accounted for about half of this $14 million. The congressman's and President's name: Lyndon B. Johnson.

LBJ's line during his 1964 campaign, which only *Wall Street Journal* reporter Louis M. Kohlmeier and a few other reporters questioned, was that his wife, who owned radio station KTBC in Austin, Texas, had turned an asset she bought for $17,500 into a property worth millions by working hard. Not quite. Instead, as biographer Robert Caro dramatically documents in his masterful biography *The Years of Lyndon Johnson: Means of Ascent,*[3] LBJ was the one who worked hard—at using his political influence. Between December 1939 and January 1943, despite countless attempts, KTBC's owners were unable to get permission from the FCC to let them sell the station. But on January 3, 1943, Mrs. Johnson filed her application to buy the station and just 24 days later, after having previously waited over three years, the owners were allowed to sell. In June 1943, Mrs. Johnson applied for permission to operate 24 hours a day, up from daylight hours only, and at a much better part of the AM frequency, and was granted permission just one month later. While all this was happening, the FCC was under attack by a powerful congressman, Eugene Cox of Georgia. Lyndon Johnson strategized secretly with FCC official Red James and used his influence with House speaker Sam Rayburn to deflect the attack. In fact, James later admitted that he had recommended to Mrs. Johnson that she apply for the license. Lyndon Johnson further enhanced the station's value by doing political favors in return for ad revenues. With the Office of Price Administration (OPA) creating shortages by imposing wartime price controls, scarce goods were often allocated to businesses with political influence. LBJ used his influence to get higher allocations for those who advertised on his station. Months after grocery retailer Howard E. Butt started advertising on KTBC in 1943, for example, Johnson intervened with the OPA to allocate to Butt 150,000 extra cases of grapefruit.

The case of LBJ is one of the more dramatic instances of a government official using his power, when property rights are absent or ill-defined, to make himself rich at others' expense. But it is also very common. When government hands things out or underprices them, politically well-connected people inside and outside government will take advantage of this and capture much of the value that would have otherwise been captured by property owners.

Of course, to be powerful protectors of people, property rights must be respected. Yet even though the vast majority of people respect each other's property rights in the most important ways—only a small percent of people, for example, would ever try to steal your car or break into your house—the various levels of government in the United States are increasingly disrespecting our property rights. Under various federal, state, and local laws, governments can now seize our cars, houses, and money if they even suspect that those assets were somehow involved in a drug crime, for example. The government agents don't even need to charge you with a crime in order to keep the assets. To get your assets back, you need to prove that you are innocent, a complete inversion of the usual presumption of innocence absent proof of guilt. And your court and legal costs will not be covered even if you prevail. No wonder that innocent people, when the government seizes their cars worth only a few thousand dollars, don't bother to get their cars back. Joe McNamara, a colleague of mine at Hoover, told me that one year, while he was police chief in San Jose, California, he noticed that there was no money in his proposed budget to buy cars. When he asked why, one of his budget people told him that they didn't need to budget for that because they would probably seize assets under the asset forfeiture laws to give the department enough new cars.

Another way in which governments increasingly disrespect our property rights has to do with land use. Take the sad case of Poletown.[4] Poletown was a section of Detroit in which General Motors decided, in 1980, that it wanted to build a Cadillac factory. There was only one problem: Poletown had 4,200 residents, many of whom owned the modest houses they lived in, and many of these residents didn't want to move. Now if I ask you to sell me your briefcase and you say no, that seems like the end of the discussion, doesn't it? Well, that wasn't the end of the discussion. In fact, if GM and the high-ranking politicians in Detroit had had their way, there would have been no discussion. The city government, run by Coleman Young, a former socialist, decided to use its power under Michigan's Uniform Condemnation Act of 1980—the aptly named "quick-take law"—to grab the land, force the owners to sell without their consent, and mow down their houses. To make matters worse, owners were often paid a below-market price. When residents complained loudly, U.S. Senator Donald Riegle criticized them, refused to meet with them, and said that their resistance "borders on the irresponsible." Michigan's other U.S. Senator, Carl Levin, complained that Ralph Nader's request for hearings on the issue was "audacious." The only Michigan politician who showed any sympathy for the residents was U.S. Representative John Conyers. As a result, the Poletown residents lost their houses, and a neighborhood was destroyed.

Nor is this case unusual. When the Brooklyn Dodgers were enticed to move to Los Angeles in the late 1950s, one of the attractions was the chance to build Dodger Stadium in Chavez Ravine. Chavez Ravine, at the time a largely Mexican community of single-family houses, was destroyed and the house owners were paid a fraction of their houses' value. Urban renewal, which the federal government used in the 1950s and 1960s to tear down homes in poorer areas and build homes for higher income people, depended crucially on the government's ability to take the homes rather than buy them from willing sellers. Federal regulations on wetlands prevent private owners from using their land as they wish. Because there is no fixed legal definition of *wetland,* the ambiguity gives the government discretionary power over people's lives. Robert J. Pierce, an Army Corps of Engineers official who helped formulate a 1989 definition of *wetland,* admitted as much. He wrote: "For regulatory purposes, a wetland is whatever we decide it is."[5] One victim of this discretion, Bill Ellen, actually went to prison for building duck ponds on his own property. Even though Ellen had gotten all the necessary permits, a change in the definition of *wetland* led the Army Corps of Engineers to tell him to stop. He did stop within 48 hours, but was prosecuted anyway. The Army Corps proceeded to dynamite his duck ponds, destroying the wetland.[6] But I guess by their definition, since *wetland* means whatever they want it to mean, they didn't destroy his wetland.

One of the biggest insights economists have ever had about the beneficial effects of property rights and the harmful effects of their absence is summarized in something labeled "the tragedy of the commons." The label was coined, not by an economist, but by a famous ecologist named Garrett Hardin in a 1968 article in *Science*.[7] But the insight he laid out was from William Forster Lloyd, an economist who lived over 100 years earlier, who noticed that common lands in Britain were overgrazed and private grazing lands were not. The reason, explained Lloyd and later Hardin, is that when no one owns the land, each user has an incentive to overuse it. So as not to destroy the grass, I may hold back for a while on the number of cattle I graze on the land in common. But my holding back doesn't work. I don't get more grass for my cattle later, because meanwhile you or other cattle owners decide to graze more cattle to take advantage of the grass I save. Even if the vast majority of us exercise restraint, it takes only a few of what Hardin calls "non-angels" to overuse the land. Once the rest of us figure out that by restraining our use, we are acting like suckers, we start overusing too.

We see instances of the tragedy of the commons all around us. In the office building on my campus, I have quasi-ownership of my office, as do my colleagues of theirs. But not so for the hallways. A favorite technique that many of us have used when we want to get rid of old furniture is to dump it in the hall and hope that someone will come and take it. In essence, we treat the hallway as common property. The streets of a city are essentially a commons, which is why they're much dirtier than the stores and houses that are on them.

The tragedy of the commons can explain many other phenomena, big and small. It explains why many species of animals have disappeared or are in danger of disappearing. Often, for example, governments turn species into "commons" by banning ownership of them. But making it impossible to own a fish or an animal alive means that the only way to own it is to kill it, legally or otherwise. Thus we have overfishing and overhunting of various fish and animals, with consequent threat of extinction. By contrast, the reason cows are not about to become extinct is that people can own them. And the countries in Africa that allow communities to profit from having elephants on their land have expanding elephant populations for one main reason: The communities have a strong incentive to reduce poaching.

As you may have gathered by now, the best way to solve the tragedy of the commons, if at all feasible, is to convert it from a commons to private property. When people own things, they become stewards of those things, taking much better care of them than when they don't own them. Thus the statement that we often hear people say when they lend something precious, "Treat it as if it were your own." Everyone past about age five understands, deep down, that we treat things better when we own them—which makes the contemporary hostility to property rights puzzling.

I was reminded of the power of property rights when I was recently at the cottage in Minaki that I now co-own with my cousin. He and I were both preparing late one day to leave early the next day, when a sudden wind whipped up and blew a tree over our cabin, punching two big holes in the roof. For a few minutes, I fantasized about being a renter. As a renter, my only obligation would have been a moral one to call the owner; then I would have been able to go back to the really important thing: packing. But my cousin and I are owners, and so that night we spent three hours with a chain saw cutting the branches and tree away and made a list of everything we would need to repair the roof. Early the next morning we drove into the nearest city, purchased the necessary materials, and spent about ten hours, until 8:00 in the evening, fixing the roof. Ownership transforms the tragedy of the commons into the wonder of stewardship.

The example of my cottage seems basic, right? Why do I bother giving you an example that contains no surprises and is just common sense to everyone? Because, somehow, that common sense deserts many people when they start thinking about private property more generally. Otherwise, how can you explain the attraction that socialism has for many people? Imagine a whole economy in which almost nothing is privately owned. Actually, we don't need to stretch our imaginations very far, because in the Soviet Union and other socialist countries, almost no production plants, farms, or other physical assets were privately owned. And the results could have been predicted, although few people other than Hayek and von Mises predicted them. When no one owns anything, the resources of the country become one vast commons, with very little incentive to take care of things. Why bother to make sure that the product you produce is a good one when you don't get rewarded for producing a better product, because your boss doesn't get rewarded, because the factory owner—there is no owner—doesn't get rewarded? Or, to take another example, why would you bother to take care of the environment when you can't keep the benefits of preserving the environment? Khrushchev and Brezhnev, high officials in the Soviet Union in the 1950s and 1960s, poisoned the Aral Sea with run-off herbicides and insecticides in a futile attempt to turn the Kara Kum Desert into a rich farmland.[8] The wonder is that for 70 years people claimed that socialism was some kind of ideal. How can it be ideal to set up a system that takes away people's protections, destroys their incentive to work, and consigns hundreds of millions of people to grinding lifetime poverty and early death?

Not only do property rights give people a strong incentive to invest to steward their property, making themselves richer in the process, but they also resolve many problems and prevent many conflicts. We don't often realize this, because the conflicts prevented are...prevented. To see what happens when people aren't allowed to own property, visit any Indian reservation in Canada or the United States. On my vacation described above, I spoke to a man who runs a store on a Canadian reservation. I made the point that the inability of people on that reservation to own their own houses strictly limited the amount they were willing to invest in improving "their" houses. He responded that the fundamental problem was that various factions on the reservation are always at each other's throats. But this wasn't a fundamental problem; it was a derivative problem. Imagine what would happen if you had to get a coalition together every time you wanted to paint your house. You would start complaining about "factions."

Property rights also resolve other issues. Should, for example, people be allowed to petition for various causes on the parking lots of supermarkets? The Supreme Court ruled in the early 1970s that they should, because petitioning is a free speech right. But the venerable justices showed a fundamental misunderstanding of free speech. My right to free speech doesn't give me a right to speak in your house without your permission any more than it gives me a right to a working larynx. My right to free speech simply gives me the right to use my own resources to speak. What the justices literally ignored was the property rights of the owners of the supermarket parking lot. Free speech means I have the right to have my speech protected if I'm speaking where I have a right to be.

That misunderstanding among the Supreme Court justices goes back to the early twentieth century. One of the most famous statements from a Supreme Court justice is Oliver Wendell Holmes's statement, "The most stringent protection of free speech would not protect a man in falsely shouting fire in a theatre and causing a panic."[9] But, as the late economist Murray Rothbard has pointed out, private ownership solves the problem. The theatre owner has no interest in allowing someone to shout "fire" in a crowded theatre unless there is in fact a fire. Someone who falsely yelled "fire" in a crowded theatre would be liable for damages caused. Few people who quote the line know its context. Holmes used the fire analogy to justify the Court's decision, in *Schenck v. United States,* to deny the free-speech rights of two socialists who were critical of conscription during World War I. In their pamphlets, these war protesters wrote that the Thirteenth Amendment prohibited involuntary servitude and therefore the World War I draft was unconstitutional. Holmes apparently saw quoting the Constitution as being similar to misleading theatre-goers about fire.

Take another issue: Should people be allowed to smoke in restaurants or bars? Government officials in California have answered "no" and enforce their answer with threats of fines. But they completely ignore the wishes of the people who own the restaurants and bars. The crucial question is not whether secondhand smoke has long-term health consequences for nonsmoking customers and waiters. Even if the secondhand smoke has no harmful health effects, most of us nonsmokers find smoke incredibly unpleasant. But if the restaurant or bar is privately owned, the owner has the incentive to trade off, in an unbiased way, the wishes of smokers and of nonsmokers. If, by allowing smoking, he or she must give up the business of some nonsmokers and pay nonsmoking waiters slightly more, the owner will do so if he or she can more than offset the loss if revenue and increase in costs with higher revenue from smokers. The rights of nonsmokers are not violated; they never had the right to require someone to cater to their wishes. Of course, most restaurant owners find that the optimal strategy is to have smoking and nonsmoking sections. But this strategy is made illegal in California and other places whose governments use their edicts to violate owners' property rights.

ENDNOTES

1. Quoted in Michael Barone, "The law and a little boy," *U.S. News & World Report,* May 8, 2000, p. 29.

2. Quoted in Jim Powell, , *The Triumph of Liberty,* Free Press, 2000, p. 345.

3. Robert A. Caro, *The Years of Lyndon Johnson: Means of Ascent,* New York: Alfred A. Knopf, 1990, pp. 82–111.

4. The story is told in Jeanie Wylie, *Poletown: Community Betrayed,* Urbana: University of Illinois Press, 1989.

5. Robert J. Pierce, "Redefining Our Regulatory Goals," *National Wetlands Newsletter,* November/December 1991, p. 12, as quoted in James Bovard, *Lost Rights,* New York: St. Martin's Press, 1994, p. 34.

6. James Bovard, *Lost Rights,* p. 36.

7. Garrett Hardin, "The Tragedy of the Commons," *Science* 162 (1968), pp. 1243–48.

8. This issue is discussed in Jim Rogers, *Investment Biker,* New York: Random House, 1994, p. 45.

9. Quoted in Louis H. Pollak, ed., *The Constitution and the Supreme Court: A Documentary History,* Vol. 2, Cleveland: World Publishing Co., 1966, pp. 8–9.

6

FREEDOM
OF ASSOCIATION

⬜ ne morning in March 1980, I woke up to the sun streaming into the bedroom of my Oakland, California apartment. "Wouldn't it be nice," I thought, "to wear my bright yellow t-shirt to work?" I wanted to wear something that reflected my disposition, but another thought immediately darkened my mood. I realized that I couldn't wear the t-shirt because that wasn't allowed where I worked. My boss had made it clear that a tie, dress shirt, and jacket were required. Suddenly I felt like a slave (other aspects of my job besides the dress code had been getting to me lately). Then I had a new thought: I can wear whatever I want; it's just that I couldn't dress that way and keep my job.

That new thought was both scary and exciting. Suddenly I felt very powerful. What I had just discovered, in a very personal and tangible way, was freedom of association. I was free to associate, or not, with my employer.

With my newfound power, I felt incredible clarity. My head no longer clouded by fuzzy thinking about what I *couldn't* do, I thought through the pros and cons of my job and decided to quit. Whether or not it was the right move—I think it was—is beside the point. The point is that I was able to think more clearly when I understood that I was *freely choosing* my job. And you are where you are because of your own choices; unless you are reading this in prison, you are free to make different choices if you'd rather be somewhere else.

You can quit your job at any time, but that doesn't mean there won't be consequences. Freedom isn't the power to make decisions without bad consequences. If there were no consequences, then freedom would be a lot like one of those little cars for 3-year-olds, the ones whose steering wheels can turn without affecting the direction the car goes. Instead—to extend the analogy—freedom is a *real* car; feel free to turn the steering wheel toward that big tree, but expect to pay for the damage to your car. Freedom is, simply put, the power to make decisions and bear the consequences. Even though you may dislike some aspects of your job, you might want the money, the companionship, or the on-the-job learning you're getting enough to put up with the things you don't like. You make tradeoffs.

Since I quit that job in 1980, I've had negative feelings about other jobs. In one case, I left the job, but not right away, because I still had more to learn before I left. In another case, I kept the job—it's the one I have now—because I figured out how to make it in my employer's interest to give me some of the things I wanted. When you want something from an employer, the easiest way to get it is to let your employer benefit too. The best jobs, as job counselors will tell you, are created by employees; employers rarely hand you the ideal job on a platter. If you want to create a job you'll love, you do best at designing such a job when you are clear that both you and your employer are free to associate.

I said that when I considered quitting my job in 1980, I discovered, in a personal way, the freedom of association. That's not quite accurate. What I did was *re*discover freedom of association. As I mentioned in Chapter 1, in the summer of 1968, I quit a well-paying job with the federal government because I concluded that my employer had no right to be involved in the activity it had hired me for. I consciously exercised my freedom not to associate with that particular employer.

I tell this story because sometimes, when I tell people that they are, or should be, free to associate with others, they reply, "That's easy for you to say. You're sitting in a cushy job and you're wealthy. But people with very low incomes are forced to work for employers they don't like." Even when I was 17 and had a net worth of less than $1,000, I didn't see it that way. Having or exercising freedom of association doesn't depend on wealth. Of course, if you're wealthy, choices tend to be easier. But even if you're dirt poor, you can choose whether or not to work for a particular employer. In fact, realizing that fact and acting on it are the start to getting out of poverty.

Virtually all of us understand and appreciate freedom of association in our personal lives. Think about friendship. Although some people may have strong negative opinions about your choice of friends, they are just that—their *opinions*. These people have no legal power to prevent you from becoming friends with anyone you choose. Friendship is truly the area of our lives in which laissez-faire—a fancy French phrase for freedom—is honored most.

Freedom of association always has two parts. One part is the freedom to associate with someone. The other, just as important, part is the freedom *not* to associate with someone. I can choose to be your friend or not to be your friend. And we can't associate with each other unless we both choose to.

FREEDOM TO CHOOSE A ROOMMATE

Imagine that you're a homosexual and would like to live with a homosexual roommate. Or imagine that you're a heterosexual and would like to live with a heterosexual roommate. Guess what? Some governments in the United States claim that you don't have the right to make such a choice. In Madison, Wisconsin, recently, the government fined a woman for refusing to accept a lesbian roommate. The woman took her case all the way up to the U.S. Supreme Court, which, in May 1997, refused to hear the case.[1] By doing so, the Supreme Court upheld this extreme intrusion on the freedom of association. Is freedom to choose your friends the next area that, with the Supreme Court's blessing, governments in the United States will assault?

SEXUAL FREEDOM AND ROMANTIC FREEDOM

Freedom of association also applies to dating and sex. People are free to say no to those who ask them out on dates or who ask them for sex. In fact, everyone knows the word for the violation of another's freedom to say no to sex. We call it rape. My impression is that governments in the United States completely respect half of the freedom of association in sex, the freedom to say no. It was not always so. In the nineteenth century and before, when a man raped his slave, the courts did not step in and punish him. Back then, judges, and indeed most people, believed that rape did not violate a slave's freedom of association because they didn't consider slaves human beings with rights.

Governments still, however, don't consistently respect the other half of freedom of association in sex, the freedom to say yes and to act on it. In some states, certain forms of sex are illegal. Georgia's government, for example, says that a "person commits the offense of sodomy when he performs or submits to any sexual act involving the sex organs of one person and the mouth or anus of another."[2] If you find this language distasteful, welcome to the club, but don't blame me. Instead, put the blame where it properly falls, on the Georgia state legislators who felt the need to define sodomy so they could ban it, and backed their definition with a prison sentence of up to 20 years. And, remember, we're talking about consensual, not forced, sex. In 1986, incidentally, the U.S. Supreme Court, in *Bowers v. Hardwick,* upheld Georgia's sodomy law by a 5–4 vote. So even in such an intimate area as sex, we have a long way to go to get to complete freedom of association.

I would like to say that freedom to choose our marriage partner is just as accepted and understood as freedom to choose our friends. I would like to, but I can't. It took until 1967, hardly ancient history, for the Supreme Court, in *Loving v. Virginia,* to strike down a state law that banned interracial marriage. And as I write this, in the fall of 1998, serious people with political power advocate that a man not be allowed to marry the man of his choice and that a woman not be allowed to marry a woman.[3] So, even though freedom of association in our friendships, in our sexual relations, and in our choice of marriage partners is respected, it is by no means *completely* respected. I hope this changes, but we're not there yet.

FREEDOM OF ASSOCIATION FOR WORKERS AND EMPLOYERS

Government's official disrespect for freedom of association in sex and marriage pales when compared to the way it tramples on freedom of association for workers and employers. Governments in the United States, in Europe, in Latin America, in most of Asia, indeed in most countries, legally prevent employers and employees from associating with each other in many ways. This happens no matter how much the employers and employees would gain from associating with each other.

HOMEWORK IN VERMONT

In 1980, the U.S. Labor Department, under President Carter, discovered a number of women in Vermont were knitting in their homes and being paid by the piece. The government charged the women with illegally doing homework (not to be confused with the kind that school children do, which, if found illegal, would lead to millions of kids dancing in the streets). Among those who were barred from working at home were young women with children, disabled women who had trouble working outside their homes, and older women. The Labor Department tried to enforce regulations that had been introduced in the early 1940s. Why would the government try to ban such work? Because the International Ladies' Garment Workers Union, to prevent competition, lobbied for the ban. Worried that their members' relatively high wages would be undercut by women working at home, and worried that the government would not be able to enforce the minimum wage law on homework, the union had persuaded President Franklin Roosevelt and his Secretary of Labor, Frances Perkins, to ban the practice outright.

But the Vermont women decided to defend their freedom. In response to their complaints, newly elected President Ronald Reagan held hearings in 1981. The reason I am so familiar with the case is that I testified at the hearings (for my testimony, go to my Web site, *www.davidrhenderson.com*). After reading that the hearings were to be held in Washington, I decided that I just had to be there. Here were these dozens and dozens of women peacefully minding their own business, literally sticking to their knitting, and the federal government was trying to shut them down. I had to help them. So I called the Council for a Competitive Economy (the predecessor of the Competitive Enterprise Institute, a Washington-based public-interest group that lobbies for economic freedom), persuaded them to let me represent their organization, got the Labor Department to put me on their witness list, and flew to Washington on the appointed date.

At the hearings, held in February 1981, both the union and the unionized companies had to hide their real reason for wanting to ban homework: to prevent these pesky women from competing. Such naked assertion of self-interest, with members of the public present, was risky. (Without the public present, it happens all the time. As I learned a year later, when I worked in the same Labor Department, union representatives and representatives of unionized firms are quite prepared to assert their naked self-interest. Interestingly, whenever the career civil servants I talked to in the Labor Department talked about getting the views of "the public," they didn't mean the public in any real sense of that word; instead, they meant representatives of labor unions and of unionized firms.) So they would argue, I figured, that the companies paying for piecework were exploiting the women. I figured right.

But the absurdity of their position was apparent. Picture the scene. Spokesmen for the union and unionized firms testified with straight faces that the women working at home were being exploited. Yet, sitting not 50 feet from them were some of these women, who had traveled all the way to Washington, on a weekday and at their own expense, to fight for the right to continue making ski caps and other items on a piecework basis. The women obviously didn't think they were exploited, as some of them in their testimony, and I in mine, pointed out. The women who testified pointed out that homework was giving them an opportunity. Many of them wanted, whether because of age, health, or desire to be with their young children, to work at home. How could they be worse off if they were *choosing* this opportunity? And if this choice made them better off, which, by their action, they were saying it did, how could this be exploitation?

Robert Rosenfeld, a Cleveland lawyer who represented unionized apparel firms, testified in favor of banning homework. One of his key arguments was that the opportunity that homework gives people to work for low wages was like the opportunity that both the poor and the rich have to sleep in the park at night. His point was that this was not a real opportunity, because only poor people would find it attractive. What he failed to recognize (or admit) was that sleeping in the park, as miserable as that might be, is far preferable to having nowhere to sleep. If the government succeeded in prohibiting these women from working at home, then they would go to a worse alternative, not a better one.

Under the rules of the hearing, anyone who testified and agreed to be questioned by even one person had to agree to answer questions from anyone in the hearing room. I saw my opening. I stood and approached Rosenfeld. "Your analogy between sleeping in the park at night and working at home for low wages is appropriate," I told him. "Are you saying," I asked, "that you would prevent poor people even from sleeping in the park?" I've forgotten his answer, but I'll never forget the look of utter surprise on his face. That alone was worth the trip. Rosenfeld had probably been so used to ending discussions with the park analogy (similar to nineteenth-century French writer Anatole France's analogy with the right of rich and poor to sleep under bridges) that he didn't know how to handle someone who turned the analogy against him.

Later that morning, union official Alex Rose testified that these women really wouldn't be out of a job if the ban on homework remained, because they could get jobs in factories where they would be paid at least the minimum wage. Not only the rest of us, but also Mr. Rose himself, seemed unconvinced. His tone suggested that he just didn't care whether these annoying women found work or not. I noticed also that whenever he happened to look over at the Vermont women, he looked angry and bitter. So I played a hunch.

"Do you know of a woman named Cecile Duffany?" I asked him.

"No," he said curtly.

"Mrs. Duffany has acute arthritis in her hips and she can't work in a factory," I explained. "If this ban stays, Mrs. Duffany will be out of work. What would you have her do?"

"If she can work in her home, she can work in a factory!" he snapped angrily.

"Thank you," I said, and sat down.

Mr. Rose had shown, to all those present, how little he cared about these women.

Unfortunately, there was no happy ending for the women. Although the Reagan administration ended the homework restrictions in six of the seven apparel industries in which they had existed, a federal appeals courts later overturned that decision. The court argued that enforcing the minimum wage law trumped the right of people to work in their homes.[4] In the United States of America, you can still be busted—if you're selling to someone who pays piece rate—for knitting ski caps in your home.

THE MINIMUM WAGE

Another way the U.S. government violates workers' freedom of association is with the minimum wage law, the law that requires employers to pay at least the minimum, currently $5.15 an hour, to employees unless they are legally exempt.

Try this experiment. Go to the library and pull out any introductory economics textbooks you find. Look under the heading "minimum wage" and see what the textbooks say. Here's my prediction: In more than 90 percent of the textbooks, and maybe even in 100 percent, you'll find a statement that the minimum wage hurts some unskilled workers by pricing them out of their jobs. Economists have done hundreds of studies of the minimum wage and all but a few have found that the law destroys jobs for those who are least skilled.

The first federal minimum wage in the United States was passed in 1938. Within a few years, economists were writing about its harmful effects. The first well-known analysis of the minimum wage appeared in a 1944 book that is still available. The book *The American Dilemma*, thought of as a classic in sociology, was written by economist Gunnar Myrdal, a Swedish socialist who shared the Nobel Prize for economics in 1974 along with Friedrich Hayek. *The American Dilemma* was the end product of a study that the Carnegie Corporation had commissioned on what was then delicately called the "Negro question." Although it is better known for Myrdal's critique of the "separate but equal" doctrine that played a large role in the Supreme Court's famous 1954 school desegregation ruling in *Brown v. Board of Education of Topeka*, the book also contains solid economic reasoning. "When government steps in to regulate labor conditions and to enforce minimum standards," wrote Myrdal, "it takes away nearly all that is left of the old labor monopoly in the 'Negro jobs.'"[5] What Myrdal was saying was that the minimum wage destroys black people's jobs.

Not much has changed. The minimum wage still destroys jobs for unskilled workers, a disproportionate number of whom are black. In 1994, David Card and Alan Krueger, two economists at Princeton University, conducted a study of a minimum-wage increase in New Jersey.[6] Supposedly, the increase did not reduce employment of unskilled teenagers in New Jersey fast-food restaurants relative to employment in Pennsylvania restaurants, where the minimum wage had not been increased. The Clinton administration, particularly Clinton's labor secretary Robert Reich, leaned heavily on this study in justifying its 1996 increase in the minimum wage. There's only one problem, as I pointed out in "Rush to Judgment," my review of their book: The study was based on poor data.[7] The authors surveyed managers of fast-food restaurants and asked them the number of full-time and part-time employees without ever specifying what they meant by "part-time" or "full-time." But two other economists, David Neumark of Michigan State University and William Wascher of the Board of Governors of the Federal Reserve System, redid the Card-Krueger study, using more reliable payroll data, and found that employment in New Jersey fast-food restaurants did, indeed, decline relative to employment in Pennsylvania fast-food restaurants.

Of course, the minimum wage does raise wages for many workers, but this doesn't mean that those workers are better off. Higher minimum wages don't suddenly make unskilled workers more productive. Employers often respond by cutting other components of the compensation package, whether in the form of health benefits, free or subsidized meals, or training.

REASONING FROM PRINCIPLE

You can do a sophisticated economic analysis of the minimum wage to reach a conclusion about its merits—or lack of them. But you can reach the same conclusion by simply applying the basic principle embodied in freedom of association: No one should be allowed to interfere in the exchanges of anyone else. And that's exactly what the minimum wage does. This is not a coincidence. It comes about because of a very powerful fact, one of the most important facts economics has come up with: Both parties gain from an exchange. If people didn't see themselves as gaining, they wouldn't keep trading. A corollary of the principle of gains from exchange is that when someone inter-feres in an exchange between you and someone else, you will likely be worse off; and if the person interferes enough to *pre-vent* the exchange (as the minimum wage often does), you will *definitely* be worse off. I'm taking as given, of course, some-thing that is usually, but not always, true—namely, that each person is the best judge of his or her own best interests.

I've often seen how clearly people with no economics back-ground can think when they just latch on to, and apply with-out compromise, some simple principles. Freedom of associa-tion is one such principle. It clarifies and cuts through so much of the fuzz that surrounds discussions of people's legal rights and obligations in the workplace.

Take the case of a woman in Bangladesh who wants to work for a few dimes an hour making clothing. Freedom of associa-tion says that she should be free to do that. Economics says that her choice of that job means that she sees herself as bet-ter off in that job than in the other jobs available to her. Therefore, preventing her from taking the job, or preventing a multinational company from hiring her, would make her worse off. Again, whether we follow the principle of freedom of asso-ciation or the principle of gains from exchange, we reach the same conclusion: The woman should be allowed to work for a very low wage if that is what she chooses. Indeed, the British charity Oxfam reported that when some factory owners in Bangladesh were persuaded a few years ago not to hire some children, the children either starved or became prostitutes.[8]

In 1996 I wrote an article in *Fortune* magazine[9] making these points about so-called "sweatshops" in poor countries. I also pointed out that interviews of the "sweatshop" workers quoted in the *New York Times* found, as could have been pre-dicted, that these workers liked their jobs better than the even harder, less well-paying jobs they had left. One worker in Honduras told the *Times,* "This is an enormous advance, and I give thanks to the *maquila* [factory] for it." I criticized then U.S. Labor Secretary Robert Reich and a U.S. labor-union-funded organization called the National Labor Committee for trying to get these workers put out of work while feigning con-cern for them. In response, Reich wrote a sarcastic letter to

Fortune,[10] beginning, "It's hard to romanticize the exploitation of child labor, but in 'The Case for Sweatshops' David Henderson tries." Interestingly, though, Reich didn't challenge my facts or my reasoning. He seemed to think that sarcasm would be enough to divert his readers' attention from the real issues. For some readers, it may have worked. I pointed out in my response to Reich's letter that he and some other letter writers "have no answer to my point that you hurt people, not help them, by stripping them of the best of their bad choices."

Imagine my surprise, then, when I later learned that Reich had defended child labor long before he attacked my views. In his book, *Locked in the Cabinet,*[11] Reich recounted the story of a 14-year-old batboy named Tommy McCoy, who, in 1993, worked for the Savannah Cardinals, a Class A farm team for the Atlanta Braves. Reich's Labor Department enforcers of the child labor laws had discovered that the Cardinals were using his services after 7:00 p.m., a practice that was illegal under U.S. child-labor laws. After Reich's department threatened the baseball team with a stiff fine, the team fired Tommy. Interestingly, his enforcers' big argument for making sure Tommy could not get his job back was that, in Reich's words, "if we don't support our investigators, they'll become demoralized." In other words, the enforcers' trump card was to defend enforcement on the grounds that it made *them* better off. Reich's explanation might sound unusually candid, but, as I had learned when I worked in the Labor Department ten years earlier, it wasn't. When the cameras and tape recorders aren't turned on, government regulators will often admit that they make many of their decisions to suit themselves.

To his credit, Reich told his enforcers to back off and insisted on changing the regulations so that Tommy could work. But his reasoning on that case, three years before he attacked child labor in *Fortune,* is interesting. Here it is, in Reich's words:

> They [the Labor Department regulators] say there's nothing we can do. The law is the law.
>
> "Nonsense," I say. "We can change the regulation to make an exception for kids at sporting events."

But then we'll invite all sorts of abuses: Vendors will exploit young kids on school nights to sell peanuts and popcorn; stadiums will hire young children to clean the locker rooms; parking lots will use children to collect money.

"Okay," I coax them, "so we draw the exemption tighter—limiting it to batboys and batgirls."

With this fix in place, Reich proudly called ABC's producers of *World News Tonight* to announce that, in his words, "I've decided to let Tommy keep his batboy job."

Notice what Reich did. He altered the regulations as little as possible so that one particular person, who was creating a lot of negative publicity for the Labor Department, could keep his job. Why didn't that reasoning apply to other children who, even when uncoerced by their parents, wanted to work at jobs that Reich wanted to keep off-limits? And notice, also, Reich's Louis XIV, *l'etat c'est moi* celebration of his power over people's lives: "*I've* decided to let Tommy keep his batboy job."

THE CASE OF THE CORNROW BRAIDS

Freedom of association also means that anyone should be free to offer his or her services to anyone else. Take the 1998 case of Sabrina Reese, a 28-year-old entrepreneur who owned two African hair-braiding salons that offered a competitive alternative to traditional hair salons. In July 1998, the state government of California mounted a sting operation against Ms. Reese. Her crime? She was operating her business without a cosmetology license. Ms. Reese had gone to cosmetology school for a while, but she found that braiding was neither included in the curriculum nor tested in the licensing exam. So, for her, cosmetology school was useless. It was also expensive. She would have had to attend for 1,600 hours and spend $9,000. So she set up her business without a license. It thrived, and so she set up a second location and, at this writing, has nine employees. For practicing cosmetology without a license, even though she didn't practice cosmetology, Reese faced fines and even a possible jail sentence of up to one year. Fortunately, the Washington-based Institute for Justice brought a federal lawsuit against the state government of California and won.

If you think that government regulation via licensing is needed to ensure that people in various jobs and professions are competent, then notice something interesting: In the last 20 years, it has been government, through court decisions and legislation, that has made it difficult for employers to fire, or refuse to hire, competent people. The Americans with Disabilities Act, for example, voted for by Congressman Newt Gingrich, Senators Orrin Hatch, Strom Thurmond, and Phil Gramm, and virtually all "liberal" Democrats in Congress, and signed by President George Bush in 1990, virtually requires that incompetent and even dangerous people be kept in their jobs. The proponents of the law steadfastly, and successfully, refused to define a disability, and the only conditions they excluded from the list of protected disabilities were pyromania, kleptomania, compulsive gambling, and other conditions related to sexual behavior and gender identity.[12] Explicitly *not* excluded were alcoholism and schizophrenia. Thus, one of the uses of the ADA law has been to make it hard for employers to fire alcoholics and others who are dangerous to customers and fellow workers. Take the case of Northwest Airlines, one of whose pilots, Norman Lyle Prouse, went to prison for flying an airplane while drunk (he had a blood-alcohol content of .13 percent, well over the legal limit in any state). But after his release from prison, Prouse was rehired and, in July 1995, was flying airplanes again.[13] And under a Michigan discrimination law, a suburban Detroit hospital was ordered to pay $610,000 for discriminating against a narcoleptic surgeon.[14]

But haven't customers pushed for licensing laws in various occupations so they can be assured of quality service? Actually, I can find no instance of a customer group lobbying for licensing. The main people who have always instigated occupational licensing laws are people already in that occupation. Various medical societies, for example, have tried to prevent nurse practitioners from performing certain medical procedures.

Of course, the people defending privilege will rarely admit that their main reason is to prevent competition. But their stated reasons rarely make sense. For example, in opposing the granting of hospital privileges to qualified nurse midwives, psychologists, podiatrists, and other nonphysician health professionals, the Washington, D.C., Medical Society speculated in its newsletter that "pretty soon a boy scout with a rusty knife will be permitted to perform brain surgery."[15] Or take another case cited by University of Washington economist Paul Heyne. Heyne tells of the executive director of a state board of examiners in veterinary medicine, who said that pet groomers who were not licensed veterinarians should not be allowed to invade a dog's gums because they might cause unnecessary pain. Heyne asks: "Do you think people with their hand in a dog's mouth are likely to cause the dog unnecessary pain?"[16]

Sometimes, when the enforcers arrest people who are practicing without a license, they reveal that their goal is not consumer protection. For example, when Dennis C. Vacco, Manhattan's Attorney General, announced the arrest of 10 people in Chinatown for providing medical care without a license, he stated, "Their level of training and expertise is irrelevant."[17]

FREEDOM OF ASSOCIATION FOR EMPLOYERS

Freedom of association applies not just to employees, but also to employers. Just as you and I should be free to work, or not to work, for anyone we wish, so employers should be free to hire, or not to hire, anyone they choose. There should be no legal privileges; freedom of association applies to all.

Employers and employees do not receive equal treatment today. Whereas employees are free not to work for an employer, and can have even the most capricious reason for choosing not to, employers do not have that freedom. A gay man, for example, had better not tell a straight man that he won't be hired because he is heterosexual; if the gay employer says that, he can be sued. Similarly, although it is not in law today, many gay groups would like to see a law preventing straight employers from discriminating against gays. Interestingly, though, I have never seen any of these groups call for laws to prevent straight employees from refusing to work for gay employers. Don't get me wrong. I'm not saying there should be such a law. But my position comes from principle. I don't advocate laws preventing *employers* from discriminating, either. What I don't understand is how those who want to use laws to prevent employers from discriminating never seem to want to use laws to prevent discrimination by employees.

LABOR UNIONS

What does freedom of association say about labor unions? Two main things. First, anyone who wants to join a union should be free to do so. Second, anyone who wants to hire only nonunion workers, or who wants to hire union workers but not deal with the union, should be free to do so. Freedom of association means that both sides—union and employer—can agree whether or not to deal with each other. This simple principle solves literally all of the problems that people think of when they think of unions. Take two contemporary examples.

First, take the issue of quality circles in unionized firms. Many nonunion firms have adopted quality circles, in which workers and managers meet to find better ways of working. But the federal government's National Labor Relations Board has threatened legal action against unionized firms that have tried to adopt this innovation. Their reason: In quality circles, workers deal with managers without being represented by the union. Workers having to think for themselves? "Oh my God!" say the unions and the National Labor Relations Board. "We can't have that!" But freedom of association says that, as a matter of fact, we can have that. If workers and employers want to get together without the union involved, they should be allowed to do so. This assumes, of course, that the workers have not agreed in their contract with the union to have the union represent them in all interactions with the employer. But that's a good assumption. Workers who join unions by choice are unlikely to hand over to the union that much power. If a union with voluntary membership attempted to use its power to hamper quality circles, it would likely lose members.

A second example is one that arose in 1982 when I was working at the U.S. Department of Labor. Bunker Hill Co., a unionized mining and smelting firm in Idaho, was on the verge of going out of business. If that happened, about 2,000 Idaho steelworkers would have lost their jobs. Because the only way they saw to save their jobs was to accept a 25 percent cut in their high union wages, the union local voted, by a wide margin, to accept such cuts.[18] But, within 15 minutes of the vote, the local officials resigned, apparently due to pressure from the parent union, the United Steelworkers of America. The parent union then hand-picked the local's new leaders to do its bidding. The United Steelworkers of America didn't care about the 2,000 workers. It cared only about maintaining high wages for the workers who managed to keep their jobs. It probably feared that Bunker Hill's products would be produced at a lower cost, giving it a competitive advantage over products produced by high-wage union workers elsewhere. Applying the principle of freedom of association would have solved this. The local workers in Idaho should have been free to make their own deal with the steel company. The Reagan administration didn't even speak out against this injustice, and it let the United Steelworkers Union roll right over the Idaho workers. The workers lost their jobs. Being part of an administration that claimed to champion freedom, but failed to defend it in this case, was very disheartening.

If freedom of association were implemented in the United States, wouldn't the strength of unions be drastically reduced? Well, yes. But the Idaho case eloquently illustrates what the key source of union power is: the ability to prevent other workers from competing. Although unions like to portray wealthy firms as their opponent, their real competition comes from nonunion workers, who are much less powerful than the unions. Unions use the law to hobble these competitors.

Their power to prevent competition derives from two things. First are U.S. labor laws that grant and enforce the unions' monopoly. If 51 percent of voting workers in a plant choose to join a union, then the other workers at the plant, no matter what their wishes, must accept the union as their representative.

The second source of unions' power is local government's frequent unwillingness to protect the basic physical safety of people who wish to work for a lower wage while unions are on strike. Local police often rationalize their refusal to protect nonunion workers by claiming that to do so would be to take sides in the strike. But the only side they would be taking is in favor of carrying out their duty to protect people from violence. People don't suddenly give up their right to protection from violence because they choose to continue working when the labor union tells them that they shouldn't. Protecting nonunion workers from union workers' violence is no different in principle from protecting union workers' freedom from violence. Union strikers often use a disgusting word to refer to their fellow human beings who wish to compete for their jobs: They call these nonunion workers "scabs." By dehumanizing them in this way, they rationalize their own cruelty and lack of regard for their rights. But the right not to be physically assaulted is universal and does not depend on whether you belong to a union.

Interestingly, the articulate defenders of union privilege admit that unions have monopoly power. The late Arthur Goldberg, former Justice of the Supreme Court, Secretary of Labor under President Kennedy, and counsel for the United Steelworkers Union, said it plainly: "Technically speaking, any labor union is a monopoly in the limited sense that it eliminates competition between workingmen for the available jobs in a particular plant or industry."[19] Economists Armen A. Alchian and William R. Allen, commenting on this revealing quote from Goldberg, asked,

> Why did he write *"technically speaking"* and "in the *limited* sense"? Is there some other mode of speaking, and is there an unlimited sense of monopoly? [Italics in original.]

While clearly admitting that unions have a government-enforced monopoly, Goldberg was trying to soften the harsh reality. Here's what Harvard economists Richard B. Freeman and James L. Medoff, who both *favor* legal privileges for unions, wrote in their book, *What Do Labor Unions Do?*: "Most, if not all, unions have monopoly power, which they can use to raise wages above competitive levels."[20] There you have it.

If freedom of association were respected, labor unions would lose their monopoly power. But if you feel inclined to mourn that loss, first understand what the consequences of their power have been. Unions have not raised wages generally. On this there is widespread consensus among the scores and scores of economists who have studied unions' effects on wages. In 1985, the late H. Gregg Lewis, one of the country's leading labor economists, summarized the results of 200 studies of unions' effects on wages. On average, he found, union members' wages were about 15 percent higher than the wages of similarly skilled nonunion workers. Employers respond to higher union wages by decreasing their employment of union workers, and the people put out of work find jobs in the nonunion sectors of the economy, driving wages down there. Therefore, the gains in wages for the seventh of the labor force that is unionized come mainly at the expense of nonunion workers. Even if all workers could be organized into one big union, so that workers put out of work could not bid wages down in nonunion occupations, the gains to unionized workers would then come at the expense of the many workers put out of work. This "one big union" scenario, though unlikely, is an extreme version of what's happening in France, Germany, and some other Western European countries: Unions get their high wages and 20-year-olds have terrible trouble finding jobs. In France the unemployment rate averaged 11.3 percent in the 1990s, and in Italy, it averaged 10.2 percent. Compare that to the United States, where it averaged 5.8 percent. Moreover, early in their development in the United States—and even today in their effects if not their intent—unions used, and continue to use, their power to exclude blacks from some of the best jobs. We'll see more about this in the next chapter.

THE FUGITIVE PLANT LAW

In the United States, companies greater than a certain size must give their employees at least 90 days' notice before shutting down. This requirement violates employers' freedom of association. It is no different in principle from a law that would require employees to give 90 days' notice before quitting. Freedom of association means that employers and employees should be able to enter any contractual agreement they wish, as long as it does not violate anyone's rights. Therefore, if an employer agrees in advance to notify employees when he plans to close a plant, he should have to keep his contractual commitment. But if he doesn't agree to do so, he shouldn't have to prenotify. He shouldn't be forced to carry out someone else's idea of his obligation unless he undertook this obligation contractually.

Forcing an employer to give 90 days' notice before closing a plant will make potential employers less likely to open plants in the first place. Also, when employers are forced by law to take on such obligations, then wages and other forms of compensation will fall to offset this added cost of employing workers for the additional 90 days. Both of these facts mean that the prenotification requirement is not a freebie for employees. But those are not my main reason for opposing the federal government's prenotification law. My main reason is that I believe in freedom of association.

Now, you might say that prenotification is typically not very costly for employers and that, therefore, I shouldn't make such a big deal about it. But it is a big deal. Requirements that employers notify their employees before closing, although not always financially arduous, may require the employer to stay in business against his wishes. They are, literally, a form of employer slavery. Just as laws requiring the return of escaped slaves were called "the fugitive slave laws," so laws requiring employers to keep their plants in business should be called "fugitive plant laws."

Similarly, laws that prevent employers from setting mandatory retirement ages for their employees are also wrong. No one I know of advocates forcing employees to work past the age at which they want to quit. The vast majority of people would see this as a form of slavery for those employees. You might say that they are not slaves because they are paid, but this ignores the history of slavery; some slaves, especially the more productive ones, were paid also. When the obligation is put on employers to keep employees beyond the point at which the firm wishes to, why is that not slavery for employers?

FREEDOM TO ENTER ENFORCEABLE LONG-TERM LABOR AGREEMENTS

There is one freedom that the employer has and the employee doesn't: The employer can commit to a long-term employment contract that U.S. courts will enforce. The employee can't. How do courts justify their decision not to hold employees liable for their contracts to nongovernment employers? They claim that such contracts are involuntary servitude. But they're not. They're *voluntary* servitude; the people who made them did so voluntarily. My obligation to show up at work, if I committed to doing so, is no different in principle from my obligation to pay my mortgage. But the courts don't refuse to enforce mortgage contracts.

You might think this a picky point. Who would want to enter a contract obligating himself or herself to work five years for somewhat lower-than-normal wages at IBM or GM? I'll tell you who. Prospective college students. Many of my students at the Naval Postgraduate School joined the ROTC at age 18 so that Uncle Sam would pay their college expenses in return for a 4-year commitment once they graduated. And one option in Americorps, the federal government's national service plan, is for young people to go to college first and have some college expenses paid for, and then to pay off the obligation by serving for two years in a government agency or nonprofit firm. Similarly, medical students often have their medical training expenses paid by the federal government in return for their commitment to work a given number of years in some otherwise unattractive area, such as Alaska. This last is the premise of the popular TV show "Northern Exposure." In all these cases, the federal government is the other party to the contract. But why should young people be able to enter those contracts only with the federal government? Why shouldn't they be allowed to do the same thing with IBM or Microsoft or Procter & Gamble? Such contracts would be a straightforward way out of poverty for many of America's more productive youth. For young, promising workers from low-income families who have trouble paying for college, long-term employment contracts would be a tremendous boon. But the federal government won't allow them unless, of course, the government is the employer.

DRUG TESTING

Should employees have to submit to mandatory drug testing? Following the principle of freedom of association gives the answer. Employers should be free to enter agreements with employees under which employees can be tested for drugs, and employees should be free to enter, or not to enter, such contracts. Such tests carry three costs: the out-of-pocket cost of the test itself, the time spent testing, and the indignity inflicted on employees, whether drug-free or not. Employers have to decide whether this cost is worth it. I am confident that airlines will decide that it is worthwhile for their pilots. On the other hand, employers who hire people in jobs where the damage done by a drug-using employee is low may decide not to test their employees.

But doesn't mandatory drug testing violate the freedom of association of people who must submit to the tests? If they *had* to submit, then yes. But they don't. They freely choose those jobs and, therefore, freely, if often begrudgingly, choose to submit to those tests. Just as my employer did not violate my freedom by requiring a dress code that I hated, so employers who require drug testing do not violate their employees' freedom. An old Spanish saying fits here; it translates to "Take what you want and pay for it." If you want to use drugs, then don't bother trying to be an airline pilot. If you want to be an airline pilot, then learn to get along without drugs.

ENDNOTES

1. Leonard Novarro, "Roomies: Trouble May Move in When All You Wanted Was a Roommate," *San Diego Union-Tribune,* Sunday, August 17, 1997, pp. H-1, H-4.

2. The definition of sodomy in Georgia is quoted in *Bowers v. Hardwick,* 478 U.S. 186 (1986), dissent of Justice Blackmun, joined by Justices Brennan, Marshall, and Stevens.

3. Moreover, in 1996, two thirds of U.S. voters believed that marriage should be limited to a man and a woman. See "Washington Wire," *Wall Street Journal,* September 20, 1996, p. A1.

4. See "Federal Appeals Court Reinstates Ban on Homework in the Knit Outerwear Industry," *Daily Labor Report,* November 30, 1983, A-9–A-10.

5. Gunnar Myrdal, *An American Dilemma,* Vol. 1, New York: McGraw-Hill, 1964 (first published in 1946), p. 397.

6. David Card and Alan Krueger, *Myth and Measurement: The New Economics of the Minimum Wage,* Princeton: Princeton University Press, 1995.

7. David R. Henderson, "Rush to Judgment," *Managerial and Decision Economics,* Vol. 17, May–June 1996, pp. 339–344. For a shorter review, see David R. Henderson, "The Squabble Over the Minimum Wage," *Fortune,* July 8, 1996.

8. "Our view: Banning imports made by child labor won't help kids," *USA Today,* June 12, 1996.

9. David R. Henderson, "The Case for Sweatshops," *Fortune,* October 28, 1996, pp. 48–52.

10. Robert Reich, "No Case for Sweatshops," *Fortune,* December 9, 1996, p. 24.

11. From Locked in the Cabinet by Robert B. Reich © 1997 by Robert B. Reich. Used by permission of Alfred A. Knopf, a division of Random House, Inc.

12. Walter K. Olson, *The Excuse Factory,* New York: Free Press, 1997, p. 126.

13. Olson, *Excuse Factory*, pp. 119–122, and references on p. 334.

14. Olson, *Excuse Factory,* p. 136, and Daniel Seligman, "Keeping Up," *Fortune,* April 11, 1988.

15. Paul Heyne, *The Economic Way of Thinking,* 9th edition, Upper Saddle River, NJ: Prentice-Hall, 2000, p. 228.

16. Heyne, *The Economic Way of Thinking*, p. 229.

17. Garry Pierre-Pierre, "Arrested in Chinatown for Practicing Medicine Without Licenses," *New York Times,* August 9, 1996, B1.

18. For further details, see Erik Larson, "Steelworkers in Idaho Bitter at Union Stand," *Wall Street Journal,* March 15, 1982, p. 29.

19. From Exchange and Production, 2nd edition, by Alchian & Allen, © 1977. Reprinted by permission of South-Western College Publishing, a division of Thomson Learning, fax 800-730-2215.

20. Richard B. Freeman and James L. Medoff, *What Do Labor Unions Do?,* New York: Basic Books, 1984, p. 6.

7

FREE MARKETS VERSUS DISCRIMINATION

Imagine you are a member of a group that is often discriminated against. You might not have to imagine. You might be facing real prejudice right now in your life. Say you have a choice between two kinds of political/economic systems: one in which the government has lots of power to make decisions that affect people's everyday lives and one in which the government has much less power, and people are responsible for their own decisions. Under which of the two systems would you like to live? To get the most out of the rest of this chapter, take a minute to answer the question before reading on.

Racism. It happens in degrees, sometimes subtly, sometimes not. Everyone notices differences, but only beyond a certain age do they seem to *care* about those differences. White children notice that black children look different, and black children notice that white children look different. In itself this awareness of differences is not a problem. Children on the playground are more interested in having enough playmates for a game of tag than they are in the color of their playmates' skin.

I remember when my daughter Karen, then about four years old, asked my wife and me why people with *brown* skin are called *black*. Good question, and not one for which we had a satisfying answer. Karen then took the next logical step.

"What are we? Pink?" she asked. When we told her that we were called *white*, she looked puzzled and asked, "Why?"

"Now that I think about it, there's not a good reason," I said, thoroughly confused myself. This 4-year-old's ability to see clearly and to ask good questions had shown me what an absurd structure adults—black and white, or brown and pink—have built around the issue of skin color.

So, a simple awareness of differences is not a problem. But when people start to correlate those differences in skin color with differences in behavior, to generalize to everyone of a particular race, and to base strong moral judgments about whole races on skin color—or any other superficial trait—that's when the trouble begins. We get absurd and offensive generalizations, ranging from "Blacks are stupid" to "White men can't jump" to "Jews are greedy."

FIGHTING RACISM IN OUR OWN BACK YARDS

So, how do we fight racism? There is much we, as individuals, can do. We can reach out to people of different races, religions, and ethnicities—in business, socially, through marriage, and in other ways. We can actively support those who are discriminated against on the grounds of race. That support takes various forms. One form is to organize boycotts of businesses that discriminate against, say, blacks, as many black people did in 1955, after Rosa Parks was kicked off a bus in Montgomery, Alabama, for sitting at the front of a bus. Black community leaders used this strategy very effectively to protest the law that required segregation on buses.

Another way is to give personal support to those hurt by discrimination by letting them talk about their hurt and listening to them completely, without interrupting, editorializing, or making excuses. An organization called the National Coalition Building Institute (NCBI) runs workshops at which people do just that for one another.

And, though this may be hard for many people to accept, another effective way of fighting racism is to listen to people who are racist, letting them tell about all *their* hurts. Supporting racists? Really? Yes, racists have their stories too, and they're usually stories of deep hurt, often early in life. It's important to remember that giving moral support to racists is not the same as supporting racism. Somewhere in their lives people *learn* to be racist, and, as a teacher, I have found that the best way to change people's minds is to listen and ask questions, not to lecture. "You have to be taught to hate," says a song in the movie *South Pacific,* a song that was almost cut because it was too controversial.

What else can we do in our personal lives to end racism, classism, anti-Semitism, and other prejudices? For one thing, we can stop listening in embarrassed silence when someone tells a racist joke, and instead say, "I find that joke offensive." Better yet, when people ask (I have two friends in particular who do this) if I want to hear their latest Polish (or whatever) joke, I answer with a firm "no." After a while, people will get the point and stop trying to make you laugh at someone else's expense.

Many of us fantasize about being a big hero who saves lots of people's lives. But meanwhile, in our everyday lives, we have many opportunities to do the day-to-day heroic things that, added together with other people's efforts, could change the world. That's the meaning I take from, and why I like, the bumper sticker that says Think Globally; Act Locally.

FIGHTING THE REAL ENEMY

We've all been taught well—too well. But, in spite of the fear and hatred most people have learned to harbor about people who are different from themselves, I believe we know, deep down, that blacks, Asians, Jews, Arabs, or any other group, are not really our enemies. Is there an enemy?

HOW GOVERNMENT CAUSES RACIAL DISCRIMINATION, USUALLY INTENTIONALLY

Actually, when it comes to racial discrimination, there is an enemy. The enemy is the use of naked force against people of particular races or ethnic groups. Sometimes private groups, such as the Ku Klux Klan, unrestrained by government, use force against people of other races. But by far the most common, vicious, and destructive use of force against racial and ethnic groups is by governments themselves. In many countries and at many times, governments have used force to prevent people of certain ethnic groups from practicing in certain occupations and living in certain areas. In extreme cases, the government has systematically tried to murder entire races.

Government use of force against ethnic groups is far more effective than private use of force against these same groups. I remember that when I first heard about Hitler at about age eight, and asked my mother who he was, I was told that 15 years earlier he had used tanks and other weapons to try to take over the world. I pictured a nut with some tanks he had bought coming down our highway and invading our small town in rural Canada. I didn't understand at the time why Hitler was such a threat; I had been raised to believe that the police would protect us. Imagine the shock and sudden surge of overwhelming fear I had when, years later, I learned that Hitler employed the police and, indeed, ran a whole *government*. That was scary. Even as a child I knew that the government, any government, had more power than anyone who was not in the government, and that when the government passed and enforced a law, you couldn't legally fight back. That's when the true terror of Hitler dawned on me. Which brings us to Exhibit A of the government's enforcement of racial discrimination: Nazi Germany.

Nazi Germany

Nazi Germany is the clearest case of government-enforced racial discrimination. Hitler began by stepping up the previous German governments' policies of preventing Jews from participating in certain occupations, kicking them off university faculties, for example, and forbidding Jewish doctors to serve non-Jewish Germans. Hitler confiscated the property of Jews simply because they were Jews, and in the late 1930s, began a systematic policy of murdering Jews, a policy that continued until his death.

South Africa

South African Apartheid was another recent flagrant example of racial discrimination imposed by government. The explicit purpose of Apartheid, which lasted from 1948 until the early 1990s, was to have blacks and whites live and grow separately. Blacks were not free to work where they wished, even if employers were willing to hire them. Blacks were not free even to live where they wished, even if someone was willing to sell them a house or rent to them in one of the restricted areas. Apartheid as an economic system was thus a fundamental violation of basic human rights to live and work in peace. It is Exhibit B for the view that the worst forms of discrimination are caused by government.

Interestingly, Apartheid and its precursor, the Colour Bar, resulted from the South African government's desire to help white workers avoid having to compete with black workers. Apartheid was, in essence, an extreme form of affirmative action for whites.

"Workers of the world unite, and fight for a white South Africa." The first part of this slogan sounds socialist. The second part sounds racist. So which is it? Both. The slogan was used, with deadly seriousness and no hint of irony, by striking white South African workers in 1923. They struck to oppose white mine owners' plans to replace expensive white workers with cheaper, yet skilled, black labor. The powerful white Mine Workers' Union received support for this strike from its allies in the South African Labour Party (SALP), formed in 1908 with the explicit goal of carving out a privileged place for white workers. The SALP was modeled intentionally on the British Labour Party, which was, even then, an avowedly socialist party.

Apartheid was, in the words of economist Thomas Hazlett, "socialism with a racist face."[1] The socialist roots of Apartheid are a secret in plain sight. Although these roots are well known to scholars who have studied Apartheid, they have received little publicity in the West. That so few Western intellectuals have been unwilling to look seriously at Apartheid's socialist roots is not surprising. After all, a serious examination of these roots could easily lead to doubts about the goodness of socialism. And, as most of us know, questioning strongly held beliefs in which we have a lot invested is usually painful.

But avoiding pain is never a good enough reason to avoid thinking and understanding, especially when the issue is so crucial. I began this chapter by asking in what kind of society you would want to live if you were in an unpopular group. One of the two choices was a society in which the government takes responsibility for people's well-being and uses a great deal of control to carry out that responsibility. Let's see how that choice worked out in South Africa. Let's examine the roots of Apartheid.

Start with the Colour Bar. The Colour Bar, laws that prevented black people from holding certain jobs in South Africa, began with the Mines and Works Act of 1911. The intent and effect of this Act was to decertify non-Europeans for work in hazardous occupations such as mining. Non-Europeans were deemed "unqualified." Who pushed for this law? Not employers. Indeed, employers *wanted* to hire the many black workers who were as qualified as the white workers and who were often willing to work for lower wages. *The main people who pushed for laws enforcing racial discrimination in workplaces were the white union workers.* Their reason was simple: They did not want to have to compete with black workers. By passing laws to make work by blacks illegal, the white union workers could restrict the supply of labor and drive up their own wages. To this end, the white unions succeeded in passing a series of laws in the 1920s and 1930s to strengthen their monopoly power by further restricting competition from blacks.

Imagine how a white employer must have viewed the Colour Bar. He didn't have to be a big fan of black people to want to hire them. What made white employers want to hire from a pool of qualified black labor was what makes virtually all employers hire the people they do: the desire to make money. Most employers will hire someone if their earnings from the person's output exceeds the cost, in wages, other compensation, and monitoring, of employing the person. So an employer would do far better if he could get around the law. Hazlett says it well: "Industrialists, eyeing low-wage blacks anywhere in their neighborhoods, found them irresistible."

That, from the viewpoint of many white workers, was the problem. The employers' profit motive and the black workers' desire for better-paying jobs created constant pressure for racial discrimination to break down. Moreover, blacks working alongside whites led to social integration, and social integration led to further economic cooperation, thus breaking down the Colour Bar even more. Many white workers, wanting to maintain their privileged position, saw only one possible solution: The labor force would have to be segregated, not just on the job, but outside the workplace as well. So in 1948, the National Party was elected to implement Apartheid, which means apartness, a comprehensive social policy of "separate development." Under Apartheid, the government dictated where members of various races could live, and its infamous Pass Laws regulated travel within the country.

So there you have it. Apartheid did not come about simply because South African whites didn't like South African blacks or because whites considered blacks inferior. Those factors were necessary and were present, but the impetus for Apartheid came almost solely from white workers who used government regulation to prevent blacks from competing with them. Without government as the enforcer, the believers in Apartheid would have been seen as a bunch of cranks and would have had their own little racist sects, but would not have been able to determine where blacks and whites worked and lived for over 40 years. The main opponents of Apartheid were not just the black people who wanted better jobs, but also the white employers who wanted to hire them.

IT CAN'T HAPPEN HERE?

Let's look closer to home. In the United States, just as in South Africa, the worst forms of racial discrimination have been caused or strongly aided by government.

The worst discrimination against black people in the United States was the introduction of slavery. Short of murder and torture, slavery is the greatest possible violation of people's rights. It is essentially legalized kidnapping. The U.S. government helped maintain slavery in three main ways. First, the government *allowed* slavery. By doing so, it failed to perform one of government's few legitimate functions: protecting people's basic liberty. Slaves were not free to live and work where and for whom they wished. Second, the government used force to make people maintain slavery. In his book, *Emancipating Slaves, Enslaving Free Men: A History of the American Civil War,* economic historian Jeffrey Rogers Hummel shows that governments in the South, at the behest of slave owners, made many white non-slave owners bear the cost of enforcing slavery. Most able-bodied white males were required by law to man the slave patrols, which apprehended runaways, monitor the rigid pass requirements for blacks who were traveling, break up any large gatherings of blacks, and suppress slave uprisings. Without this compulsory service, slavery would have been harder to maintain. The federal government, too, aided slavery. It enforced the fugitive slave clause, part of the U.S. Constitution, allowing slave owners to retrieve their slaves who had escaped to northern states. Indeed, until 1842, governments in northern states were required to help hunt down runaway slaves. The third main way that governments maintained slavery was by making it illegal for slaves to learn how to read and write. Slave owners understood well that an educated slave was a threat to slavery.

Even after slavery ended, governments in the South severely restricted blacks. In his book *Black Reconstruction,* W. E. B. DuBois, the famous black activist, writes about the infamous Black Codes, also known as Jim Crow laws, that threw legal obstacles in the way of blacks seeking jobs. A black person found traveling from one job to another, for instance, could be charged with vagrancy even if he could show proof that he was on his way to a new job.

Local governments in the South also regularly refused to provide the most rudimentary protection to blacks threatened by lynch mobs. And in the 1870s, at the behest of the Ku Klux

Klan and other white supremacists, southern states passed some of the nation's earliest gun control laws, prohibiting blacks, but not whites, from owning or handling firearms. Commenting on that era, Don B. Kates, Jr., a lawyer who has written or edited a number of books on gun control, writes, "Alabama, Arkansas, Mississippi, Missouri, and Texas deprived the victims of the means of self-defense, cloaking the specially deputized Klansmen in the safety of their monopoly of arms."[2]

Government discrimination against black people continued well into the twentieth century. Laws in the South required segregation of restaurants and other privately owned facilities, whether or not the owners desired it. These segregation laws were thus a direct attack on the property rights of the owners. And, although local governments did not give blacks a break on property taxes, they used the revenue from these taxes to subsidize schools for whites. In 1886, for example, Mississippi's legislature passed a law allowing state funds allocated to black schools to be diverted to white schools. Later the law was revised to give discretion to county school boards about how much money could be diverted. By 1910, according to economist Finis Welch, governments in counties with a black majority, and therefore with more funds to tap, spent from 7 to 30 times as much on white as on black students; white-majority counties spent "only" 2 to 3 times as much on white students.[3]

UNICONS

The union man, he decide whether I live or die.

—FROM A SONG SUNG BY FOUR YOUNG BLACK WOMEN
AT AN ANTIWAR RALLY IN SAN FRANCISCO, FEBRUARY 1980

An observer traveling across the United States by train in the first few decades of the twentieth century would have noticed a conspicuous absence of black railway conductors, commercial telegraphers, locomotive firemen, and boilermakers. Why would this be? After all, slavery had ended much earlier, and the infamous Black Codes that black activist W. E. B. DuBois wrote about early in the twentieth century no longer existed. The answer: early in the twentieth century, the railroad business was highly unionized. Just as in South Africa, employers often wanted to hire black people. But unions run by white people excluded blacks from membership and often committed acts of violence against black workers who tried to get such jobs. Interestingly, my information comes not from an anti-union source, but from President Jimmy Carter's secretary of labor, F. Ray Marshall, who favors the legal privileges that U.S. unions have. Before entering politics, Marshall, an economist, made his academic reputation by documenting U.S. unions' sorry record of race relations. In his 1967 book, *The Negro Worker,* Marshall lists unions that barred blacks in 1930.[4] They included

American Federation of Express Workers (AFEW)
American Federation of Railway Workers (AFRW)
American Train Dispatchers Association (ATDA)
American Wire Weavers Protective Association (WWPA)
Boilermakers, Iron Shipbuilders and Helpers Union (BIS)
Brotherhood of Dining Car Conductors (BDCC)
Brotherhood of Locomotive Firemen and Enginemen
    (BLFE)
Brotherhood of Railroad Trainmen (BRT)
Brotherhood of Railway Carmen (BRC)
Brotherhood of Railway Conductors (BRC)
Brotherhood of Railway Station Employees and Clerks
    (BRSEC)
Brotherhood of Railway and Steamship Clerks (BRSC)
Commercial Telegraphers (CT)
International Association of Machinists (IAM)
National Organization of Masters, Mates and Pilots of North
    America (MMP)
Neptune Association (NA)
Order of Railway Expressmen (ORE)
Order of Railway Telegraphers (ORT)
Order of Sleeping Car Conductors (OSCC)
Railroad Yard Masters of America (RYA)
Railway Mail Association (RMA)
Switchmen's Union of North America (SNA)

Unions didn't just prevent blacks from holding jobs; they sometimes assaulted, and occasionally murdered, black workers who tried to compete with them. During the 1911 strike against the Illinois Central, Marshall notes, whites killed two black strikebreakers and wounded three others at McComb, Mississippi. Marshall also tells of white strikers killing 10 black firemen in 1911 because the New Orleans and Texas Pacific Railroad had granted them equal seniority. Small wonder, then, that early twentieth-century black leaders Booker T. Washington and W. E. B. DuBois, whose disagreements with each other are legendary, agreed on unions. Washington, a lifelong foe of labor unions, wrote in a 1913 article in the *Atlantic Monthly*,

> The average Negro who comes to town does not understand the necessity or advantage of a labor organization which stands between him and his employer and aims apparently to make a monopoly of the opportunity for labor.[5]

DuBois summed it up quite succinctly: "[Unions are] the greatest enemy of the black working man."[6]

How Unions Got Their Clout

So unions in the United States have traditionally oppressed African Americans. But how did they become so powerful? That can be answered in one word: government. As I noted in the previous chapter, there is nothing wrong with unions per se. Unions are simply associations of workers who get together to bargain with employers. What gives unions virtually all their negative characteristics is one legal privilege: their ability to use force against workers who tried to compete with them.

Unions' legal power to be the sole bargaining agent for workers in a bargaining unit prevented workers from making their own deals with employers, and thus made it hard for many black people to get jobs. In the United States, just as in South Africa, blacks competed by being willing to work for lower pay. The high union-negotiated wages that were the same for everybody hampered black workers' ability to compete.

The amount of explicit discrimination by unions against blacks decreased during World War II, presumably because many white workers went off to war, creating enough openings for everyone, including blacks. The civil rights movement of the early 1960s and the antidiscrimination laws that it led to made explicit discrimination—discrimination as a written-down policy—illegal. But much discrimination remained and still remains. F. Ray Marshall points out, for example, that the craft unions (the plumbers union, for example) could discriminate more than the industrial unions (the auto workers) because the craft unions could determine literally who could join and who could not. Craft unions run union hiring halls and therefore are the gatekeepers who decide who works and who doesn't—this was almost certainly what the four young black singers quoted previously had in mind when they sang, "the union man, he decide whether I live or die." By contrast, *employers* of workers in industrial unions usually make the hiring decisions. Marshall lists a number of "informal" means that U.S. unions could use to bar black people from high-paying jobs, including

> agreements not to sponsor Negroes for membership; refusal to admit Negroes into apprenticeship programs or to accept their applications, or simply to ignore their applications; general "understandings" to vote against Negroes if they are proposed (for example, as few as three members of some locals can bar applicants for membership); refusal of journeyman status to Negroes by means of examinations which either are not given to whites or are rigged so that Negroes cannot pass them; exertion of political pressure on governmental licensing agencies to ensure that Negroes fail the tests; and restriction of membership to sons, nephews, or other relatives of members.[7]

As a result, many large union locals, even in areas where many black people lived, continued to discriminate against blacks. In Pittsburgh in 1963, for example, the Steamfitters had 1,400 members and the Plumbers had 886 members, but neither had even one black member.

Unions also have discriminated against other races. The "look for the union label" ad campaign was started in the

1880s as a way to tell customers that a product was made by white laborers rather than by Chinese. Unions also were strong supporters of the Chinese Exclusion Act of 1882, whose purpose, as the name implies, was to prevent Chinese people from immigrating to the United States. They also supported the Immigration Act of 1924, which restricted Japanese people from immigrating.[8]

Civil rights laws today can be, and are, used against labor unions that discriminate against blacks and other minorities. This seems just, given the unions' legal privileges that have been a major source of racial discrimination.

The most just solution is to go to the root of the problem and remove the legal privileges that unions now have. This solution is the only one that respects people's freedom of association. If unions could no longer coerce workers who wish to make their own arrangements with customers and employers, black people who want to be, say, plumbers would not have to get *anyone's* permission. People could still join unions if they wished to, and employers could still bargain with unions. But don't force anyone to join, and do protect the rights of those who wish to work for employers no matter who tries to prevent them from working.

The Minimum Wage

Unions also have made it harder for black workers by lobbying for, and achieving, minimum wage laws. A minimum wage of, say, $5.15 an hour makes it unprofitable for an employer to hire someone whose productivity is worth only $4.00 an hour. Because a higher percentage of black workers than of white workers is unskilled, black workers are more likely to be put out of a job by the minimum wage. In his book *An American Dilemma,* Gunnar Myrdal quoted an estimate that minimum wages set under FDR's National Industrial Recovery Act of 1933 had put half a million blacks on relief by 1934,[9] before that law was found unconstitutional. Similarly, the minimum wage law, originally imposed by the Fair Labor Standards Act of 1938 and still in force today, destroys jobs for hundreds of thousands of workers, a large percent of whom are unskilled young blacks. Of black males between the ages of 16 and 19, 37 percent were unemployed in 1995, a year during which the overall unemployment rate averaged only 5.6 percent. Compare that whopping rate—two out of every five black teenagers out of work and looking for work—to the 15.6 percent unemployment rate for white males between the ages of 16 and 19. Similarly, while white females aged 16 to 19 had a 13.4 percent unemployment rate, their black counterparts had a stunning rate of 34.3 percent. While not all of this high unemployment was due to minimum wages, some of it was. According to Charles Brown, a labor economist at the University of Michigan who was head of economic research for President Carter's Minimum Wage Study Commission, the consensus estimate among economists is that a 10 percent increase in the minimum wage reduces teenage employment by 1 to 3 percent. The minimum wage may currently be preventing 250,000 to 800,000 teenagers from finding work.

The 1 to 3 percent estimate comes from a published staff study done for President Carter's Minimum Wage Study Commission by Charles Brown, Curtis Gilroy, and Andrew Kohen. That they dared do this study is a strong tribute to them because the study must not have been welcomed. In spite of their evidence on the minimum wage, the Commission advocated indexing the minimum wage to inflation, and also advocated ending some of the exemptions from the minimum wage[10] that are a safety valve for unskilled workers whose productivity is not worth the minimum.

The loss in jobs caused by the minimum wage is not an accidental byproduct of higher minimum wages. It is the consequence intended by those who most avidly support increasing minimum wages. Unions don't support minimum wage increases because their own members are working at the minimum wage. Virtually all union employees—I've never heard of an exception—work at wages above the minimum. Northern unions and unionized firms, for example, have traditionally supported higher minimum wages to hobble their low-wage competition in the South. In the late 1960s, Otis Elevator pushed for an increase in the minimum wage in New York state because it had begun to specialize in converting human-operated elevators to automatic elevators and wanted an increase in demand for its services.

Forty years ago, the politicians who pushed for the increased minimum wage did not hide their motives. Nor, in an era of state-sanctioned segregation, did they feel the need to hide their knowledge of who the intended victims of minimum-wage increases would be. In a 1957 Senate hearing, minimum-wage advocate Senator John F. Kennedy of Massachusetts, who just four years later would be President of the United States, stated,

> Of course, having on the market a rather large source of cheap labor depresses wages outside of that group, too—the wages of the white worker who has to compete. And when an employer can substitute a colored worker at a lower wage—and there are, as you pointed out, these hundreds of thousands looking for decent work—it affects the whole wage structure of an area, doesn't it?[11]

The witness he was addressing, Mr. Clarence Mitchell, then director of the Washington Bureau of the NAACP replied,

> I certainly think that is why the Southern picture is as it is today on the wage matters, that there is a constant threat that if the white people don't accept the low wages that are being paid to them, some Negroes will come in [to] work for a lower wage. Of course, you feel it then up in Connecticut and Massachusetts, because various enterprising people decide to take their plants out of your states and take them down to the areas of cheap labor.

Kennedy's colleague Jacob Javits, then a U.S. Senator from New York, was similarly blunt. He said,

> I point out to Senators from industrial states like my own that a minimum wage increase would also give industry in our states some measure of protection, as we have too long suffered from the unfair competition based on substandard wages and other labor conditions in effect in certain areas of the country—primarily in the South.[12]

Although probably no northern senator today would dare admit it, many who vote for increases in the minimum wage understand that one consequence will be to destroy jobs for the least skilled workers, a disproportionate number of whom are black.

KEEPING BLACK WORKERS
OUT OF CONSTRUCTION

Just as the minimum wage prices unskilled workers out of jobs, the federal government's Davis-Bacon Act prices less-skilled workers out of construction jobs. The Act, which requires that the government pay "prevailing wages" on all construction projects receiving more than $2,000 in federal funds, was passed in 1931. The Labor Department's regulations to implement the law interpret prevailing wages to mean union wages. So, for example, electricians covered by Davis-Bacon in Philadelphia in 1993 had to be paid $37.97 an hour in wages and fringe benefits, while the average wage paid to electricians working for private contractors on uncovered projects in Philadelphia was $15.76.[13] An employer required to pay $37.97 an hour will want a highly skilled employee for that money. Thus, unskilled and less skilled workers, who are disproportionately black, are much less likely to get construction jobs.

Mark Simmons, a builder in Troy, New York, saw these results up close in 1985. When renovating 82 buildings with federal funds, he won a waiver from Davis-Bacon. Halfway through the project, the Labor Department ruled that the Act applied and withdrew the waiver. The result: "We had to fire over 100 laborers, nearly half of them minority," Simmons told the *Wall Street Journal*. To finish the project, he hired local union workers, 95 percent of whom were white.[14]

The Davis-Bacon law has similar effects economy-wide. In their study done for Washington University's Center for the Study of American Business, now the Weidenbaum Center, economists Richard Vedder and Lowell Gallaway found that black people were overrepresented in other blue-collar occupations in 1990, but underrepresented in construction.

Specifically, 25.5 percent more blacks were employed in other blue-collar occupations than would be predicted on the basis of the population of blacks and whites, and relative to equal proportionate representation, 29.6 percent fewer black people were in construction.[15] Economists have long understood the harm that Davis-Bacon does to black workers, which is one reason why no economists I know of, other than those hired by unions, have ever defended the law.

Even if the hurt that Davis-Bacon inflicts on black people were unintentional, there would still be a good reason to repeal it. But the hurt was intended. When the law was passed in 1931, blacks and immigrants were the acknowledged target of two congressmen named Robert Bacon and James J. Davis.[16] Bacon, a Republican from Long Island, first submitted the bill in 1927 after an Alabama contractor won a bid to build a federal hospital in Bacon's district and, in Bacon's words, "brought some thousand nonunion laborers from Alabama into Long Island, N.Y., into my congressional district." According to Ethelbert Stewart, the commissioner of labor statistics in 1928, the contractor brought with him "an entire outfit of Negro laborers from the South."[17] Stewart's boss at the time was Labor Secretary James J. Davis, a Democrat and a strong supporter of racial restrictions on immigration. Davis was later elected to the U.S. Senate.

Representative Bacon and Senator Davis couldn't tolerate these uppity blacks, nor, apparently, could a majority of their colleagues in the House and Senate who, backed by the white-dominated American Federation of Labor, passed the Davis-Bacon Act in 1931. Some of the congressmen who favored the bill gave an explicitly racist rationale for their support; one, Representative Clayton Allgood, complained of "cheap colored labor" that was "in competition with white labor throughout the country."[18]

Back of the Bus, or Government in the Driver's Seat

Most Americans have heard the story of Rosa Parks, the heroic black woman who, tired after a long day's work, refused to move to the back of a Montgomery, Alabama, bus. Less well known is why buses and streetcars in the South were segregated in the first place. It wasn't because the streetcar companies wanted it that way, but because local governments required it. In fact, owners and managers of private streetcars strongly opposed racial segregation. Before the law required segregation, most streetcar companies voluntarily segregated tobacco users, not blacks. Nonsmokers of either race were allowed to ride where they wished, but smokers were relegated to the back or the outside platform. Even after segregation laws were passed early in the twentieth century, streetcar companies dragged their heels for as long as they could before complying. Their objection was very simple: Racial discrimination cost them money. One railroad manager complained that racial discrimination required his company to "haul around a good deal of empty space that is assigned to the colored people and not available to both races." In Augusta, Savannah, Atlanta, Mobile, and Jacksonville, streetcar companies refused to enforce segregation laws for as long as 15 years after the laws' passage. But as the government stepped up the legal pressure, the streetcar companies finally had to comply with the law, and the United States stumbled further into government-enforced segregation.[19]

GOVERNMENT INTERVENTION HELPED CAUSE THE DETROIT RACE RIOT OF 1967

During a five-day period in July 1967, 43 people were killed during a riot in Detroit's inner-city. President Johnson then appointed the National Advisory Commission on Civil Disorders, the so-called Kerner Commission, named after the then-governor of Illinois who headed it, to look into the causes of that and other riots during the summer of 1967 and to make recommendations that would prevent such riots in the future. Its 1968 report made a big splash. The report stated that black poverty was a big cause of the Detroit riots, and its recommendations for more government jobs and housing programs for inner-city residents were explicitly based on that assumption. These recommendations are what received much of the publicity at the time and are what most people took away from the report. Too bad more people didn't actually read the report. The Commission's own account of the Detroit riot tells a different story. Here's the report's first paragraph on Detroit:

> On Saturday evening, July 22, the Detroit Police Department raided five "blind pigs." The blind pigs had their origin in prohibition days, and survived as private social clubs. Often, they were after-hours drinking and gambling spots.

These "blind pigs" were places that inner-city black people went to be with their friends, to drink, and to gamble; in other words, they were places where people went to peacefully enjoy themselves and each other. The police had a policy of raiding these places, presumably because the gambling and drinking were illegal. The police expected only two dozen people to be at the fifth blind pig, the United Community and Civic League on 12th Street, but instead found 82 people gathered to welcome home two Vietnam veterans, and proceeded to arrest them. "Some," says the Commission report, "voiced resentment at the police intrusion." The resentment spread and the riot began.

In short, the triggering cause of the Detroit riot, in which more people were killed than in any other riot that summer, was the government crackdown on people who were going about their lives peacefully. The last straw for those who rioted was the government suppression of peaceful, albeit illegal, black capitalism. Interestingly, in its many pages of recommendations for more government programs, the Commission never suggested that the government should end its policy of preventing black people from peacefully drinking and gambling.

The government's fingerprints show up elsewhere in the Commission's report. Urban renewal "had changed 12th Street [where the riot began] from an integrated community into an almost totally black one..." says the report. The report tells of another area of the inner city to which the rioting had not spread. "As the rioting waxed and waned," states the report, "one area of the ghetto remained insulated." The 21,000 residents of a 150-square-block area on the northeast side had previously banded together in the Positive Neighborhood Action Committee (PNAC) and had formed neighborhood block clubs. These block clubs were quickly mobilized to prevent the riot from spreading to this area. "Youngsters," writes the Commission, "agreeing to stay in the neighborhood, participated in detouring traffic." The result: no riots, no deaths, no injuries, and only two small fires, one of which was set in an empty building.

What made this area different was obviously the close community the residents had formed. But *why* had a community developed there and not elsewhere? The report's authors unwittingly hint at the answer. "Although opposed to urban renewal," the Commission reports, "they [the PNAC] had agreed to co-sponsor with the Archdiocese of Detroit a housing project to be controlled jointly by the archdiocese and PNAC." In other words, the area that had avoided rioting had also successfully resisted urban renewal, the federal government's program of tearing down urban housing in which poor people lived and replacing it with fewer houses aimed at a more upscale market. Economist Martin Anderson, in his 1963 book, *The Federal Bulldozer*, showed that urban renewal had torn down roughly four housing units for every unit it built. The Commission, instead of admitting that urban renewal was a contributing factor, recommended more of it. Their phrasing is interesting, though, because it admits so much about the sorry history of the program:

> Urban renewal has been an extremely controversial program since its inception. We recognize that in many cities it has demolished more housing than it has erected, and that it has often caused dislocation among disadvantaged groups.

> Nevertheless, we believe that a greatly expanded but reoriented urban renewal program is necessary to the health of our cities.[20]

In short, the commission's remedy for poison was to increase the dosage.

HOW FREEDOM REDUCES RACIAL DISCRIMINATION BY MAKING IT EXPENSIVE

When I was the John M. Olin visiting professor at Washington University in St. Louis, an emeritus sociology professor named Murray Wax told me a story. Wax had been a young member of the Communist party in the United States in the late 1940s. While earning his graduate degree in the early 1950s, he applied to the city college system in Chicago for a teaching job and was hired to teach at Wright Jr. College. But just before the academic year was to begin, he received a call from the City of Chicago's superintendent of education, asking him to come for a visit. At the meeting, the superintendent showed him a thick dossier that the FBI had gathered on him about his earlier political activities, and told him that the teaching offer was withdrawn. Figuring that all the government-run colleges in the Chicago area would now be similarly off limits, Wax got a job as a freelance market researcher for two years, and then went to the Toni Company for an additional few years. Neither his clients nor, later, the Toni Company asked, or seemed to care, about his political background. Says Wax, "I had absorbed all this Marxist teaching, but until then I hadn't realized this paradox: The corporations didn't care about my Communist background, but academia—which I had thought of as mine—was willing not to hire me for reasons totally unrelated to my teaching ability."[21]

The government-run City Colleges of Chicago could discriminate against a high-quality applicant because no one owned the university and, therefore, no one bore a cost for this discrimination. But the ad agency was a for-profit company. If the company passed up the opportunity to hire someone who would do a good job, it wouldn't do as well. By taking longer to find someone as good or settling for someone less skilled, the company would pay for its decision to discriminate, which is why the company that hired him didn't ask him about his political background—it didn't care enough to put its profits at risk.

That's how markets work. Employers care mainly about people's productivity relative to their compensation package. Employers who want to discriminate on grounds other than productivity may do so, but they pay a price—they pass up the opportunity to hire people whose productivity exceeds their wage rate. As a former economist colleague of mine, Linda Gorman, once told her female students after one of the male students had made a disparaging remark about females, "Don't worry; the market will get him." Her point was that markets break down discrimination.

Her point is beautifully illustrated in Steven Spielberg's 1994 movie *Schindler's List*. In Poland during World War II, a businessman named Oskar Schindler, who was well connected with the Nazis running Poland's government, employed hundreds of Jews, many of whom would otherwise have been carted off to concentration camps.

The Nazis' Reich economic office made money off the Jews the same way Fidel Castro makes money off Cuban workers hired by foreign companies; the Nazis charged out skilled Jewish men at a wage rate of seven marks a day and unskilled Jewish women at five marks a day and kept for itself all the money they earned. (Fidel lets them keep a small fraction of what they earn.) Non-Jewish Poles were paid more. Schindler saw an opportunity to start a factory and hire Jews cheaply. Schindler's thinking was clear: "Poles [non-Jewish Poles] cost more. Why should I hire Poles?" he tells his accountant, Itzhak Stern, a Jew. So Schindler paid the government for the Jews' labor.

By hiring Jews from the Krakow ghetto, Schindler provided them with some degree of safety and shelter inside the walls of his factory. But his true motive was clear. When Schindler tells his wife that he has 359 workers on the factory floor with one purpose, she asks, laughing, "To make pots and pans?"

Replies Schindler, "To make money. For me."

Schindler cared about keeping good workers, not because he cared about the workers per se, but because he could make good money by hiring skilled labor for low wages. This narrow goal even led Schindler to save one of his most valued employees from certain death. In one scene, Schindler learns that his accountant had been picked up by the Nazis to be shipped off to one of the Nazi death camps. Schindler angrily rushes to the train station and cleverly intimidates a petty Nazi official into letting him retrieve Itzhak Stern from the death train.

What makes the bigger point—and what ultimately makes the movie so satisfying—is Schindler's transformation into someone who cares intensely about the Jews, enough to put his whole fortune and even his life at risk. But simply by employing them and keeping them out of harm's way, Schindler did them a big favor. Schindler's story shows the power of the profit motive in reducing discrimination, even in extreme cases where vicious lethal discrimination is official government policy.

Throughout history, governments have generally been much less tolerant of racial differences than private employers have been. This is because the government officials who discriminate incur no cost for doing so, as long as discrimination is politically acceptable, which it often has been. Economist Thomas Sowell points out that between 1910 and 1930, when blacks were making gains in the private sector, racial animosity by whites increased. The federal government, responsive to the concerns of whites, increasingly hired on the basis of race.[22] Writes Gunnar Myrdal, "Segregation was introduced into Washington offices where it had scarcely occurred before."[23] During that period, a rule was added to civil service hiring that allowed federal agencies to choose among the three applicants with the highest ratings. This made it easier for agencies that did not want blacks to turn them down. Later, the requirement that every applicant supply a photograph made exclusion of blacks even easier.

The federal government's discrimination against blacks in the civil service looks positively tolerant compared to its record on hiring blacks in the military. There were no blacks at all in the Marine Corps during World War II. At the end of World War I, the Navy discharged all blacks and accepted no more until 1932, and even then hired only for kitchen jobs. How many black combat officers did the Army have in 1940? Two. Not 2 percent. Two.[24]

Governments in other countries, whose officials do not personally bear the cost of discrimination, discriminate against unpopular groups also. India's government has traditionally imposed hiring quotas based on caste, while Sri Lanka's government has imposed quotas that favor people of Sinhalese extraction. Government-imposed caste and racial quotas in those countries have actually provoked civil wars.

THE FREE MARKET HELPS BREAK DOWN DISCRIMINATION IN ALL ECONOMIC TRANSACTIONS

In 1992, I went to San Francisco's Candlestick Park to see the Giants play the Cincinnati Reds. To get into the baseball spirit, I wore my blue L.A. Dodgers helmet. (I root for both the Giants and Dodgers, but I figured why buy a Giants helmet when I already had a Dodgers one?) I was sitting in the stands when a young man came by selling hot dogs. Because he was about 40 feet away, rather than try to shout above the din, I put up one finger for one hot dog. The young man looked at me, noticed my helmet, pointed to his own head symbolizing my helmeted head, and shook his head as if to say, "No, I won't sell you a hot dog because you're a Dodgers fan." Then he grinned and I grinned, and he passed the hot dog down the row. We both knew that he would sell me the hot dog. There was no way he was going to refuse to make money off me even if I was a Dodgers fan.

This story of how the free market broke down discrimination may sound trivial. If it just had to do with my hot dog, it would be. But the story illustrates a much wider and crucial point: Markets are especially good at breaking down discrimination when what is exchanged is goods rather than labor. Think about how little you know about the politics, race, gender, or even nationality of the person who makes the bread you buy. You don't know because you don't care. What you care about is getting the best deal on bread, and even if this means buying it from someone whom you would hate, you'll still buy the bread. That's why, for example, even book stores whose owners and employees detest Rush Limbaugh still displayed his books prominently. By trying to hide the books, which apparently some stores did for a short time, they would pass up precious sales.

One of my favorite lines in a movie is in the scene of *The Magnificent Seven,* where Yul Brynner tries to persuade the local hearse driver to risk getting shot while taking a dead Indian to be buried in dignity in boot hill. When the driver declines, Brynner asks, "Are you prejudiced?" The driver answers, "When it comes to saving my life, I'm downright bigoted." The market illustrates the opposite point. When it comes to saving their economic lives, even otherwise prejudiced people are downright tolerant.

Neither Steven Spielberg nor I originated the idea that free markets break down discrimination. Actually, the French writer Voltaire made the point over two centuries ago after observing the London Stock Exchange. He wrote,

> Go into the London Stock Exchange...and you will see representatives of all nations gathered there for the service of mankind. There the Jew, the Mohammedan, and the Christian deal with each other as if they were of the same religion, and give the name of infidel only to those who go bankrupt.[25]

As economist Gary Becker of the University of Chicago made clear in his book, *The Economics of Discrimination,* free markets make discriminators pay for discriminating, but that doesn't mean that people in a free market will never discriminate; the most extreme racists and bigots will often be willing to pay the price for discriminating. Becker's insights were cited by the Swedish Academy when it awarded Becker the Nobel prize in economics in 1993. The bottom line is that in a free market, any employer who discriminates on grounds that have nothing to do with productivity will pay a cost for doing so. The economic system that removes the props from racism is free markets.

In his book, Becker pointed out that the wage differential between black and white workers of a given ability and experience is a measure of the remaining discrimination against black workers; the larger the differential, other things equal, the more discrimination black workers face. This insight has been abused in two ways in discrimination lawsuits in the United States. The statistical abuse is to assume that the whole wage differential between blacks and whites is due to discrimination rather than to other factors that the researcher has failed to measure. Yet, as virtually every economist who studies wage data will admit, you can never account for all factors, especially those that you can't even observe. The idea that you could sum up the earning power of a person simply by knowing that person's age, experience, union affiliation, education, and little else is absurd. Many people are the same age as Bill Gates and are similar in all other respects; no one else with those same characteristics has close to his level of wealth. One study of wage differentials between men and women found that women's wages were either 61 percent *lower* or 19 percent *higher* than those of comparable men, depending on how one controlled for unobservable characteristics.

The second abuse of Becker's insight has been an even more fundamental breach of justice. Workers who feel that they have been discriminated against bring lawsuits against those who employed them and often ask for compensation for the lower wages they were paid. But even if you grant that their wages were lower because of discrimination, they are suing the wrong people. They are suing employers who actually hired blacks and other minorities, but to the extent they hired them at lower wages, they are helping to *eliminate* discrimination. To the extent lower wages are due to discrimination, they are caused by those *not* hiring people in the discriminated-against group. By going after those who hire minorities, the people suing and the judges and juries that find in their favor are acting like the minister who harangues those attending his service for the low turnout. Both the legal system and the minister are attacking the very people who are helping to solve the problem. Moreover, just as berating loyal church attendees discourages some of them from attending in the future, requiring higher pay for minority workers discourages employers who already hire minority workers.

That freedom breaks down racial and other kinds of discrimination is one reason many people don't like free markets. Politicians Davis and Bacon understood very well that free markets were causing black people to be employed where they wanted whites employed, and that's why they pushed the Davis-Bacon Act. Senator John F. Kennedy understood that free markets were shifting textile industry jobs to Southern blacks, and that's why he wanted an increase in the minimum wage. Some people probably aren't happy about the fact that a former member of the Communist Party could make it in a U.S. business. But that's how freedom works: When people are free, some people whom others don't like will do well because they are productive. And in the vast majority of cases, the result of freedom will be racial tolerance and tolerance of differences generally. If you don't want a society in which people are tolerant of others, then you might not like freedom. But consider this: Even if your group dominates now, it is unlikely to dominate forever. And when your group is not dominant, oh how you'll value tolerance.

When people are free to decide, some *will* discriminate on racial grounds and on other grounds that most of us think are wrong. But to say that such discrimination is wrong is not to say that people should be forcibly prevented from discriminating. Freedom of association means that people should be free to hire or not hire, or to work for or not work for, whom they please. That means that gay employers will often discriminate in favor of gay employees, a phenomenon that some visitors to San Francisco have noted. It means also that straight employers will sometimes discriminate in favor of straight employees, that white employers will sometimes preferentially hire white employees, and that black employers will sometimes discriminate in favor of black employees. And that's their right. I say this even though I have been a victim of racial discrimination. A few years ago, an editor of the business section of a major U.S. newspaper who wanted to have me as a regular columnist told me explicitly that there was one problem: I was the wrong color. I found that newspaper's racial discrimination against me despicable. I still do. But at no time during this conversation did I question that the newspaper had a right to discriminate by any criteria it chose.

Moreover, laws against discrimination seem invariably to get out of control in two ways. First, the government often starts to require discrimination. The Civil Rights Act of 1964, for example, made it illegal for employers to discriminate on grounds of race. One of its strongest supporters, Minnesota

Senator Hubert Humphrey, who had fought for similar laws the whole of his political life, swore during the Senate debate that the law could never be interpreted to require quotas and that if he thought it could, he would oppose the Civil Rights bills. Guess what? Within a few years, the federal government used its power to insist on quotas. To adhere to such quotas, employers must often discriminate in favor of blacks and other minorities. In 1995, the Congressional Research Service found 160 federal programs that used race and gender criteria. That same year, two half-white, half-Asian five-year-olds were denied admission to a public school as Asian applicants, but were told they could reapply as whites. In short, various levels of government have turned many decisions into issues of racial spoils. Comments author David Boaz, "Soon we may need to send observers to South Africa to find out how their old Population Registration Act worked, with its racial courts deciding who was really white, black, 'colored,' or Asian."[26] Justice is strictly a secondary consideration.

The second major way that antidiscrimination laws get out of control is by making even sensible discrimination illegal. Many employers would want to know, for example, whether the person working for them ever stole anything. Yet, it is now illegal for many employers to refuse a job to an employee for having a criminal record unless the crime was "job-related." The Equal Employment Opportunity Commission has actually ruled against a company that refused to rehire a crane operator who was released after serving time for first-degree murder. After all, he didn't murder anyone on the job.[27] An employer cannot discriminate on the basis of age, even though age is often very relevant. If you were an employer, would your expected revenues from training a 70-year-old be as high as your expected revenues from training a 25-year-old? Employers often cannot legally turn down pregnant women for jobs, even though they have good reason to believe that pregnant women will want time off for their pregnancies and are more likely to quit after their babies are born. As one frustrated employer having to contend with this law told me, "I advertised this job so I can find someone who will work for me for a few years, not someone who won't." No one would accuse a worker of being unfairly discriminatory if she declined a job offer from a firm that she thought likely to go bankrupt. She is legally able to discriminate against that firm, as well she should be. Why shouldn't an employer be allowed to do the same against an employee who is likely to quit or want time off?

Laws beginning as modest antidiscrimination measures inevitably evolve into laws that require discrimination or ban reasonable discrimination. Why is this evolution inevitable? Because even antidiscrimination laws that ban discrimination that most of us see as offensive are based on the assumption that a person who otherwise would be discriminated against has a right to a job or a right to shop at a particular store. He doesn't have those rights because such rights would deny the right of the employer to hire whom he wants and of the store-owner to deal with whom he wants. Once people in the society accept the premise that someone has a right to a job or the right to shop at a store, it's not long before they begin to think of that pseudo-right as a fundamental right that everyone has, independent of anything the person has done before. That certainly appears to be the way more and more judges and politicians have thought in ruling, for instance, that employers can't discriminate against people with certain kinds of criminal records.

Think back to the question I posed at the beginning of this chapter. I asked you to imagine that you are in a group that is often discriminated against, and to choose which kind of society you would like to live in, one in which government exercised a lot of control over people's lives or one in which they were free. In a government-run society, unpopular groups are often discriminated against, often as a matter of government policy. In a free society, on the other hand, freedom removes the props from discrimination.

Government penalties against discrimination by business make headlines. Yet market penalties against discrimination are much more forceful and consistent than government penalties. These market penalties almost never make headlines, and few people even know about them. But a free-market economy exacts a stiff penalty from employers who discriminate against people on any basis other than productivity.

For all their holier-than-thou talk about the evils of racial and other discrimination, government officials have been the main enemies of unpopular groups, and profit-maximizing business-men have been their main saviors. Indeed, the market penalty for discrimination has been so strong that businessmen are often tenacious champions of fair treatment, even when doing so is unpopular and even when the businessmen would them-selves prefer to discriminate.

ENDNOTES

1. The story of Apartheid and the accompanying quotes are from Thomas W. Hazlett, "Apartheid," in David R. Henderson, ed., *The Fortune Encyclopedia of Economics,* New York: Warner Books, 1993, pp. 97–104.

2. Don B. Kates, Jr., "Handgun Prohibition in the United States," in Don B. Kates, Jr., ed., *Restricting Handguns: The Liberal Skeptics Speak Out*, Croton-on-Hudson, NY: North River Press, 1979, p. 19.

3. Finis Welch, "Education and Racial Discrimination," in Orley Ashenfelter and Albert Rees, eds., *Discrimination in Labor Markets*, Princeton: Princeton University Press, 1973, p. 56.

4. The list of unions is in F. Ray Marshall, *The Negro Worker,* New York: Random House, 1967, pp. 165–166. Marshall's was taken from Abram L. Harris, *The Negro Worker,* New York: Conference for Progressive Labor Action, 1930.

5. Booker T. Washington, "The Negro and the Labor Unions," *Atlantic Monthly*, June 1913, p. 756.

6. DuBois is quoted in Morgan Reynolds, *Power and Privilege: Labor Unions in America*, New York: Universe Books, 1984, p. 223.

7. F. Ray Marshall, *The Negro Worker*, New York: Random House, p. 63.

8. The facts in this paragraph are taken from Morgan Reynolds, *Power and Privilege*, p. 220.

9. Myrdal's data are quoted on p. 398 and are from Virginius Dabney, *Below the Potomac*, 1942.

10. *Report of the Minimum Wage Study Commission*, Vol. 1, May 24, 1981, pp. 121–138.

11. From U.S. Senate, Labor and Public Welfare Committee, Proposals to Extend Coverage of Minimum Wage Protection, Hearings before the Subcommittee on Labor, 85th Congress, 1st session, March 20, 1957, p. 856.

12. Congressional Record, Feb. 23, 1966, p. 2692.

13. Data on Philadelphia are from John Frantz, "Davis-Bacon: Jim Crow's Last Stand," *The Freeman*, February 1994, p. 68.

14. The Simmons story is from "Davis-Bacon Meets Jim Crow," *Wall Street Journal*, May 22, 1992, p. A10.

15. Richard Vedder and Lowell Gallaway, "Cracked Foundation: Repealing the Davis-Bacon Act," Center for the Study of American Business, Policy Study Number 127, November 1995, p. 15.

16. The story of the origins of the Davis-Bacon Act is told in David Bernstein, "The Davis-Bacon Act: Let's Bring Jim Crow to an End," Cato Institute Briefing Papers, No. 17, January 18, 1993; Scott Alan Hoge, "Davis-Bacon: Racist Then, Racist Now," *Wall Street Journal*, June 25, 1990; and John Frantz, "Davis-Bacon: Jim Crow's Last Stand," *The Freeman*, February 1994, pp. 66–70.

17. The statement from Ethelbert Stewart is from a letter reprinted in U.S. Congress, House Committee on Labor, *Hearings on H.R. 7995 & H.R. 9232*, 71st Congress, 2d Session, March 6, 1930, p. 17, and quoted in Bernstein, "Davis-Bacon Act," p. 11.

18. The Allgood quote is from *Congressional Record*, February 28, 1931, p. 6513.

19. For a slightly more detailed account, see Linda Gorman, "The Market Resists Discrimination," in David R. Henderson, ed., *The Fortune Encyclopedia of Economics*, Warner Books, 1993, pp. 474–475. For a much more detailed account, see Jennifer Roback, "The Political Economy of Segregation: The Case of Segregated Streetcars," *Journal of Economic History*, Vol. 56, No. 4 (December 1986), pp. 893–917.

20. *Report of the National Advisory Commission on Civil Disorders*, New York: Bantam Books, 1968, pp. 479–480.

21. Phone interview with Murray Wax, August 29, 2000.

22. Thomas Sowell, *Race and Economics,* New York: David McKay Company, 1975, p. 182.

23. Gunnar Myrdal, *An American Dilemma,* Volume 1, New York: McGraw-Hill, 1964, p. 327.

24. Myrdal, *American Dilemma,* p. 420.

25. Quoted in David Boaz, *Libertarianism: A Primer,* New York: The Free Press, 1997, p. 38.

26. David Boaz, *Libertarianism: A Primer,* New York: Free Press, 1997, p. 101.

27. Walter K. Olson, *The Excuse Factory,* New York: Free Press, 1997, p. 26.

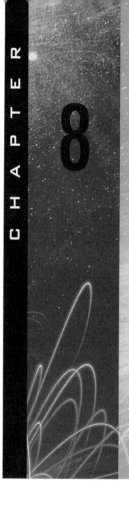
THE JOY
OF CAPITALISM

Why did men die of hunger, for six thousand years? Why did they walk, and carry goods and other men on their backs, for six thousand years, and suddenly, in one century, only on a sixth of this earth's surface, they make steamships, railroads, motors, and are now flying around the earth in its utmost heights of air? Why did families live thousands of years in floorless hovels, without windows or chimneys, then, in eighty years and only in these United States, they are taking floors, chimneys, glass windows for granted, and regarding electric lights, porcelain toilets, and window screens as minimum necessities?

—ROSE WILDER LANE, *THE DISCOVERY OF FREEDOM: MAN'S STRUGGLE AGAINST AUTHORITY*, 1943, FOX & WILKES, 1993. REPRINTED WITH PERMISSION.

Ultimately, capitalism will beat socialism because capitalism is more fun.

—ROY A. CHILDS, JR., 1988

One night, while rounding a curve on the wet pavement in my Toyota, I asked myself, "Why do I trust my car not to skid?" The answer, I realized, is that I am confident in the free market. I know that engineers in Akron or Yokohama or Tokyo or Detroit persisted day after day and week after week to design a car that I could operate safely in the rain without having to be an ace driver. That trust gave me a warm, fuzzy feeling.

One of the most amazing things about this focused effort of the engineers and others to create my car is that they did all that without even knowing me, yet acted as if they cared a lot about me. Why did they care? Partly because they took a lot of pride in their work and wanted to solve the technical problems that must be solved to produce a good product. But the other, usually bigger, reason was that they cared about themselves and their families. They wanted their families to live well, and they knew that unless they robbed a bank or hit the lottery, the only way they could make that happen was to be competent in their jobs because they were rewarded to the extent of that competence.

When you first realize that the vast majority of people from whom you get things on which your life depends care about you only derivatively, it can be quite unnerving. You can drive yourself crazy with the "what ifs." What if that grocer who smiles at me really doesn't like me? Maybe the meat he's selling me is older than he claims. What if the auto mechanic is jealous of the fact that my car is nicer than his—will he purposely make the car run worse? And on and on. But after a while, you start to get it: The main reason people sell you good products and good service is not that you're likable but that they need you as much as you need them. A very comforting thought.

When I was young, I didn't travel much, and when I did, I always worried. How will I get where I'm going? When I leave the airport, how will I get to the hotel? Who will take care of me? This fear was similar to the fear I had—growing up in Carman, Manitoba, population not quite 2,000—of traveling to Winnipeg, which to me seemed to be a giant city with its population of over half a million. Now that I've traveled, I understand that taxi drivers, hotel bellmen, and a host of others will take care of me because *their* well-being depends on it. When traveling in a strange country, you have to be cautious, of course. But what was striking to me was how much my caution exceeded my need for it.

Greg Christiansen, a master teacher of economics at California State University in Hayward, illustrates the incredible effectiveness of free markets: "Put me in any town in America with a population of over 20,000," he says, "and I can, within an hour, find a high-quality blue dress shirt with my neck and sleeve size." I have a similar story. When I was at the annual meetings of the American Economics Association in

Boston a few years ago, I woke up the first morning and found I had failed to pack the nice pants that go with my blue blazer. I went to the first session of the day wearing my blue blazer— and blue jeans. I was to have breakfast the next morning with Murray Weidenbaum, who, as chairman of President Reagan's Council of Economic Advisers, had hired me to be a senior economist in 1982. Now Murray was interested in hiring me as a visiting professor at Washington University for the following academic year. Blue jeans just wouldn't quite make the impression I wanted. Although it's easy to buy pants I like, I've rarely found a pair that, right off the rack, fits well. I would have to get the pants altered, which takes time. While pondering my dilemma that first morning, I ran into an economist friend, who, having a similar build, easily understood the fix I was in. "Too bad it normally takes a few days for alterations," he said. Then suddenly I saw the solution to my problem. "How long it takes depends on what I'm willing to pay," I responded, and I immediately went off to find a men's clothing store. One was attached to the hotel, and within five minutes, I had found a pair that was better than the ones I'd left at home and that cost only about $100, a full $50 below what I had expected. I asked the retailer what I would have to pay to get the pants in two hours. I got lucky: He wasn't busy that day and offered to do it for the standard charge of $15. I had the impression that even on a busy day I could have gotten them in two hours if I had offered to pay $50.

THE JOYOUS SCIENCE

I pointed out in Chapter 1 that British author Thomas Carlyle called economics "the dismal science" because the free-market economists around him were strongly opposed to slavery. For me, economics is the joyous science. I started off believing in economic freedom (sometimes called capitalism) as a moral imperative, as something that should exist because it is the only system in which people deal with each other on the basis of choice rather than on the basis of force. But the more I learned about economics, the more I saw that economic freedom was also enormously practical, that it delivered the goods better than any other system, and not just better, but incredibly better.

Capitalism's incredible productivity wasn't so easy for me to appreciate when I was in my teens and my early 20s. This was so for two reasons. First, starting at age 16, I was on my own financially and lived on a shoestring budget until I got my first full-time academic job as an assistant professor at age 24. Second, and more important, I was incredibly ignorant of economic history. Most of the history I learned in school was of the "who fought what war when and for what four reasons" variety. I learned very little about the day-to-day lives of ordinary people centuries ago.

In the last 20 years, though, I have found it easier and easier to appreciate capitalism. That's in part because my income, adjusted for inflation, has risen a lot. But it's also because the awesome technological revolution that has been going on around us has increased virtually everyone's real income—even those people whose incomes, adjusted for the government's faulty inflation measure, have been stagnant.

Think of what we can do nowadays, even those of us with modest incomes. If we miss a movie when it's in the theaters, we don't have to wait, the way we used to, until either it comes around again (unlikely) or is shown, years later, on TV, interrupted by ads and missing some of the best parts courtesy of network "censors." Instead, we can see the uncut version at our convenience on a video recorder that costs less than the earnings from three days of work at the minimum wage. We can rent the movie for a price that is often less than half of what we would have had to pay to see it on the big screen. I know we often take this for granted. One of the joys of capitalism is that we *can* take its awesome productivity for granted. But it's good, every once in a while, to have some wonder about the many things that are wonderful. A lot of "wonder robbers" out there think it's not "cool" to have wonder. But don't ever let anyone rob you of your sense of wonder. If you've already lost it, here's your chance to reclaim it.

Actually, even when I was a college student living on a very tight budget, I should have appreciated capitalism's productivity—

and would have if I had been more aware of the writings of an early twentieth century economist named Joseph Schumpeter. In his 1942 book, *Capitalism, Socialism, and Democracy,* Schumpeter wrote,

> Queen Elizabeth [queen of England from 1558 to 1603] owned silk stockings. The capitalist achievement does not typically consist in providing more silk stockings for queens but in bringing them within reach of factory girls in return for steadily decreasing amounts of effort.[1]

Strip away the sexist language and Schumpeter was on to something. What only kings and queens could have even 200 years ago, let alone 400, almost everyone in the United States takes for granted. Those kings and queens could get music by snapping their fingers and commanding an orchestra to play. Now, anyone who owns a CD player or a tape player can get music on command.

Although powerful nobility were almost the only people with enough to eat, almost all Americans today have ample food, which is much more varied and, due to the invention of canning, preservatives, refrigerators, and freezers, much, much safer to eat. Virtually the only people who traveled great distances in those days were the aristocracy. Today, the vast majority of people can travel a few thousand miles in under six hours for a price, with a discounted air fare, that is less than two weeks' pay for a typical worker.

Or take books. *Forbes* magazine writer Peter Brimelow has pointed out that in 1776, Adam Smith's *The Wealth of Nations* sold for $7.99, or about $650 in year-2000 dollars. The high cost of books is the reason the most famous university in the United States is named Harvard.[2] Brimelow notes that it was named after John Harvard, a man who donated 400 books to start the university's library. But relentless technical progress has brought down the cost of books so that the cost of an average hardcover book is now less than five percent of the 1776 price. So, a library of 400 books doesn't sound like much today: Tens of millions of people around the world have libraries with at least that many books. And the Internet has made thousands of books available free, via the Gutenberg project *(www.gutenberg.com)*.

Now here's the kicker. Although Schumpeter was one of the most pro-capitalist economists of his day, he actually *understated* capitalism's achievements. He focused on capitalism's awesome ability to deliver to ordinary people the goods that kings and queens had had access to for centuries. But even the most powerful king had to give the orchestra members a few hours' notice when he wanted to hear music. I, on the other hand, with a simple push of a button, can get an orchestra to play for me at any time of day or night. So can you. If I'm not in the mood for that orchestra, I can push another button to command another orchestra, or a rock band, or a string quartet to play, and I can do so whether I'm at home, at my office, or in my car. And the musicians get it note perfect every time.

Although that king who wanted to travel a few thousand miles might have been able to do so, he was subjected to the elements in a way that we are not today, and it took him about six weeks. Our idea of a serious complaint about flying is that we had to sit in a cramped space beside someone with body odor *for 6 hours.* Back then, everyone had body odor. I make myself remember that every time I find myself fuming in coach class. I remember that I have something that the most powerful king couldn't have had even 100 years ago. And I also realize that I could still have what I have, just less often, if my income fell by half.

Maybe you think of music and travel as inessential. But life is pretty essential. Edward Gibbon, the famous historian who wrote *The Decline and Fall of the Roman Empire,* was one of seven Edwards his parents had. Why did his parents give the same exact name to seven of their sons? Because they wanted the name Edward Gibbon to continue, and in the early eighteenth century, when Gibbon was born, parents could expect that in the normal course of events, most of their children would die before becoming adults. If you had been born in the eighteenth century or earlier, you would probably have been wiped out early in childhood by starvation, disease, or infection.[3] Life expectancy for someone born in the United States today is about 76, more than double what it was in the eighteenth century and earlier. The improvements in our health and our life expectancy are not due mainly to medical care. They are, rather, the result of better nutrition, safer food, safe drinking water, and modern sewage systems. As recently as 1900, one out of every 2,000 people in the United States died of tuberculosis. In 1990, tuberculosis killed only one out of every 140,000, a 99.6 percent decline.[4]

You don't even need to look over centuries to see how capitalism has delivered huge benefits. Again, consider health. I see the differences simply by looking at my own family's history, as you probably would by looking at your parents' and grandparents' histories. In 1993, I interviewed my father on videotape so I could learn more about his life. (I strongly recommend that you do the same with the older people in your life.) I asked him why, although he had lived a block from the Assiniboine River in Winnipeg, Canada, he had never mentioned swimming in the river. I will never forget his matter-of-fact answer: It was out of the question because the river carried raw sewage that had been dumped upstream. Also, my father and my older sister had polio; do you know anyone who has gotten polio in the last 30 years?

Consider clothing. In 1960, when I was 10, we spent Christmas with another family. One of their daughters, Dru, a precocious 5-year-old who had a crush on me, chased me around their house until my pants split. So I walked home, changed pants, and returned. Dru chased me again and my second pair of pants split. I was out of options—two pairs of pants were all I had. Fast forward to today. When a newly married friend recently showed me how neatly his wife had organized his clothes closet, I commented, "We are so incredibly wealthy." He had 5 to 10 suits, about 20 nice shirts, and the same number of nice ties. Even a friend of mine whose income of under $15,000 put him just above the poverty level had 6 to 10 pairs of pants and about 20 shirts all neatly stacked or hanging in his closet. When I was a child, I had one pair of shoes and one pair of Converse sneakers. Now children, even those in lower income brackets, often have more than two pairs of shoes, and the shoes are of much higher quality.

The quality of almost everything we get is higher than it was 30 or 40 years ago. The only things I can think of that have gotten worse are our protection from crime and the quality of education our children receive in schools. Each of these, interestingly, is provided by the government.

But don't we hear again and again that, under capitalism, the rich get richer and the poor get poorer? We do hear that. The statistic usually cited to back up this belief is the *percent* of income that goes to the households in the lowest fifth of the U.S. income distribution: 4.3 percent in 1980 and, in the U.S. Department of Commerce's most recent finding, 3.6 percent in 1998. The top quintile, on the other hand, received about 49.2 percent of all income in 1998, up from 43.7 percent in 1980. But this doesn't mean that the rich are getting richer and the poor poorer, for three reasons. First, the government data reflect shares of income, not absolute income. A slightly lower share, if it's a share of a much higher total, is still a higher income. And the total *is* much higher. Between 1980 and 1998, household income, as measured by the Department of Commerce, rose from $3.43 trillion to $5.39 trillion, all in 1998 dollars. But the measure that the Commerce Department uses to adjust incomes to 1998 dollars is the Consumer Price Index (CPI), which, over that time period, overstated annual inflation by about one percentage point. So total income over those 18 years really rose, not from $3.43 trillion to $5.39 trillion, but from 2.96 trillion to $5.39 trillion. The income of the lowest quintile in 1998 dollars, therefore, was 4.3 percent of $2.96 trillion, or $127 billion, in 1980 and 3.6 percent of $5.39 trillion, or $194 billion, in 1998. Due to a growing population, there were 20.8 million households in the 1998 quintile, up from 16.5 million households in the 1980 quintile. Per household, therefore, average real income in the lowest quintile rose from about $7,700 in 1980 to about $9,300 in 1998, an increase of over 20 percent.

Because of the problems with measuring income and adjusting for inflation, there's a better way to judge the well-being of a household: See what's in the house. Is there a washing machine, a color television, a VCR? In their book, *Myths of Rich and Poor,* W. Michael Cox, the chief economist at the Federal Reserve Bank of Dallas, and his coauthor, journalist Richard Alm, used this method to estimate how households officially defined as "poor" fared between 1984 and 1994. Their bottom line was that, on average, such households were doing much better. In 1984, 70.3 percent of poor households had a color TV; by 1994, 92.5 percent had one. While 3.4 percent of households had a VCR in 1984, 10 years later, 59.7 percent did. And 71.8 percent of poor families had one or more cars in 1994, up from 64.5 percent in 1984. Microwaves were unheard of in the early 1960s. By 1994, 60.0 percent of poor households had one. In one striking table, Cox and Alm show that a higher percent of poor households in 1994 even had more than the average household in 1971, whether measured by washing machines, clothes dryers, dishwashers, refrigerators, stoves, color televisions, or air conditioners.[5]

Second, to call someone rich or poor, you have to know that person's wealth, not his or her income. A retiree who receives only $10,000 annually in Social Security benefits but who owns a $300,000 house with no mortgage would be counted in the lowest fifth and, based on income, would be thought of as poor. But that person is clearly wealthy. The correlation between wealth and income, though positive, is far from perfect, particularly for the elderly.

The third reason the line between those getting richer and those getting poorer becomes blurred is the incredible income mobility that exists in the United States. Imagine that you could take a picture of everyone in the lowest quintile; nine years later, you take another picture of that quintile. How many people would be in both pictures? Surprisingly few.

This was the finding of a study done in 1992 by the U.S. Treasury. Using before-tax income for 14,351 taxpayers between 1979 and 1988, the Treasury economists found that of the taxpayers in the bottom quintile in 1979, only 14.2 percent—one in seven—were still there in 1988. Meanwhile, 20.7 percent had moved to the next higher fifth, 25 percent to the middle fifth, 25.3 percent to the second-highest fifth, and 14.7 percent—again one in seven—to the highest fifth. Thus, a taxpayer in the lowest bracket in 1979 was about as likely to be in the highest fifth nine years later as to have stayed in the lowest fifth.[6]

Why is mobility so high? The most important factor is age. Heavily represented in the bottom quintile are young people, the majority of whom have recently graduated from, or dropped out of, high school or college and are living on their own. Their current earnings are low, but as they age and gain skills, their earnings rise. Similarly overrepresented in the lowest quintile are retirees, who are wealthier than the average household—people over age 65 have the second-highest wealth of any age group—but don't have high incomes. Other factors matter too. A worker who lost a job may have had a low annual income one year, but then he's found another job. Or a newly divorced mother may be in the lowest quintile, but nine years later she is remarried or has acquired new work skills and more job experience.

There is an underclass of people who are born into poverty and live their whole lives that way, but it's much smaller than you might think. For most of the people classified by the government as poor based on their income, poverty is temporary. In the 10 years from 1969 to 1978, for example, only 2.6 percent of the population were classified as poor for eight years or more. During that same period, 24.4 percent were classified as poor for at least one year. Of the "poverty spells" experienced by the non-elderly, 43 percent occurred when a marriage ended in divorce, a child was born, or someone in the family set up an independent household.[7]

Many people in the welfare establishment have believed that so many welfare recipients are poor because they lack the skills to make a living. One such person is Thomas Fraker, an economist who uses survey data to study the effects of government policy. An alternative view, held by many economists who have studied the details of the welfare system, is that the poor are "trapped" because of the disincentives built into the welfare system. When you're on welfare, you aren't legally allowed to save more than a few thousand dollars without forfeiting your benefits. Also, when you're on welfare, your benefits fall by as "little" as 67 cents and as much as one dollar for every additional dollar you earn.[8] In other words, when you're on welfare, you face about a 67 to 100 percent implicit marginal tax rate. This is a strong disincentive for anyone to work. The welfare reform of 1996, voted in by Congress and signed reluctantly by President Clinton, who had promised in his

1992 campaign to "end welfare as we know it," put both views to the test. The reform law put a time limit on welfare benefits, after which those on welfare would be kicked off. On the one hand, those who believed that people on welfare lacked basic job skills predicted that people who lost their welfare benefits would become destitute. On the other hand, those who believed that people remain on welfare because of the strong disincentive to work expected that people who lost benefits would do all right. Fraker conducted a study for his Washington, D.C. employer, Mathematica Policy Research. In the study, which was funded by the federal government and some nonpartisan foundations, Fraker examined 137 families in Iowa that had recently lost welfare benefits. The results? About half had incomes slightly higher than or equal to their previous cash welfare benefits; the other half had slightly lower incomes.[9] Said Fraker to the *Wall Street Journal*, "We thought we would find a lot of people living on the streets. They're not."

The fact is that incentives work. When welfare recipients lose almost a whole welfare dollar for every work dollar they earn, many of them simply won't bother earning any income (or won't bother to report it). But tell them credibly that their welfare will end soon, or kick them off, and they'll come up with ways of earning a living. The government could make it easier for them to find work by getting out of the way. It could and should end the minimum wage, which prices low-skilled workers out of the market, and end other government-imposed rules that prohibit them from owning taxicabs, dressing hair, cutting down trees, selling food out of kiosks, and doing other productive work. Fortunately, even with these barriers in place, former welfare recipients are making it.

But isn't wealth in the United States becoming increasingly concentrated? The economist whom people cite on this is New York University's Edward Wolff, who claims that in 1992, the wealthiest 1 percent in the United States held 35.9 percent of wealth, up from 31.9 percent in 1983. Yet another economist, John Weicher of the Hudson Institute, claims that this share actually fell, from 31 percent in 1983 to 30 percent in 1992. I don't know who's right. I haven't looked at Wolff's or Weicher's data carefully enough to say, because whether

wealth is becoming more or less concentrated is far less important to me than whether everyone is getting wealthier. And
Wolff doesn't address that issue. When I went to Wolff's book,
*Top Heavy: A Study of the Increasing Inequality of Wealth in
America,* I wanted to find things like the median wealth of families in the United States, the median wealth of people in various age and ethnic groups, and how those had changed over
time. Unfortunately, I couldn't find them. I couldn't find any
data on the wealth of anyone. The reason is that Wolff didn't
report people's wealth. The only wealth data he reported in his
widely cited book is the *ratio* of various people's wealth to various other people's wealth. To compute these ratios, he had to
have the actual wealth data on various groups. But, presumably, he didn't find these data important enough to present in
his book. You can read his book and have no idea—literally no
idea—whether the United States is getting wealthier or poorer.
If you didn't know the title of his book, you could read it without knowing at the end whether you were reading about wealth
in the United States or in Bangladesh. Wolff writes as if all that
matters is relative wealth rather than whether people are doing
well.

But virtually everyone in the United States *is* getting
wealthier. As Cox and Alm have established, the cost of almost
every good people buy in the United States, measured in the
number of hours people must work to get those goods, is
declining. In 1916, they note, a refrigerator cost $800, which
took a manufacturing worker 3,162 hours to earn. In 1970, a
vastly-improved fridge cost $375 and took 112 hours of work
at the average manufacturing wage. Today, an even-more-
improved fridge costs about $900, which takes a manufactur-
ing worker only 68 hours to earn. Cox and Alm reach similar
conclusions about clothes, food, cars, air travel, cameras, elec-
tricity, you name it. Even houses of a given size with given
amenities have become slightly cheaper when measured in
hours of work. Actual new houses cost more, measured in
time, than they did, but that's because they contain more and
nicer "stuff"—garages, more bedrooms, air conditioners,
garbage disposals, garage door openers, storm windows, and
insulation, to name a few.[10]

Few people disagree any longer that capitalism is much better than government at delivering the goods. But many of capitalism's critics—and even many of its defenders—subscribe to the age-old belief that capitalism hurts culture and the arts. Does it? Actually, a strong case can be made that capitalism nurtures culture.

Of course, to discuss capitalism's effect on culture, you need to make a basic value judgment: What is good culture and what is bad culture? I am not a cultural relativist who believes that no standards can be used to judge culture. I do think, though, that judging the goodness or badness of a culture is an order of magnitude more difficult than judging the goodness or badness of generosity (good) or murder (bad). But here's what I can say unequivocally: Whatever your criterion for culture, the odds are extremely high that, with capitalism—that is, with free markets—you will get more of the kind of culture you want than you will get when government rules the economy with a heavy hand.

Go back to the fact that capitalism "delivers the goods," that is, produces goods of such quality and abundance that even the worst off are better off than in earlier times. This widespread prosperity gives people the means to buy books and other forms of art. In the so-called good old days, books were prohibitively expensive partly because people's incomes were low and partly because the cost of paper and printing was high. But capitalist-initiated improvements in mass production and mass marketing and increases in general wealth changed that. In his 1998 book, *In Praise of Commercial Culture,* Tyler Cowen, an economist at George Mason University, points out that, in 1760, a common laborer had to work two whole days to earn enough money to buy a cheap book, while today the cost of a paperback is slightly more than the minimum wage. As wealth has increased relative to the cost of books, people have bought more books. In 1989, for example, the average American bought eight books, up from three in 1947.[11] Presumably also because of increased wealth, in 1997, 35 percent of Americans visited an art museum, up from 22 percent in 1982.[12]

Now, if you don't regard a Tom Clancy novel as a work of art, then being able to get his novels cheaply might not seem a major cultural benefit. But that's all right, because those same productivity improvements in production and marketing, and that same improvement in prosperity, are what allow you to buy any books you care to buy more cheaply than at any time in the past. Contrary to many people's impression that only a few works account for a large part of all sales, the fifteen best-selling books in the 1980s accounted for less than 1 percent of the total number of books sold.[13] Today's superstores, Borders and Barnes and Noble, and the Web have helped niche writers.

And just as the Gutenberg press revolutionized book publishing by making books much cheaper to produce, the Internet is making publishing even cheaper. Two years ago, neo-conservative historian Gertrude Himmelfarb wrote that, although someone could put *Paradise Lost* online, "more likely is that something like a *Cliff Notes* version is online." But with cyberspace virtually costless, that tradeoff is nonexistent: There's room for both. In fact, *Forbes ASAP* writer Virginia Postrel, responding to Himmelfarb, noted that a Yahoo! search turned up five full-text versions of Milton's great poem.[14]

Capitalism has also allowed minority groups to achieve access to markets, despite the widespread discrimination they face. When, for example, black rhythm-and-blues musicians were turned down by the major record companies, they marketed through independent labels such as Chess and Motown. When radio stations hesitated to play R&B, musicians got their product advertised through jukeboxes. Chuck Berry's record company used payola—paying disk jockeys to play new records—to promote his first hit, "Maybellene." Interestingly, although a House Committee attacked the practice as scandalous, payola was not illegal until Congress outlawed it *after* its famous 1959 hearings. According to Cowen, the payola investigations were essentially a witch hunt against black music.[15]

Capitalism also helped women authors. A few centuries ago, when the high cost of books made it hard for authors to survive by selling their books to readers, men received nearly all the patronage support. But when writers competed for readers rather than for favors, men's advantage was nil. Privately run, for-profit circulating libraries, which did for books what

Blockbuster now does for videos, ordered novels for a largely female readership; they were women authors' biggest market. That's how Jane Austen and Charlotte and Emily Bronte flourished. By the nineteenth century, half of the English novelists published were female.[16]

The increasing wealth from capitalism also made it easier for artists, painters, and musicians to make a living at their craft, without having to depend on a king or other aristocratic patron. Early in his career, for example, the composer Franz Joseph Haydn was in a long-term contract with Austrian Prince Esterhazy. He was required to wear white stockings and powdered hair and could not travel without his employer's approval. He also composed many musical pieces for the baryton, an awkward version of the viola, simply because the prince played that instrument. But Haydn renegotiated his contract and started selling his music, achieving financial security equivalent to that of a millionaire today. When Nicolaus II, son of the earlier Esterhazy, criticized Haydn's conducting, Haydn replied, "Your Highness, that is my business."[17]

What about the idea that culture starves because artists starve? Again, widespread prosperity has made that less and less true. Over 250 years ago, J. S. Bach made an annual income that would translate into over $70,000 a year today.[18] At its worst, Mozart's income was three times greater than that of the head doctor at a Vienna hospital, and whatever financial hardship he suffered was due more to his profligate spending than to a lack of earning.[19] Nor were many of these artists shy about making money. Mozart wrote, "Believe me, my sole purpose is to make as much money as possible; for after good health it is the best thing to have."[20]

Of course, it's true that even nowadays artists work at other jobs to finance their art. U.S. poet Wallace Stevens published an impressive body of poetry while working full-time in the insurance industry. "He [Stevens] was a very imaginative claims man," said one former insurance colleague.[21] Interestingly, Stevens turned down an endowed chair to teach and write poetry at Harvard University. Even many moderately successful painters, musicians, and writers do make their living from their art.

Many cultural pessimists, people who think the culture is going downhill, make a simple statistical error. If there were 10 good songs a year for the last 40 years, and if there are 10 good ones this year, then this year is as good as any other. But people make the mistake of comparing all of this year's songs to the best of the last 40 years. Of course, this year comes up short; but so would, say, 1969 compared to all other years between 1960 and today. So next time you find yourself rejecting new songs, books, or paintings, remember this: Whereas everyone agrees that William Shakespeare's work is high culture, critics at the time considered him "lowbrow." And we have Shakespeare's plays today because they were in popular demand in the sixteenth century. Shakespeare and so many other famous artists thrived because their products were popular in the free market.

Whereas a few decades ago, someone could rightly complain that TV was a vast cultural wasteland, that claim is hard to sustain today. Most TV programming is still junk, at least by my standards. But cable and satellite television have multiplied the number of channels and programs so that almost no matter what your taste, you can find a program to satisfy it. Interestingly, the reason cable took so long to develop was that the Federal Communications Commission and local regulators held it back. Had unfettered capitalism been in place for the airwaves, we would have had much better choices years earlier. Also, municipal regulators around the country have generally granted legal monopolies to cable companies. These monopolies still exist, but satellite television, another capitalist innovation, has undercut their power.

How I Got Culture

A stereotype that many intellectuals hold strongly is that television and radio are the enemies of culture. Yet, popular television and radio shows gave me my earliest experience of classical music. I, like most other Americans over age 45, first heard Rossini's "William Tell Overture" as the theme song to the radio program, and later the television show, "The Lone Ranger." When my brother Paul and I used to hear it on the radio, we would gallop around the house, hitting our own backsides with our hands to spur on our imaginary horses, which is one reason I will never forget the "William Tell Overture." Of course, it wasn't until I was in college that I bought the record and heard the whole overture, but I never would have been interested in it had it not been for the radio and TV programs.

Similarly, my interest in Rossini's "The Barber of Seville" was first piqued by a Bugs Bunny cartoon in which Bugs sings a song to the tune of Rossini's opera.

ENDNOTES

1. Joseph A. Schumpeter, *Capitalism, Socialism, and Democracy,* New York: Harper & Row, 1942, p. 67.

2. Peter Brimelow, "Why they call it Harvard College," *Forbes,* March 9, 1998, pp. 50–51.

3. Mabel C. Buer, *Health, Wealth, and Population in the Early Days of the Industrial Revolution, 1760-1815,* London: George Routledge & Sons, 1926, p. 30.

4. These data are taken from Aaron Wildavsky, "Riskless Society," in David R. Henderson, ed., *The Fortune Encyclopedia of Economics,* New York: Warner Books, 1993, pp. 426–432, who, in turn, got them from *The 1991 Information Please Almanac,* Boston: Houghton Mifflin, 1991, pp. 817, 820.

5. W. Michael Cox and Richard Alm, *Myths of Rich and Poor,* New York: Basic Books, 1999, p. 15,

6. David Wessel, "Low-Income Mobility Was High in 1980s," *Wall Street Journal,* June 2, 1992, A2.

7. The data in this paragraph are from Isabell Sawhill, "Poverty in the United States," in David R. Henderson, *The Fortune Encyclopedia of Economics,* 1993, pp. 56–61. Shortly after writing this article, Sawhill, an economist with the Urban Institute in Washington, D.C., became an associate director of the Office of Management and Budget in President Clinton's administration.

8. See Hillary Hoynes, "Work, Welfare, and Family Structure: What Have We Learned?" National Bureau of Economic Research, Working Paper No. 5644, July 1996.

9. Fraker's study is quoted in Christopher Georges, "On Their Own: Most Iowans Taken Off Welfare Do Get By, Legally or Illegally," *Wall Street Journal,* May 16, 1997, p. A1.

10. For these data, see W. Michael Cox and Richard Alm, "Time Well Spent: The Declining Real Cost of Living in America," in Federal Reserve Bank of Dallas, 1997 Annual Report, pp. 2–24.

11. Cowen, *In Praise of Commercial Culture,* Cambridge: Harvard University Press, 1998, p. 51.

12. Douglas A. Blackmon, "Metamorphosis: Forget the Stereotype: America is Becoming a Nation of Culture," *Wall Street Journal,* September 17, 1998, p. A1.

13. Tyler Cowen, *In Praise of Commercial Culture,* Cambridge: Harvard University Press, 1998, p. 47.

14. Virginia Postrel, "A Net of Plenty," *Forbes ASAP*, April 6, 1998.

15. Cowen, *Commercial Culture,* pp. 166–168.

16. Ibid., pp. 62–64.

17. Ibid., pp. 137–138.

18. Ibid., p. 134.

19. Ibid., p. 139.

20. Ibid., p. 18.

21. Ibid., p. 17.

CHAPTER

9

WHOSE INCOME? WHO'S DISTRIBUTING?

As I mentioned in Chapter 5, when I was a kid, we spent every summer vacation at our cottage in Minaki, Ontario, Canada. Almost everyone else who had a cottage there was better off than our family, whether measured by income or wealth. To get around the system of lakes and rivers, you needed a canoe or a motorboat. Every other family I knew there had a motorboat; we had to make our way around in a canoe that my father had bought in 1931. Also, everyone but us—at least it seemed that way—was a member of the yacht club, a fancy name for an organization that had a few small sailboats and a cocktail lounge. My father strongly resented this "conspicuous consumption" of "the rich" around him. His working definition of "the rich" was anyone whose income was at least 30 percent more than his, and included almost everyone else who owned a cottage at Minaki. My father often talked as if he thought "the rich" had somehow obtained their income dishonestly or, at least, dishonorably. It also bugged me that some of my friends had their own motorboat or at least occasional access to their parents' boat. Some of my hardest times were when I would see my cousins out on the lake, water skiing, and not having invited us.

Yes, I shared my father's deep resentment of people who had more than we had. And given that about half the families in Canada had an income higher than ours, I had a lot of resentment. I adopted, subconsciously at least, my father's view that those with much more than us had come by it dishonestly. I had no evidence, of course. Sure, I had a few stories about wealthy people who had taken advantage of others, but I had no basis for my grudge against the millions of people I resented. Because I couldn't have some of the material possessions other kids had, I felt left out, and that was enough.

Then, in my late teens, I started to learn economics. I started to understand that the vast majority of income in a relatively free society is *earned*. It's true that a small number of wealthy people did get their money by fraud or dishonesty. More common, especially in societies with lots of government controls, were people who got wealthy by using political pull. But I started to see that the *typical* high-income person in a relatively free society gets his or her income the old-fashioned way—by *earning* it.

This resentment over the good fortunes of others is not unique to me. Often, when one person tells another that he or she won a prize or is going on a great vacation, the other person responds, "I hate you." It's generally said jokingly, but the fact that it is said at all speaks volumes.

My resentment didn't vanish instantly. It took years and wore away bit by bit. I remember going for a walk one time in Brentwood, a wealthy section of Los Angeles. As I walked north through Brentwood and got into the hillier sections, the homes I saw were nicer and nicer. Even though this was a full four years after I had realized that the vast majority of "the rich" get their money relatively honestly, I felt the old resentment at these people who had what I could not imagine myself ever being able to afford. I looked down at my fists and saw that I had clenched them in anger.

Even at my most resentful, though, I didn't see any basis for rejecting my belief in human freedom, which includes people's right to keep what they earn or are given. That was one reason I felt so upset after my walk in Brentwood: I didn't even have the consolation of being able to say, "I'll get you" or "Your taxes should be raised and your wealth expropriated." But imagine how easy it would be, if you had no strong belief in people's freedom, for your resentment of the rich to lead you to conclude that the government should take what they have. In 1969, I heard Will Herberg, a prominent American Communist in the 1930s and 1940s who had later become a strong anticommunist, speak at a conference. My friend Clancy and I asked him how he had come to be a Marxist. Immediately, his eyes lit up. He talked passionately about growing up with very few possessions, but because he was smart, being hired as a teenager to teach the dumb kids of wealthy parents. He told us of his intense resentment of the fact that he was smart and had nothing, while they were dumb and had a lot. "That," he said, "is how I became a Marxist. I hated the rich." We were shocked. We had thought that virtually all intellectuals came to their views via their intellect, not via their resentments. Herberg must have read our faces, because he added that his route to Marxism was a very common one. "The number of people who became Marxists by reading Marx," I still remember him saying, "can be counted on the fingers of one hand."

My resentment toward "the rich" has declined over the years. That's fortunate, because envy is very self-destructive. Three things have helped me become less resentful, and I recommend all three to you if you sometimes envy those who have more.

First, when I feel envious of those who are wealthier than I, I remind myself to take deep breaths, look around me, and think. When I start thinking, I realize how incredibly wealthy I am and how incredibly wealthy almost everyone in the industrialized world is. As I detailed in the previous chapter, the modern world, compared to the world of 200 years ago and even compared to the world of 30 years ago, is a world transformed.

Second, I remind myself that, in the long run, I am the person most responsible for where I've gotten and, if I really want things to be different, I can take responsibility for making them different. A few years ago I complained to my friend Tom Nagle that, although I was as smart as many of the Harvard faculty, I was not at nearly as prestigious a school.

"You chose not to teach at Harvard," shot back Tom.

"What do you mean?" I said, stunned, hurt, and defensive, all at the same time.

Tom replied, "I mean that if you had decided in graduate school that you wanted to teach at Harvard, you could have committed to working 12 hours a day, six and a half days a week, you could have had three articles published in top academic journals, and you could have had a shot at Harvard. To get tenure there, you would have had to keep up that same pace for another five to ten years. You chose not to do that."

Now, whenever I feel bad about not teaching at Harvard, I remember that discussion and I feel better almost instantly. I've made a choice. I like working "only" nine hours a day, five to six days a week, and having a life with my wife, my daughter, and my community.

Looking back, I realize that I was responsible for my own outcomes even when I was a kid. When I saw that everyone at our summer resort but us had a boat, I decided to make enough money to buy a used motorboat. At age 13, I spent a large part of my summer, and a large part of my free time during the school year, at various odd jobs and entrepreneurial ventures. By the start of the next summer I had almost enough to buy a boat. I decided not to after all, but that's another story. While I was working for the money to buy the boat, my resentment of others vanished. I enjoyed working towards a goal.

I've had people tell me that it's easy for me to talk this way because I have many high-paying skills, such as writing and speaking. But even people of very modest means who live in the industrialized world can accumulate net worths of half a million or more. Dwight Lee and Richard McKenzie, economists at the University of Georgia and the University of

California at Irvine, respectively, recently wrote a fascinating book, *Getting Rich in America,* in which they laid out eight simple rules for becoming rich.

EIGHT SIMPLE RULES FOR GETTING RICH IN AMERICA

These rules are taken from Dwight Lee's and Richard McKenzie's book, *Getting Rich in America: 8 Simple Rules for Building a Fortune and a Satisfying Life.* I've added short explanations, illustrations, or quotes for each, some of which are taken from Lee's and McKenzie's book.

1. *Think of America as a land of choices.*

   "If you want your prayers answered, get off your knees and hustle." —Ron Jones, owner of Handy Andy Janitorial Services, Plano, Texas

2. *Take the power of compound interest seriously—and then save.*

   Famous physicist Albert Einstein, when asked what the most powerful force in nature is, is reputed to have answered "compound interest." If you invest $2,000 a year and earn an 8 percent real (i.e., inflation-adjusted) rate of return, after 30 years you will have $207,932; after 40 years, you will have $477,882.

3. *Resist temptation.*

   If, three times a week, you substitute a $1.00 bag lunch for a $6.00 restaurant lunch and invest the amount saved at 8 percent a year, after 30 years you will have saved over $28,000.

4. *Get education.*

   Remember, *education,* not just schooling. (For the difference, see Chapter 16.)

5. *Get married and stay married.* Married people live longer.

6. *Take care of yourself.* Exercise, eat, and drink in moderation.

7. *Take prudent risks.*

If you're not planning to touch your funds for at least 15 years, invest them in index funds—funds that track the stock market. Also, invest in funds, such as Vanguard, that have low management fees.

8. *Strive for balance.*

Don't just build wealth; build your character also, and add a component of service to others.

When I reviewed their book for the *Wall Street Journal,*[1] I realized that I had been living by these rules. And it worked. Starting with a net worth of less than $1,000 (counting all my possessions, including my car) at age 31, and helped by a booming stock market and housing market, by my late 40s I was well over half way to having a net worth of $1,000,000. And I plan for this book and another book in the works to put me over the top. Lee's and McKenzie's eight rules make it virtually a sure thing that you'll get rich if you don't die early or get some horrible disease—and following their rules will help you live long and not get a horrible disease. But I realized that you could boil the rules down to the two rules I gave a friend who worried that the information revolution would jeopardize his journalism career: Live below your means, and invest in stock-index funds.

The third thing that helps me when I feel envious is to realize that the language of economics has set me up, along with many others, to feel envious. Pick up any basic economics textbook and you'll probably find a section on the distribution of income. The distribution of income is simply a statistical measure of how many people earn or receive various amounts of income. However, people, including many economists, often mistakenly talk as if society is "distributing" income and people are passively receiving it. When I think of someone distributing income, I imagine a truck backing up to a crowd of people, the tailgate coming down, and someone on the truck throwing out wads of dollar bills. If you think someone is just handing out money, then the most natural thing in the world is to think that everyone should get the same amount and that it's unfair if they don't.

I have news for people who think that society is distributing income: *No one is distributing*. In a free society, we *earn* our income. Society didn't wake up one morning and decide that Michael Jordan deserved $10 million for playing basketball and $30 million for advertising consumer products. Instead, Michael Jordan woke every morning for more than 15 years with a fierce determination to stay in tremendous physical shape, to practice for hours a day, often with weights on his arms and legs, and to be the awesome athlete that he was. And millions of basketball fans and buyers of consumer products didn't "distribute" to Mr. Jordan. Instead they decided, one by one, to spend a little more time watching Jordan on TV, or to spend a few pennies or dollars more for products that he advertised. That's how his income was determined: not by society distributing, but by Jordan earning.

So, whenever you hear that the top 20 percent *receive* 45 percent of all income or that the top 5 percent *receive* 20 percent of all income, remember what that really means. It means that the top 20 percent *produced* 45 percent of all output and that the top 5 percent *produced* 20 percent of all output. Also, the connection between the number of family members producing and the income they generate is a major factor in the inequality of family income. An average household in the top fifth has about 2.5 times as many workers as an average household in the bottom fifth.[2] The bottom fifth includes many single mothers, a lot of them on welfare. The top fifth includes a high number of two-earner married couples along with, presumably, some working teenagers or young adults.

You might think I exaggerate when I say that the word "distribution" misleads people into thinking that someone is distributing. But if people aren't misled, then why, when we talk about government taking from some and giving to others, do we use the word *redistribution*? If no one is distributing in the first place, then such government measures should simply be called *distribution*. Where does the "re" in redistribution come from? It must come from the mistaken assumption that someone distributed wealth in the first place. Of course, the idea that someone is distributing is ludicrous. But our language makes many of us think that way, with highly destructive consequences.

Fortunately, there is a lot of clear thinking on this issue, especially by people who have not received a lot of formal education and therefore have not been corrupted by what almost all American universities teach. One incident in particular was one of the first things that made me want to move to the United States. While running for the Democratic presidential nomination in 1972, George McGovern proposed a 100 percent tax—complete confiscation—on all inheritances over $500,000 (about $2.5 million in year 2001 dollars). Gordon L. Weil, one of McGovern's advisors who favored the plan, later wrote,

> McGovern was completely comfortable with the admittedly radical proposal, because we all shared the belief that most people had a strong bias against great concentrations of inherited wealth. The proposals would directly affect only a handful of people.[3]

But the good Democratic citizens of New Hampshire, from whom McGovern was seeking votes, were not at all comfortable with the proposal. Weil writes,

> I remember sitting one day in the Lafayette Club in Nashua with a group of workmen who opposed the idea of a confiscatory inheritance tax. Although none of them stood to be penalized by it, they argued that it was unfair to take away all that a man had received. McGovern was receiving similar reactions in the plants we visited and believed that all men nourished the hope of receiving a large inheritance or of winning a lottery.[4]

Notice that McGovern assumed that these workers held out unrealistic hopes of "winning a lottery," instead of believing that what they said upset them really was what upset them, namely that they simply found McGovern's confiscatory tax unfair.

Americans still think the way these New Hampshire workers thought. In 2000, when Congress passed a bill to repeal the estate tax and President Clinton vetoed it, a *Wall Street Journal* reporter found people opposing the tax who knew that the direct effect on them would be nonexistent. Luisa Olear, for example, a high-school teacher in Rockledge, Florida, joked that she would never pay the tax unless she appeared on "Who Wants to Be a Millionaire?" But then she added, "I think that's money that has been earned by somebody and that person has already paid taxes on it. I don't think that's right."[5] Contrast that with Treasury Secretary Lawrence Summers' claim, while he was deputy secretary, that efforts to repeal the tax were based on "selfishness."[6] Americans in general show a better understanding of basic principles of fair play than do many of America's leading politicians.

When we discuss income distribution in my class, I often ask the students to tell me all the rules about fairness or justice that they learned when growing up. I then write them down on the board. Invariably, I get something like the following:

> Do unto others as you would have them do unto you. (The Golden Rule).
> You reap what you sow.
> What goes around comes around.
> Don't steal.
> An eye for an eye, and a tooth for a tooth.
> Share with others.

The other rules tend to be variations of these. Philosophers have two main ways of judging whether something is fair. One is the end-state view of fairness: The outcome is fair based only on the outcome and not on how we got there. The other is a process view of fairness: The outcome's fairness can't be judged independently of the process used to get there. I then go through the list on the board and classify the rules my students gave me according to whether they're *E,* an end-state view of fairness, or *P,* a process view. Typically, about 80 to 90 percent of the rules are process-based. Take, for example, the rule "Don't steal." According to this rule, it doesn't matter how much the person you steal from has and how little you have; stealing is wrong. In other words, you don't even look at the outcome. That is straight P. To contrast the two types of rules, consider two people, each with one million dollars. One made the million by working hard on a product that he sold to customers, and he never lied to or cheated any customer or employee. The other designed a clever piece of computer software that stole one dollar from each of 1 million people's bank accounts. Which of the two got his money justly? Virtually all of us would answer that it was the guy who made the money honestly. In other words, *how* the person made the money matters a lot. Yet a straight end-state view would say that how the money was made doesn't matter at all. What this shows is that virtually all of us hold a process view of justice. Incidentally, so do all the major religions that I know of. The one I'm most familiar with, having grown up with it, is Christianity. Look at any of the Ten Commandments, which also apply to Judaism. Each of them, from "Thou shalt not steal" to "Thou shalt not kill," is pure process. Islam and all the other great religions of the world have similar strictures against theft and murder. Also, the Tenth Commandment says, "Thou shalt not covet thy neighbor's house, thou shalt not covet thy neighbor's wife, nor his manservant, nor his maidservant, nor his ox, nor his ass; nor anything that is thy neighbor's." As political writer P. J. O'Rourke has noted, isn't it interesting that God saw the issue of envy as so important enough to list as one of only 10 commandments?

Which view—process or end-state—do the vast majority of economists talk about when they talk about a just distribution of income? Here's a hint. They tend to judge how just or "equitable" an income distribution is by how equal it is; they don't ask *how* people got what they got. In short, the vast majority of economists have a purely end-state view of justice. Typical, for example, is economist Joseph Stiglitz, formerly the chairman of President Clinton's Council of Economic Advisers, who, in his textbook *Economics of the Public Sector,* writes,

> Consider again a simple economy with two individuals, Robinson Crusoe and Friday. Assume initially that Robinson Crusoe has ten oranges, while Friday has only two. This seems

inequitable. Assume, therefore, that we play the role of government and attempt to transfer four oranges from Robinson
Crusoe to Friday, but in the process one orange gets lost.
Hence Robinson Crusoe ends up with six oranges, and Friday
with five. We have eliminated most of the inequity, but in the
process the total number of oranges available has been dimin-
ished. There is a trade-off between efficiency—the total number of oranges available—and equity.[7]

Notice that Stiglitz doesn't even bother to tell the reader
how Crusoe and Friday got what they got. He doesn't tell
because the process is irrelevant to him; all that matters is the
end state. He hedges himself by saying it "seems" inequitable
rather than it is inequitable, but by the end of the paragraph,
the hedge is gone and Stiglitz comes right out and says that
inequality is inequitable.

While many economists and philosophers write about just
distributions of income based solely on degree of inequality, I'll
bet they don't raise their children that way. They are not indif-
ferent about whether their children earned or stole what they
have; it matters greatly to them how the end state was reached
because ends alone are not enough to justify the means. And if
their kid treated another badly, I doubt the kid would be able
to justify his behavior by saying, "But I did it because he's
rich!" So, on decisions that really matter to them—how they
raise their kids versus what they publish in economics and philosophy journals—I would bet dollars to doughnuts that they
turn out to believe in the process view. The problem is not that
these people don't practice what they preach. What they
preach—the end-state view of justice—is horrible. What I
would like is for all these economists and philosophers to
preach what they practice.

I can't leave this topic without highlighting something else
that Stiglitz writes about income distribution, something that
also represents the mainstream economics viewpoint. Stiglitz
writes,

Thus, if we don't like the income distribution generated by
the competitive market, we need not abandon the use of the
competitive market mechanism. All we need do is redistrib-

ute the initial wealth, and then leave the rest to the competitive market.[8]

Oh, is that "all"? Stiglitz makes it sound as easy as changing a graph on a blackboard. But, in fact, to "redistribute the
initial wealth" in any substantial way would probably lead to a
bloody civil war. A lot of people whose main wealth is in their
house, for example, would fight to keep their wealth. Stiglitz,
who is almost certainly a multimillionaire, would probably be
one of them. Moreover, once people figured out that every time
"we" (Stiglitz's euphemism for the government) don't like the
income distribution, "we" will intervene to change it, they will
be less likely to do things to earn that wealth. And you can be
sure that the government will want to intervene a lot because,
even if we achieved total equality, the market would upset that
pattern. In Louisiana, for example, a mother gives birth to a big
baby who grows up to be bigger than all his classmates. He also
has an aptitude for basketball and he hones his skills in high
school and college. Then, when the Orlando Magic basketball
team hires him, even unwealthy people are willing to pay to see
him play. Therefore, teams that want lots of customers are willing to pay him to play for them. Thus does Shaquille O'Neill get
rich. So do many other less visible people who have aptitude for
business, or who have any rare skill that is in great demand.

The free market upsets patterns. A government devoted to
enforced equality must intervene again and again to prevent
inequality. Either it must prevent wealthy people from spending their money the way they want or it must confiscate all
income above a modest level. A truly equality-oriented government might even try what the regulators tried in the
humorous yet haunting short story, "Harrison Bergeron," by
Kurt Vonnegut. In that story, the government offset the inherent advantages people had so that no one would have an
advantage. Physically powerful men had to wear weights so
that they wouldn't be able to perform better than anyone else.
Beautiful women had to wear masks to hide their beauty.
Smart people had to wear electric headgear that zapped them
whenever they started to think clearly. If "we" truly don't like
the distribution of wealth or income that results from a free
market, and if "we" insist on having the government "correct"

it, we will end up with a vicious totalitarian government.

However, if you, not "we," don't like your position in the income and wealth distribution, then put your effort where your mouth is. Follow the eight rules listed earlier and change your income and wealth.

If you're sitting reading this in a poor country, you probably already know how to get wealthier. Rule one was "Think of America as a land of choices." Rule zero is "Move to America." Or, if you can't leave, then stay in your own country but push for deregulation, private property, and cutting your oppressive government down to size.

The whole focus on income inequality is mistaken. If income distribution or wealth distribution in a country is equal or close to equal, that means either that there are no highly productive people or that the highly productive people are hemmed in by regulations and taxes. Either way, the economy will be one sick puppy. The vast majority of Americans are doing as well as we are because a few million people are making a lot of money figuring out how to create new products and new ways to increase our productivity. Show me an economy with equal incomes and I'll show you an economy that's in deep trouble.

Pundits and analysts constantly sift through the data to find inequalities in income, which are not hard to find. Then, they try to figure out how to shave off some of the inequality. That process, if taken to its logical extreme, is bound to destroy human freedom and prosperity. Instead, we should focus on ways that governments hold people down—in the United States and in the rest of the world—and figure out how to end those oppressive measures. Which brings me to the story of my friend François Melese.

ENDNOTES

1. David R. Henderson, "The Wonders of a Penny Saved," *Wall Street Journal,* May 10, 1999, p. A21.

2. Cait Murphy, "Are the Rich Cleaning Up?" *Fortune,* September 4, 2000, p. 258.

3. Gordon L. Weil, *The Long Shot: George McGovern Runs for President,* New York: W.W. Norton, 1973, p. 75.

4. Weil, *Long Shot,* p. 77.

5. Jacob M. Schlesinger and Nicholas Kulish, "Will Power: As Paper Millionaires Multiply, Estate Tax Takes a Public Beating," *Wall Street Journal,* July 13, 2000, A1.

6. Jackie Calmes, "Grave Concern: Washington Is Moving to Alter the Certainty of Death and Taxes," *Wall Street Journal,* April 28, 1997, p. A1.

7. Joseph E. Stiglitz, *Economics of the Public Sector,* 3rd ed., New York: W.W. Norton, 2000, p. 94.

8. Stiglitz, *Public Sector,* p. 60.

MEET FRANÇOIS MELESE

Give a man a fish, and you feed him for a day; teach him to fish and you feed him for life.

—OLD SAYING

Give a man a fish, and you feed him for a day; allow him to fish, own his net and boat, and keep what he catches, and refrain from regulating the price he charges, and he feeds himself for life.

—DAVID R. HENDERSON

One of my closest friends, and also the person I talk with most about economics, is François Melese. François grew up in an upper-middle-income household in La Jolla, California, near the University of California at San Diego, where his father was an engineer. In 1972, at age 17, he made a crucial choice, one that helped lead him to his career and his view of the world. "I felt that I wanted to do something constructive, something positive," he explains. "I saw a lot of stuff going on that wasn't positive—people taking drugs, people with too much money and not enough sense. La Jolla was sheltered from the real world. I was searching for a contribution to make, but I didn't know what it was."

That year, François and two friends learned about an organization, Amigos de las Americas (Friends of the Americas), that had been formed by doctors who felt there was an unmet need for basic medical care in Latin American countries. Amigos planned to take bright U.S. high school students, give them medical and language training, and send them down to Latin America to immunize children against three killers—diphtheria, pertussis, and tetanus. François and his friends spent the year practicing their Spanish and giving each other saline shots. "We gave each other shots everywhere—in our arms, our shoulders, our butts, everywhere," he recalls, laughing.

The next summer, after graduating from high school, François was ready. He was sent to Nicaragua for most of June and July. François landed at Managua, the capital of Nicaragua, which was then being run by the notorious dictator Antonio Somoza. He arrived just weeks after an earthquake had virtually destroyed Managua, and so his first patients were in the resettlement camps created to house those who had lost their homes in the earthquake. The typical pattern was for him and the other volunteers to go into a small village and spend a week or less, giving DPT shots to children, DT shots to teenagers, and tetanus shots to adults. Then they would move on to the next village and do the same thing.

What François noticed changed his view of the world forever: "Before going to Nicaragua, I wanted to be a doctor. While I was there, I decided that's what I *didn't* want to be." Why the change? François explained:

> I realized that there were other things causing the problem that had nothing to do with medicine. The problem was political and economic. There was a huge maldistribution of wealth, income, and opportunity. I also noticed that there were incentive problems. Farmers in the jungle told me how proud they were that they were farming on Somoza's land without him knowing. I remember thinking it was crazy that one person—Somoza—owned all this land and that here were

these entrepreneurial people who had to sneak onto his land and took a big risk doing it. That seemed really bizarre. We take for granted that if you're entrepreneurial in our country, you can own land.

I thought that if they didn't own land, they didn't have the incentive to invest. They didn't know when they might get kicked off. So they stayed near subsistence rather than taking the next step and marketing the maize and platinos [plantain—a banana-like plant]. The farmers tended garden-sized plots surreptitiously because soldiers were patrolling. They were constantly threatened by the soldiers and had to bribe them.

But wasn't he at least doing good? François says,

I thought, here's this great savior, trying to do all this good. I found out that I'm the one who benefited because they're going to die. I was giving these kids shots and they would be dead in a year. They wouldn't live long enough for the shots to work. That makes me feel like crying, even thinking about it now. It was unnecessary. I didn't see why it had to be that way. I felt that we were treating symptoms and not causes. There were a hell of a lot of symptoms. There had to be some underlying causes. That's what I needed to understand. That's why I'm glad I discovered economics. Because I found out that it doesn't have to be that way.

The next year, François went to the University of California in Berkeley. "I took biology and was thinking premed, but I was not excited. Then I stumbled across the answer to what I had seen in Nicaragua. It was in my first economics course, a course in microeconomics, in my third year at Berkeley."

Everyone around me was saying, "Save the Whales." I had a very good economics instructor. In his class, I got an explanation for the first time about why the whales were being slaughtered. It was because nobody owned them. The professor who taught the class was brilliant at applying economic principles to real life. I realized that property rights mattered and incentives mattered. I realized that the cost of doing anything productive in Nicaragua was high because you had to pay people off—soldiers, government officials, and so on. That cut off a lot of productivity that would have got people above subsistence. For the first time, I started to develop an explanation of what I had seen in Nicaragua.

Once a week, my class of 500 divided into smaller groups, each led by a graduate student teaching assistant [TA]. My TA was outstanding. He was an Iranian student who got excited about the way I was thinking. I kept testing my understanding, making connections between the economic theory we were learning and my experiences, not just in Nicaragua, but generally. The TA was pro-free market, definitely not a socialist.

Did François take any courses on the economics of developing countries?

I took a development economics course from Prenab Bardhan. At the time, there were two competing views among development economists. The dominant view from the 1950s to the early 1970s was that you needed some degree of socialism for development in poor countries to occur. The newer view, which is now the dominant one, is the exact opposite. According to this view, what poor countries need is property rights, freedom of contract, low taxes, low government spending, free trade. Bardhan had this view.

Did François ever think that socialism might be a good economic system? "I was toying with socialism and communism and trying to figure out what that was about," he says. "I took a course on the economics of socialism. I thought that this just doesn't make sense. It won't work."

In the summer of 1977, after he graduated from Berkeley, François had some real-life experience with socialism: He joined a commune.

My girlfriend at the time, Priscilla, had a junior year abroad in Spain. She had arranged to spend a month on a farm owned by a wealthy entrepreneur in Barcelona. A group of about ten people, all of whom were college students or had graduated from college, had made a proposal to revive his farm. They would run it as a commune. He bought the livestock, provided the seed grain, etc., and the group provided the labor. Priscilla invited me to join her. I did.

Hutterite communities in the northwestern United States work on the principle, made famous by Karl Marx but also based on certain passages in the Bible, "From each according to his ability to each according to his needs." Garrett Hardin, a professor of human ecology at the University of California at Santa Barbara, coined the term "tragedy of the commons" to describe what happens when that principle is applied. Each person has an incentive to shirk, noted Hardin, because each person's gain from being productive is not his own output but is only 1/n of that output, where n can be a very large number. As the size of a Hutterite colony approaches 150, wrote Hardin, "individual Hutterites tend to undercontribute from their abilities and overdemand for their needs." Below 150 people, he claims, the Hutterites can use shame to get people to be productive. Above that number, even shame doesn't work. François found the threshold for the effectiveness of shame to be much lower:

> There were a dozen people, and hardly anyone took responsibility. You could choose to do whatever task you wanted and how effective you were didn't matter. No one wanted the nasty jobs. The stables had been abandoned for 20 years and someone needed to clean them out. Priscilla and I did that. We spent two or three days at that awful job.

> No one bothered to close the chicken coop. The foxes got in and we were left with one chicken. The person who was supposed to watch the sheep, a philosophy student, let them wander off. Someone asked him why he had let it happen and he said he was playing the flute and having some great transcendental thoughts and didn't want to be interrupted. We lost three days trying to find the sheep. Disaster followed disaster. This was our livelihood. But even though Priscilla and I were there for a month, and the others were planning to be there longer term, they didn't have the same sense of urgency that we had.

There was no accountability on that commune. There were no rewards for being productive. Everyone was treated equally, and that was the problem. Whether you were effective or ineffective, you got the same reward—a piece of garlic bread at the end of the day. That's when I figured out that there wasn't a lot of hope for the Soviet Union. The Soviet system was so warped that you got strong personalities dictating and dominating. The people who contributed real substance didn't get much reward. That's why I wrote an article, much later in 1988, saying that Communism would collapse.

In 1988, François wrote an article that began as follows:

A quiet revolution is currently taking place in the Soviet Union. Mikhail S. Gorbachev has initiated a set of internal reforms which begin with nothing less than a reversal in the thought process of the average Russian citizen. Gorbachev's market-oriented economic philosophy *(perestroika)* could eventually lead to Western-style economic reforms, particularly in the civilian sector of the economy.[1]

His article was incredibly prescient. One year after it was published, the Berlin Wall came down and two years after that, the Soviet Union ceased to exist.

François now teaches at the Defense Resources Management Institute (DRMI), an organization run by the U.S. Department of Defense. His job, besides publishing economic research articles, is to teach basic economics to medium-level and high-level government officials in poorer countries around the world and, at times, in classes given in Monterey. One of the main things he teaches them is that free markets and private property are the way for them to escape poverty.

He's not alone. Serious economists at the World Bank, at the International Monetary Fund, in economics departments at U.S. and other universities, and at think tanks around the world have come to the view that what the Third World needs most for growth is economic freedom. Indeed, the story of how government regulation has kept people desperately poor in most of Africa, most of Asia, and much of Latin America is worth telling in some detail, as is the more hopeful ending, as many countries turn away from the extremes of government control. But rather than get into the details here, I recommend that you go to my Web site, *www.davidrhenderson.com,* and read it there.

The lessons that François started to understand on that commune in Spain apply to both poor and rich countries, which is why, within economics, the studies of economic growth and economic development have merged in the last few years. The basic lesson to be learned from the last 40 years is that growth's major enemy is heavy government intervention—whether through tariffs, price controls, high taxes, lavish government spending, or detailed regulation. Fortunately, people around the world have been learning that lesson in the last two decades and have been pushing their governments to implement the lessons learned. And it's working. According to the World Bank, the number of people classified as poor in East and Southeast Asia fell from 717 million to less than half that, 346 million, in the 20 years ending in 1995. As economist Charles Kadlec, citing this statistic, points out, "South Korea, Taiwan, Hong Kong, and Singapore have essentially eliminated absolute poverty as a national concern."[2]

The next big challenge is Africa, the true horror story of all the continents. Massive deregulation, tax cuts, government spending cuts, price decontrol, and tariff cuts, combined with enforcement of property rights, would turn Africa into a relatively wealthy continent within a generation.

ENDNOTES

1. François Melese, "A Quiet Revolution in the Soviet Union," *Defense Analysis,* Vol. 4, No. 4, pp. 395–398, 1988.

2. Charles W. Kadlec, *Dow 100,000: Fact or Fiction,* New York: New York Institute of Finance, 1999, p. 162.

11 MARKET VIRTUES AND COMMUNITY

Talk about free markets and capitalism to almost any intellectual and even many businessmen, and you'll get the idea that although capitalism delivers the goods, it's short on virtue. This view, more than any other, explains why advocates of government control over people's lives so often are conceded the high moral ground. Yet the exact opposite is closer to the truth. Markets teach or encourage at least three virtues: tolerance, honesty, and compassion.

MARKETS TEACH TOLERANCE

"Schindler got into [saving Jews] for the wrong reasons." These were the words of U.S. Ambassador to Japan Walter Mondale in a 1994 speech at Tokyo's Jewish Community

Center.[1] Former U.S. vice-president Mondale found Oskar Schindler, hero of the movie *Schindler's List*, less admirable than others who saved Jews from being killed. Mondale's reason: Schindler's original motive was to make money by employing Jews. But Mondale misunderstood free markets.

Why is it wrong to make money by employing people who otherwise would die? Making ourselves better off is one of the most natural human motives there is. Whenever I ask people why they think the profit motive is wrong, their reply is that it leads to bad results. But in Schindler's case, the profit motive had *good* results, and no one disputes that fact. So, if you judge the profit motive by results, isn't profit in this case a good motive and not a bad one?

The turning point in the movie comes when a young woman named Perlman comes to see Schindler. "They say you are good," she says, and she begs him to hire her parents to save them from the Nazis. He refuses. After his conversation with Perlman, Schindler says angrily to his accountant Stern,

> People die. It's a fact of life. He [Amon Goeth, the head Nazi official] wants to kill everybody. Great! What am I supposed to do about it? Bring everybody over? Is that what you think? Send them over to Schindler. Send them all. His place is a haven, don't you know? It's not a factory. It's not an enterprise of any kind. It's a haven, for rabbis, and orphans, and people with no skills whatsoever.

Schindler's anger comes from a frustration that he didn't feel earlier in the film. The Jews who work for him have taken on names and faces; he no longer sees them merely as a source of income. After his outburst, he gives the go-ahead to get Perlman's parents out of the work camp and into his factory.

Another scene, later in the movie, confirms the change in Schindler. He paces his office as Stern, seated at the typewriter, types the names of hundreds of people whom Schindler wants to ransom from the Nazis.

SCHINDLER: How many?

STERN: 850, give or take.

SCHINDLER (UPSET): Give or take what, Stern? Give or take
what? Count them. How many?

In other words, to Schindler, each person is worth count-
ing—each has value; 850 differs from 851 by one person, and
that person's life matters. This is a major transformation.
Earlier in the movie, after rescuing Stern from certain murder,
Schindler had said angrily, "What if I got here five minutes
later? Then where would I be?" He had been upset about being
without an accountant. Now he cared about all his workers.

This transformation made some movie critics call Schindler
"complicated" *(San Francisco Chronicle)* and "puzzling" and
"contradictory" *(Atlanta Journal and Constitution)*. But
Schindler's growing humanity is about as hard to understand as
warm weather in summer and should surprise only those people
who think about Marxist cardboard characters—"workers" and
"capitalists"—rather than real human beings. Schindler started to
like the people he worked with. Commerce does that. Almost all
of us care for the people we work with, whether they are our
employees, our employers, or our fellow workers. Indeed, we
think of fellow workers who don't care about anyone else as being
odd, troubled, unusual. Anyone who knows employers knows that
the part of the job many of them hate most is firing somebody.

Schindler was a hero—his actions were heroic because he
took a big risk. But what led to his heroic actions was his caring for his employees, something that is quite normal. Virtually
all of us would be willing to take some risks to help those
around us, and the bigger the threat to their well-being, death
obviously being the biggest threat, the bigger the risk we're
willing to take. So the transformation in Schindler, though
heroic, was entirely normal. The free market created an environment in which Schindler learned to value people; in a
sense, markets taught Schindler morality.

If Mondale and other critics of Schindler care about virtue,
then they also should care about the kinds of social systems
that lead to virtue. *Schindler's List* shows, in a dramatic way,
that employers can make money by resisting racism and in the
process become better people. Schindler is one example
among many. I gave other examples in Chapter 7.

The single most important factor that has broken down racial discrimination is free markets. As Gary Becker has shown,[2] when people are free to trade, it is costly to discriminate on the basis of personal characteristics that having nothing to do with productivity or with the quality of the product being exchanged. People respond by discriminating less, by paying less attention to racial characteristics that disturb them. And, as they come to see that the people against whom they had discriminated are human, then—surprise, surprise—some of them eventually don't care about differences at all. What did Mondale ever do for the so-called "right" reasons that accomplished as much?

Something implicit in these examples needs to be made explicit: Not only do markets breed tolerance, but government interference also breeds intolerance. The way it does so depends on the particular government regulation. Look back at Chapter 7 for examples. But tolerance is not the only virtue that markets engender and governments discourage.

MARKETS TEACH ACCOUNTABILITY

When I buy something at Macy's and I don't like it, I can return it. I used to hesitate to do that because I thought they would expect me to have an acceptable reason for returning the item. But my wise friend Bill Haga, who carefully observes companies and their business practices, once suggested that the next time I return something, I say literally nothing other than, "I would like a refund." Then, he said, bite your tongue and wait and see if they ask for more detail. I tried what he suggested, even though it was very hard for me to restrain myself from launching into all kinds of explanations. Sure enough, the salesperson asked for no explanation. Since then, I have followed the same strategy every time. Every once in a while, a salesperson will ask for an explanation; however, it is usually clear that the store is monitoring the quality of its own products, not second-guessing my judgment. And on those rare occasions when the salesperson does seem to be questioning my judgment, the retailer is some relatively unknown hole-in-the-wall outfit, or the salesperson seems relatively new to the job and has not yet learned the employer's practices.

This goes beyond accountability. The market has taught these companies not just to be accountable for their products, but also to care about satisfying their customers. They've learned that if they don't care, they won't last as long as companies that do.

To see the extent to which markets make private, for-profit firms accountable, compare them to government-run firms. Hold all else equal by comparing a government-run firm and a private, for-profit firm that produce, or purport to produce, a similar product. The government firm is the U.S. Postal Service, and its product is the overnight mail service called Postal Express. It guarantees that it will deliver to certain locations by the next day, but does not specify a time. The private, for-profit firm is Federal Express, and its product is the overnight mail service. FedEx guarantees that it will deliver by 9:30 a.m. or by 3:00 p.m. the next day, depending on the level of service paid for.

I never use Postal Express because when people have used it to send items to me, the items have almost never arrived on the guaranteed day. I have, however, used FedEx over 100 times and received items delivered by FedEx a few hundred times; they have never been more than 10 minutes late, and even that happened only a few times.

A few years ago, in its advertising, the U.S. Postal Service bragged of an on-time record well in excess of 90 percent. Think about that. FedEx is rarely even minutes late, and the U.S. Postal Service is bragging that less than 10 percent of the time is it *a day or more late*. Also, if Postal Express is late, try going through their government maze to get a refund.

Why the difference in accountability? The reason has to do with the profit motive in private business versus very little motive in government-run business. True, the individual person delivering for FedEx does not make more profit by performing well. But FedEx does. Therefore, FedEx makes it in the individual worker's interest to perform well—by paying or promoting for performance, or by firing for nonperformance.

But if the Postmaster General improves the efficiency of the Postal Service, this benefit goes neither to him nor to a well-defined group of stockholders.

More generally, if I have a beef with a private company, I can ask to speak to the owner. If I have a beef with a government-run organization, to whom do I speak?

When I was at Washington University in St. Louis, Nobel laureate Douglass North was one of my colleagues. North has written a lot about the problem of creating markets when most of the participants are strangers and the transactions between them are one-time. North writes,

> [R]ealizing the economic potential of the gains from trade in a high technology world of enormous specialization and division of labor characterized by impersonal exchange is extremely rare, because one does not necessarily have repeated dealings, nor know the other party, nor deal with a small number of other people.[3]

But my own experience, and that of virtually everyone I know, persuades me that the market generally handles this problem. It does so with reputations.

Just before moving from St. Louis back to Monterey, California, I told Doug North that, on my drive across the country, every purchase of gas, every purchase of a meal, and every rental on a motel room would be a one-time transaction between a stranger and me. Moreover, because I would be driving, I would not want to stick around and take someone to small claims court for cheating me on quality. So, by his theory, I said, these should be some of the toughest cases for markets to handle. I should be nervous about getting the quality I pay for. Yet, I told him, I had no fear that I would buy gas contaminated with water, buy food that had spoiled, or stay in a dirty room. As it turned out, my confidence was justified. Somehow, even in the toughest tests for markets—one-time transactions between strangers on the move—the markets had worked well.

How did the market solve those problems? With brand names and the irreversible investments in reputation that go with them—investments and reputations that are at risk if the producer shirks on quality. I bought only major-brand gas, ate at brand-name restaurants ranging from Taco Bell to Denny's, and stayed at motels certified by the American Automobile Association. Actually, because I drove late my last night on the road, I was unable to get a triple-A room, and so I stayed in a non-rated motel. There was a difference. The furniture was shabbier; the phone had no use instructions on it; there was a shower but no tub; and the room was decorated in early American graduate student. Even there, though, the quality wasn't terrible. The heater, shower, and TV all worked, and the bed was comfortable enough. So here was a non-brand and non-certified company dealing mainly with strangers, and even it had some modest incentive to produce some minimum level of quality.

Markets breed accountability and governments do not.

MARKETS, AND THE WEALTH THEY GENERATE, BREED COMPASSION AND CHARITY

As Milton and Rose Friedman have pointed out,[4] the major growth of charity in the United States took place in the nineteenth century, when real incomes were steadily increasing. Many of the most famous charities—the Society for the Prevention of Cruelty to Animals, the YMCA and YWCA, the Indian Rights Association, and the Salvation Army—date from that period. The Carnegie-funded public libraries, built in thousands of towns and cities in the United States, also date from that time. This growth in charitable giving cannot be attributed to the tax code's deduction for such gifts—there *was* no tax code. The permanent income tax was not implemented in the United States until the Sixteenth Amendment to the Constitution permitted it in 1913. The simple fact is that people give more when their incomes are higher, and as Adam Smith noted in his other book *The Theory of Moral Sentiments,* the impulse to help one's fellow human being, especially if that person is in physical proximity, is very widespread.

People often judge a society more virtuous if its government has set up programs to transfer resources from high-income people to low-income people. Think about that. To judge a society virtuous, you must make some judgment about the average virtue of the members of that society. But what makes each person virtuous? The only things that count, the only things that *can* count, are each person's own voluntary actions. I am not a moral person simply because I live in a society whose other members are virtuous. Nor am I a moral person because I live in a society where the government uses force to take from me and give to others. My morality is a function of my actions, not of other people's, and especially not of actions that I am *forced* to carry out. As John Milton wrote,[5] "If every action which is good or evil in a man of ripe years were under pittance and prescription and compulsion, what were virtue but a name, what praise would be due to well-doing, what gramercy to be sober, just, or continent?"

Moreover, a clear impact of government transfers of wealth has been to make most of us less compassionate. The government transfer system, enforced mainly with income taxes withheld by our employers, gives the expression "I gave at the office"[6] a whole new meaning. And not just at the office. With sales taxes, corporate taxes, and tariffs, I also gave everywhere I shopped.

In the Christmas season, many of us watch Charles Dickens's *A Christmas Carol*. In my favorite version, the one with Alastair Sim, the ghost of Christmas present shows Ebenezer Scrooge how his narrow selfishness has made him bereft of love and friends, and the ghost of Christmas future shows him that, unless he changes, he will be unmourned in his death. When Scrooge wakes up, he realizes that indeed he can change. In my favorite scene, Scrooge dances around in his nightshirt like a kid in a candy store, celebrating his power to change. And what is the change? Does he say, "Oh, boy, now I'll support a politician who will tax me and other people less rich than me to help poor people?" Of course not. A movie producer who tried to set up such a scene would have produced a much less compelling movie. Scrooge is excited because now *he* can change, now *he* can get pleasure from helping others who are worse off.

Economists often say that people give too little to charity because they can rely on the giving of others.[7] Here's how the argument goes: You help someone and I don't. Although I value having that person helped, I don't have enough incentive to help that person myself because you've done it for me. In other words, I "free-ride" on your efforts. If enough people think this way, goes the argument, then they won't help people even though they want people to be helped. The net result: too little charitable giving.

This argument may be correct, but it leaves out a huge part of the motive for giving. It's true that if you help someone and I don't, I may gain from your helping them. But if I don't help them, I don't gain as much as you because I don't get to feel part of the solution. I don't get the pleasure and deep satisfaction that come from knowing I made a difference in people's lives. In short, I miss out on a very important part of being human.

I say this not hypothetically, but based on real and painful experience. For a variety of reasons, the main one being that helping others was not modeled well in my family, I was not a financially generous person. Then, after I married and saw my wife and even my young daughter model a very different way of behaving, I learned generosity. And my example of *A Christmas Carol* earlier is not one chosen at random. A few years ago, on about my tenth viewing of it, I finally got it. I got that this was not a movie just to make you cry at Christmas: *A Christmas Carol* carried one of life's most important messages. I shared Scrooge's breakthrough. And I saw just how much I had missed by saying that other people—whether individuals or government officials—would take care of poor people. Indeed, the modern Scrooge, instead of asking, "Are there no prisons? Are there no workhouses?" would ask, "Is there no Medicaid? Is there no Social Security?"

In their textbooks, economists usually write that government exists to solve problems of externalities—that is, effects on others that people do not take into account when they behave in a particular way. The fact is, though, that people internalize what otherwise would be externalities by teaching and practicing virtues. As my economist friend Harry Watson once stated, "For social interaction to work, people need to self-internalize externalities."

A story from my own experience illustrates the great gulf between what economists claim as rational behavior and what we really believe in our hearts. Before going to UCLA to do graduate work, I had been reading books and articles by Gordon Tullock, James Buchanan, and Anthony Downs. They had shown that the probability of affecting the outcome of a typical election was so close to zero that the expected value of voting was substantially less than its cost. Therefore, they concluded, there was no point in voting, no matter which way you would vote, even in a close election. This was even clearer for the 1972 presidential election that was on at the time, because President Nixon was about to trounce George McGovern.

At UCLA that fall, I got into a long, heated argument with another beginning graduate student, in which I laid out Tullock's case for why it made no sense for him to vote. He understood the argument, but wasn't convinced. He said, "But if everyone thought that way and acted on it, the whole system would break down." "Wrong," I said. "If everyone thought that way, that's exactly when you should vote." We went back and forth, neither of us able to convince the other. I will admit now something that I would not even admit to myself then: Part of my reason for trying to persuade him was that I had just moved from Canada and could not legally vote, and I envied him his right to vote. Three years later, I heard that he had said that now that he was steeped in the UCLA way of thinking, he realized that I was right and he was wrong. I don't know what he thinks now, but I'm convinced that *he* was right and *I* was wrong.

What he was articulating was the way he was brought up and, for that matter, the way most of us are brought up. Most of us are taught that when we make decisions, we don't just calculate the effect on our own well-being. We don't necessarily estimate the effect on others' well-being either, because doing so is difficult and often impossible. But we do tend to ask ourselves, "What if everyone acted this way?"

If you have children, you probably raise them to believe that stealing is wrong or that they should not use other people's things without asking. I bet you say something like, "How would you feel if Johnny stole your bicycle?" Why do we say that? Because we are trying to socialize our children, to make them aware that other people count, that other people—to use a formulation from Immanuel Kant that my mentor, Clancy Smith, likes to quote—are ends in themselves also. With such devices and, even more important, with our own modeling, we turn our children into good people.

But think about that. Why should we want our children to be good people? If we totally accepted the economists' model that leads to the free-rider problem, we should want to raise our children to take advantage of other people whenever the cost to our child of doing so—and I use "cost" in the narrowest sense—is less than the child's benefit.[8] I have met hundreds or thousands of economists, and I have yet to meet one who raises his or her child that way. Well, maybe one, but I hope, I pray, for his and his child's sake, that he was kidding me. True, we have lapses. I know one economist who, when the waiter left an item off the bill, told his son not to mention it so that they could pay less. Having lapses is part of being human also. But the overall thrust of how economists raise their children is very much the way noneconomists do it: We teach, and try to model, virtues.

So, why did it take 10 viewings of *A Christmas Carol* to get me to change my behavior? A big part of it, I believe, was my father's influence. Although he was a great father in many other ways, on the issue of helping others, he fell short. (Fortunately, for the last 20 years of his life, as I discovered in going through his financial records, my father became a very generous man. Bless him.) I vividly remember leaving a restaurant with him, seeing a little container into which you could put your spare change to help an organization called Purple Heart, pulling out a quarter, and starting to put it in. My father saw me do it and, in a panicky voice, told me that I didn't have to. I knew that I didn't have to, but he made me think there was something wrong with it, and so I put the quarter back in my pocket. From then on, when I started to contribute money to a charity, I would feel shame at giving up something that was mine. That doesn't mean I wouldn't contribute, but I didn't contribute much or often.

Yet, even back then, I badly wanted to feel like a complete member of the community. One spring morning in 1966, some of the boys in my high school class came to school looking quite tired. It turned out that they had driven over to a nearby town called Morris the night before and spent the whole night setting up sand bags to protect the town from the flooding Red River. I wished that I had been part of that, but I wasn't asked. In retrospect, I think I wasn't asked because my father was not connected to the community the way their fathers were. I felt cheated.

That feeling of being cheated by not being given the chance to help others was what should have made me see through the economists' argument much earlier in my education. But it wasn't until much later in life that I saw through it. Most economists give the impression that when you help someone, the only person who benefits is the person helped. They completely disregard the benefit to the person who does the helping, the wonderful feeling of benevolence that results. Because a huge part of the reason people help each other is that they enjoy doing it, the economists' public good argument is much less powerful than its proponents believe. Although you do get the benefit of seeing other people helped even if you don't contribute yourself, what you miss are the pleasure of helping them and the feeling of being involved. To get this pleasure, most people will help others. That's why communities do so well at solving problems, whether getting together to clean up a beach or park or raising tens of thousands of dollars so that a neighborhood kid can have an expensive surgery.

The importance of community is recognized in the African expression that translates, "It takes a village to raise a child." Certainly, I saw that in the two small towns I grew up in. One reason we kids didn't (very often) destroy or steal other people's property was the sure knowledge that if we did and were seen, word would quickly get back to our parents. I will never forget the evening, when I was eight, when my father got a call from a local store owner asking him to come down to his store because he had just caught my 11-year-old brother shoplifting. I had done a little of that myself, and when my father punished my brother by making him go to every store he had ever stolen from, tell the owners to their faces, and pay them back their estimated damages (paid for by my father), I resolved that I would never shoplift again. My brother resolved the same.

Many people now scoff at "it takes a village" because Hillary Clinton used those four words as the title for her recent book. But her book distorted the true meaning of those words—instead of having communities and villages raise children, Clinton would have even more government officials than we now have interfere in the lives of families. A more accurate title of Hillary Clinton's book would have been *It Takes a Government*. But then who would have bought her book? It's important, though, to take back our language and not to let her twisted language lead the rest of us to reject a perfectly sound idea—that strong voluntary aid by people in communities has potentially huge positive effects on others, including children.

FREEDOM BREEDS COMMUNITY

One of the things I hated most about living in Washington, D.C. during the two-and-a-half years that I was in the Reagan administration was the way almost everyone there "breathed, slept, and ate" government. Of all the people in the United States, people in Washington have the hardest time understanding community because so many of them work in and/or support the most anticommunity organization in the country, the federal government. I rarely felt, for that reason, at all connected to my fellow residents. There was a coldness in many of them that I have never seen in any other community I've lived in. There's good reason for the popularity of this expression: "If you want a friend in Washington, get a dog."

Despite all this, I remember one great night when I bonded with some of my fellow Washingtonians. It was during a snowstorm, when the snow was creating ice on the road at rush hour and turning the trip across the Potomac into a huge traffic jam. On the bridge, I saw a car stuck on the ice with its wheels spinning. I got out of my car and ran over and pushed the car to get it moving again. The driver stuck his head out of the window and thanked me. In that one moment, there was a connection between us that I had never felt in that town.

I'm a relative newcomer, as I've outlined above, to the idea that communities and helping each other are important. But I'm not a newcomer to economics. And economics, it turns out, has a lot to say about what makes communities thrive and what destroys them. Isn't it interesting that we in the United States, where the welfare state is less extensive than in Europe, are more generous with others than people in Europe are. Even the British magazine, *The Economist,* which so often turns up its nose at the crassness and naivete of Americans, is impressed by Americans' generosity:

> The average American gives a little over one weekly pay cheque a year to charity, the highest rate in the world. Moreover, half the country does volunteer work, averaging more than four hours of it a week.[9]

The article also points out that, contrary to the stereotype of Americans abandoning their elderly relatives in nursing homes, "only 5.4 percent of over-65s live in an institution, fewer than a decade ago." This, points out *The Economist,* is below the proportion for most other rich countries. Moreover, eight out of ten disabled elderly people live outside institutions and 95 percent of the mentally handicapped still live with relatives.

Why does the United States exhibit more feeling of community and more generosity than other wealthy nations do? One of the main reasons is that governments in the United States take less responsibility for people's lives than governments in most other countries. This leaves room for communities to develop and support their members. People want to feel important when they help others. When governments take over, people who would help often feel that their own help is redundant and futile. Shortly after I got together money to buy diapers for residents of Watsonville, California after the 1989 earthquake, I learned that the federal government was sending government funds. I felt betrayed and marginalized. Damn their almighty gall, I thought, for taking my and other people's money by force and not letting us choose how and how much to help the earthquake's victims.

Economists have found that government aid "crowds out" private charity. Russell Roberts, an economist at the Weidenbaum Center at Washington University in St. Louis, points out that when the federal government began to hand out welfare in the early 1930s, the amount of private charity fell. Between 1929 and 1932, as the Great Depression worsened, private relief expenditures in the United States increased from $10.3 million in 1929 to $10.9 million in 1930, to $55.7 million in 1931, to $71.6 million in 1932. But as government relief expenditures grew past a certain point, private expenditures fell. By 1935, government relief expenditures were more than triple their 1932 level and private expenditures had fallen to one fifth of their previous level. People didn't stop giving, but instead started giving to other causes that the government didn't support. The New York Association for Improving the Condition of the Poor (AICP), for example, founded in 1843, gave resources to "the poor, the unemployed, the sick, the elderly, and the husbandless mother."[10] In 1932, 54 percent of AICP's spending was on poor people and 46 percent on other things; by 1938, after the federal government had established itself as the "giver" of first resort, only 29 percent was on poor people.

COMMUNITIES HAPPEN

The good news is that communities happen. (There's a bumper sticker.) One of the main virtues of Americans, which Toqueville noted as early as the 1830s, is their tremendous proclivity for forming voluntary organizations to solve various problems. No government policy is needed for communities to form. They just happen. All government needs to do is get out of the way so we can build and nurture our communities.

ENDNOTES

1. Paul Blustein, "Sugihara's List," *Washington Post,* October 3, 1994, p. B1.

2. Gary S. Becker, *The Economics of Discrimination,* Chicago: University of Chicago Press, 2nd ed., 1971.

3. Douglass C. North, *Institutions, Institutional Change and Economic Performance,* New York: Cambridge University Press, 1990, p. 12. Reprinted with the permission of Cambridge University Press.

4. Milton and Rose Friedman, *Free to Choose,* New York: Harcourt, Brace, Jovanovich, 1980, pp. 36–37.

5. John Milton, *Aeropagitica,* ("Everyman" ed. [London, 1927]), p. 18, quoted in F.A. Hayek, *The Constitution of Liberty,* Chicago: University of Chicago Press, 1960, p. 79.

6. I am indebted to Donald McCloskey for the "I gave at the office" line. See Donald McCloskey, "Bourgeois Virtue," *The American Scholar,* 63:2 (Spring 1994), p. 187.

7. Larry L. Orr, "Income Transfers as a Public Good: An Application to AFDC," *American Economic Review,* vol. 66 (June 1976), pp. 359–371; and Mark V. Pauly, "Income Redistribution as a Local Public Good," *Journal of Public Economics,* vol. 2 (February 1973), pp. 35–38.

8. See Jennifer Roback, *Love & Economics: Why the Laissez-Faire Family Doesn't Work*, Dalllas: Spence Publishing, 2001, for an extensive and insightful elaboration on these thoughts.

9. "Holding together, better than most," *The Economist,* February 22, 1997, pp. 28–29.

10. Russell D. Roberts, "A Positive Model of Private Charity and Public Transfers," *Journal of Political Economy,* Vol. 92, No. 1, February 1984, p. 143.

12

A TOUR
OF WASHINGTON

*Society is produced by our wants, and gov-
ernment by our wickedness.*

—THOMAS PAINE, AMERICAN REVOLUTIONARY,
COMMON SENSE

*It could probably be shown by facts and figures that there is
no distinctly native American criminal class except congress.*

—MARK TWAIN, *PUDD'NHEAD WILSON*

From December 1981 to August 1982, I worked as a special assistant to John Cogan, who, as an Assistant Secretary of Labor, held one of the top policy positions in the U.S. Labor Department. Then, from August 1982 to July 1984, I worked as a senior economist with the Council of Economic Advisers in President Reagan's White House. Actually, I worked in the Old Executive Office Building, separated from the White House by a driveway. When people say they work in the White House, they usually mean the Old Executive Office Building; that's where Oliver North, the originator of the Iran-Contra scandal, and where Monica Lewinsky, a famous White House intern, worked. It's also where you'll find the President's speechwriters, the Secret Service offices, and many of the President's appointees. It's just that White House sounds fancier.

One day, I was talking to a few people I worked with, one of whom was a White House fellow. (The position of White House fellow is given to about 10 or so people every year and is thought of as one of the plum jobs in Washington.) He had been asked to give a speech to a high school group on how Washington works, and he grinned knowingly to the rest of us, saying, "I wish I could tell them how it really works. It sure isn't the way it's portrayed in their civics classes."

"Why not tell them?" I wondered to myself. It would certainly be illuminating, and not just to high school students, but also to anyone who hasn't worked at fairly high levels in Washington or who thinks that popular TV shows like today's *West Wing* have much connection with reality. So, here are my observations, based on a few years of experience in Washington, many conversations with many officials in Washington, and a fair amount of reading on how Washington works, and, more generally, on how government works—or doesn't.

WHAT A SHOCK!

During the summer of 1973, I had been hired as a summer intern by the Council of Economic Advisers. The president at the time was Richard Nixon. I had applied a few months earlier, and although my professors had supported me with reference letters, two of them had made snide comments about my timing—I would be going to the White House at the peak of the Watergate scandal. One professor pointed out that most rats try to get off a sinking ship, but I was like a rat trying to get *on*. Their lack of support made me feel very lonely. Later I understood that their attitude wasn't about me, but about their contempt toward Nixon.

I was feeling vulnerable at the time, with no support from my professors and with very little money in the bank. With my last few hundred dollars, I purchased an airline ticket to Washington, D.C. and off I went. After a long red-eye flight, I finally arrived in downtown D.C. As I exited the cab and turned around to look at the Old Executive Office Building (OEOB), I was shocked to see a huge red flag with a hammer and sickle above the OEOB. Maybe it was jet lag, or maybe it was the fact that I had slept less than an hour on the plane, but I felt a second of absolute terror, thinking that the Soviets had taken over Washington in the middle of the night. I saw people around me walking normally as if nothing unusual had happened, dismissed my immediate paranoid thought about *The Invasion of the Body Snatchers,* and realized that the Soviets hadn't invaded. While I waited in the front waiting room of the OEOB to be let past the Secret Service agents, I asked one of them what the Soviet flag was there for. He answered, in an officious, self-important tone that I was to hear lots of—in every possible accent, from people at every possible level, on every day I was to be in Washington—that Soviet leader Brezhnev was visiting and that this was done to welcome him. Some welcome, I thought. I wondered which of the world's other tyrants would get such a welcome. I found out later that summer. When the Shah of Iran visited, sure enough, a huge green Iranian flag flew over the Old Executive Office Building. I learned, talking to the various secretaries and economists I met that day, that no one found it odd. Here was Brezhnev, who represented a government that had murdered tens of millions of people, more than Hitler's government had, and had never openly admitted it, let alone apologized for it, and people were matter-of-factly accepting that government's flag. Maybe there was something to my thought of the body snatchers after all. I knew literally from day one of my time in Washington that this was a strange place.

One other big shock I got during that summer of 1973 was about just how little economic policy has to do with economic reasoning. The biggest example I saw was price controls. In August 1971, Richard Nixon, going completely against his own passionately stated views, had imposed a 90-day freeze on all wages and prices in the United States. He followed up with various "phases" of price controls so that, when I arrived in June

1973, much of the U.S. economy was still under price controls. You don't have to get far in an economics course to learn that the vast majority of economists oppose price controls, whether on rents or on other prices. So-called ceiling prices, price controls that prevent the price from going above a certain level, cause suppliers to reduce quality and other services that go with the good, as a way of implicitly increasing the price of the good. Moreover, a supplier who does not reduce quality is likely to supply less of the good; and of course buyers, seeing a lower price than otherwise, want more. The result: a shortage of the good whose price is controlled. This happened with various price-controlled goods during World War II—nylons, tires, gasoline, sugar, and meat, for example—and was starting to happen all over the economy within months of Nixon's price controls. Later that year, it would happen with gasoline, when OPEC almost quadrupled the price of oil, but Nixon's price controls didn't allow gasoline prices to rise enough. The result was long line-ups and angry motorists.

MY LIFE AT THE COUNCIL

I wondered what the economists at the prestigious Council of Economic Advisers would think of the price controls their big boss had imposed. This wasn't idle curiosity. I had taken the job to get a feel for government economic policy, but I didn't want to be a part of any attempt to support the price controls. So, that first day, I wandered up and down the third floor of the OEOB looking at names of economists on doors. I searched my memory for any associations, negative or positive, with the names I saw. One name stood out: Robert Tollison. I had seen his name on a number of articles in "Public Choice," a literature in economics spawned by James Buchanan and Gordon Tullock, that began with the assumption that government officials, just like other people, act mainly on the basis of self-interest. I knocked on his door and found a 29-year-old, friendly guy with whom I had instant rapport. After a half-hour conversation, I thought I could level with him at least somewhat, and so I told him that I thought government price controls were a travesty. When I realized that he supported my views—he was worried that the coming price controls on food would cause some people to go without food—I went further and told him that I thought the government's price-control policy was incredibly immoral and that I didn't want to have any part in it. He told me that he felt the same way and that it was possible to do good work at the Council and not be involved in price controls. When I asked him what issues he was working on, he named some interesting ones and some less interesting ones, none of which involved price controls. I asked if I could work with him, and he said he'd see what he could do.

The next morning, when I showed up at work, Joel Popkin, a senior economist at the Council, gave me a table of numbers that gave the weights on the various foods in the bundle of items that is priced to get the Consumer Price Index. He wanted me to add the weights to see what percent of the CPI was accounted for by food. Not exactly a tough assignment, right? Someone with even moderate fifth-grade math skills could have done it, and I had been a math major. You'd think I could handle it. You'd think wrong.

I just knew in my gut what Popkin would do with those numbers. The Nixon administration was about to come out with the next phase of price controls, and some factions were pushing for tough controls on food prices. I went away to add the numbers and came back to Popkin a few minutes later with my sum. He said that my sum couldn't be right, and he gave me a reason that made sense. So I went away and added again and came back with a different number. Popkin angrily rejected my second addition, pointing out that it, too, couldn't be right. Again, he was right. I can't think of any other time in my life when I've done such a poor job of adding. I think that I just hated price controls so much that they got in the way of my ability to do simple arithmetic. I know that, to some people, this may seem like a failing in me as an analyst, and that's probably true, but I also think it makes me a more successful human.

Later that day, when I told Tollison, somewhat shamefacedly, that I hadn't been able to add a column of numbers correctly, he chuckled and predicted that Popkin would never call on me again the whole summer. Tollison was right.

I later learned that my gut feel about Popkin was right. As a macroeconomist who thought in terms of aggregates instead of individual markets, he favored price controls on food. He wanted to get inflation down and seemed to think that if you got the *measure* of inflation down, that was pretty good. So by controlling the prices that made up the CPI, you could make it look as if inflation was falling. I remember economist Harold Demsetz saying three years earlier that that was like thinking it was too cold outside and figuring you could solve the problem by breaking the thermometer. There was this difference: Breaking the thermometer wouldn't change the temperature, but imposing price controls would cause food shortages.

Many other economists at the Council of Economic Advisers thought price controls were a bad policy that would cause shortages. But—and this was my big disappointment— some of them defended price controls anyway. Council chairman Herb Stein, an excellent economist and one of the nicest and best bosses I have ever had, pushed for tough price controls on food and publicly defended them. In return, he got to spend a weekend at the presidential retreat at Camp David. Later that summer, Tollison and I got a good laugh when Herb came back from the White House mess complaining that they didn't have steak that day because the supplier wouldn't supply it at the controlled price. But none of what Herb knew caused him to refuse to cooperate with Nixon on price controls.

Herb would have made a first-rate comedian—his son, Ben Stein of Comedy Central fame, comes by it honestly. Near the end of the summer, Marina von Neuman Whitman (the daughter of the famous mathematician John von Neumann), one of the members of the Council, was set to leave, so there was a big party for her over at the New Executive Office Building, attended by various muck-a-mucks, including Arthur Burns, then chairman of the Federal Reserve Board, and George Shultz, secretary of the treasury, both economists who defended price controls knowing full well that they would hurt the economy. That summer, the Watergate hearings were going at full tilt, and it had been revealed just weeks before that (a) many conversations in the White House had been taped and (b) the ones the Watergate committee wanted were missing.

So, at one point in the celebration, Herb announced that "the missing White House tapes" had been found and that he wanted to play an excerpt. He turned on the tape recorder and what followed was a skit, scripted by Herb, in which Herb did his own voice, a secretary named Margaret Snyder did Marina's voice, and the other member of the Council, Gary Seaver, did Nixon's voice. One segment of that skit still stands out in my memory:

NIXON: Herb, inflation is getting higher again. What should we do?

STEIN: Let me ask our new member, Marina. Marina, what should we do?

MARINA: Impose price controls.

NIXON: But we already have price controls.

MARINA: Then abolish price controls.

People, including Burns and Shultz, laughed uproariously. I laughed too. It was pretty funny, in isolation. At the same time, I felt a strong discomfort. Herb was making fun of Nixon, price controls, Marina, and himself, and yet he knew that the price controls would cause a lot of damage. In fact, they were about to cause an energy crisis in which people would line up for hours to buy gasoline, and some disgruntled people would kill others in the violent competition that replaced peaceful market competition. Now, almost 30 years later, we still live under some of the same controls, such as the fuel economy standards for cars, that the government initiated to cope with the energy shortage it itself had caused. I still am disgusted at what I witnessed at that party: grown adults, instead of fighting something they knew to be incredibly dangerous, making fun of it.

Later that summer, I did what I could as a 22-year-old intern to fight price controls. That summer, John Dunlop, a Harvard professor who was head of the Cost of Living Council, the government agency that set the price controls, invited Harvard students in Washington for a roundtable discussion. A Harvard friend brought me along and I asked Dunlop a number of critical questions, politely but also persistently enough that he got angry and started pounding the table. There wasn't much more I could do.

At the start of that summer, I'd been harboring a thought that I hoped wasn't true; by the end of the summer, I was pretty sure it was. Now that I've observed government up close for 20 years, I'm *positive* that it's true. Government officials care very little about us. They have enormous power over us and can use this power to inflict incredible destruction on our lives, but that's all right with them as long as the destruction doesn't cause them to lose their jobs or go to jail. And what I saw very clearly that summer was that the policymakers who had inflicted great damage weren't going to lose their jobs or go to jail. They weren't even, typically, going to be fined. Had Richard Nixon not tried to cover up a burglary in 1972, or even if he had tried to cover it up but simply hadn't taped his own conversations about it and saved the tapes, he would probably have stayed in office. Even if he had been able to complete his term, the billions of dollars in damage Nixon had done to the economy with price controls would not have come back to bite him at all. That's why Bob Tollison and I celebrated when we found out that Herb couldn't get steak that day—going without steak was one of the few costs Herb bore for supporting price controls. And Herb Stein was one of the better and more courageous government officials.

This isn't to say that there aren't nice people in government. The government is loaded with nice people as well as wicked ones. One of my few positive surprises that summer, which was confirmed by my later experience in government, was that probably one in two people in government works hard: Before, I had thought it was more like one in four. This isn't always good. Some people in government are working hard at regulating people's lives and spending their money. But many people in government honestly believe in what they're doing and try hard to do it well.

A positive surprise that summer was that I had many pro-freedom allies in various departments throughout the government. When Tollison left in early July, he persuaded Herb to let me take his place as a senior economist, without the title, until his replacement arrived in late August. So I got to attend meetings on deregulating trucking and found I had allies in the Treasury, the Department of Transportation, the Justice Department, and the Office of Management and Budget (OMB). Herb, incidentally, wanted to let the issue drop, figuring that deregulation was never going to happen. I thought he might be wrong, and I persuaded him to keep the Council involved in that issue. Of course, five years later, under Jimmy Carter, trucking deregulation became a reality. It may have happened without the Council staying involved, but you never know.

Some people within the White House consistently advocated scaling back the government. One such person was Peter Flanagan, who later went on to be a very successful investor in New York. One reason his name stands out is that, at a conference I attended in the late 1970s, I heard someone quote Ralph Nader's statement that Peter Flanagan was one of the most dangerous men in government. When I heard that, I thought about a memo I had seen while I was a White House intern, in which Flanagan advocated deregulation in many industries, and spelled out the reasons why. In the early 1990s, I ran into Flanagan at a Hoover Institution conference at which he was speaking about his efforts to spend his own and other contributors' money on funding private-school scholarships for children in poor families. When I told him about Nader's quote, he had a good laugh.

AN UNSUNG HERO IN THE FEDERAL BUREAUCRACY

During my summer at the CEA, I met a senior economist at the Council named Ron Hoffman. His short stature and facial features made him look as if he could be Dustin Hoffman's brother. In fact, he is. That summer, Hoffman helped me find a good lawyer when I got in trouble with the Immigration and Naturalization Service. As a result, I kept in touch with him, visiting him a few times in the late 1970s and early 1980s, after he had moved over to the U.S. Treasury. Hoffman told me of an internal fight within the Carter administration in the late

1970s, when Joseph Califano, the secretary of the department of Health, Education, and Welfare, proposed draconian controls on health care spending, an early version of Hillary Clinton's 1993 proposal. Hoffman, working a few layers beneath Treasury Secretary Michael Blumenthal, analyzed Califano's proposal, found it to be a bad one, and argued forcefully within the Treasury that Blumenthal should oppose it. Blumenthal was persuaded and gave Hoffman the job of writing memos on the issue for his signature. Hoffman recounted for me that he formed a triumvirate with an economist in Charles Schultze's CEA and an economist in James Lynn's Office of Management and Budget. Their memos, often written for the signature of Blumenthal, Schultze, and Lynn, became known to their group as the Mike, Jim, and Charlie memos. They were successful. The Califano controls went nowhere, and the country was saved for at least a few years from a major attempt to stifle the health care sector.

In my time in Washington, I met many people like him, people who will never get public attention for saving taxpayers billions of dollars and helping delay or prevent major new restrictions on people's freedom.

PUBLIC ENEMY #1

During my stint at the Labor Department in the early 1980s, I noticed another odd thing about Washington—its concept of "the public." When I think of the public, I think of the vast majority of working, tax-paying people in the rest of the country, including everyone from the lowest paid worker to the highest paid CEO of a company. But that concept was foreign to the people who had worked in government for a while. In the Labor Department, for example, the public meant various trade associations representing unionized companies, and it meant labor union representatives who sat in offices that were as little as a few hundred feet from the Labor Department's main building. That made for a narrow perspective. When, for example, government officials discussed the public's reaction to some law that would raise production costs, they talked about the members of the public they had heard from or were likely to hear from. These "members of the public" were almost always people who represented employers or employees in the affected industry. The public was virtually never the consumers of the product who would now have to pay a higher price, except in the rare case where most of the product was sold to one large firm; in that case, you might hear from that firm, which automatically became part of "the public."

That one simple fact—that the public is thought of as the various players who lobby intensively on government policy—explains a lot. I had wondered, for example, why, when the Vietnam War ended, taxes didn't fall. Now I know. It's because the wants and needs of the taxpayers are almost invisible to everyone in Washington. Other than a few lobbies like the National Taxpayers Union and Citizens for a Sound Economy, almost no one represents taxpayers. To the various interest groups in Washington, the money saved by ending the Vietnam War was "found money," which they could, and did, easily use. Similarly, if there's no tax cut or too small a tax cut, the current surplus will not be around for long: It will be spent.

I marveled a few years ago when, based on revelations that the Internal Revenue Service had been treating taxpayers badly, Congressmen and IRS officials started talking about how the IRS should treat its "customers" better. When I first read it, I wondered what "a customer of the IRS" could possibly mean. A customer of UPS is someone who pays to send a package. A customer of GM is someone who buys a car or truck. In other words, the usual idea of a customer is someone who pays money voluntarily in return for goods or services purchased. But I don't pay the IRS voluntarily. I pay because, otherwise, I'll lose my assets and might go to prison. So how am I a customer of the IRS? If I truly am, I'd rather take my business elsewhere, thank you. Calling taxpayers customers of the IRS is like calling chickens customers of the egg farmer.

I noticed something else, both from my time in Washington and from closely following government policy for almost 30 years now. When you hear the term "government inefficiency," what often comes to mind is a comparison between the cost for the government to do something and the cost for the private sector (businesses, individuals, and nonprofit organizations) to do the same thing. It is true that government costs tend to be higher than private sector costs, and economists have amassed a wealth of evidence on this over the last 30 years. Economists have compared processing of insurance claims by Blue Cross versus the government,[1] the cost of private versus government trash collection,[2] and the costs of private versus government fire fighting,[3] to take three of the best-known examples. But these examples, as true and important as they are, leave out one of the main kinds of inefficiency created by government.

What is that inefficiency? Let me show by an analogy with a Sam Peckinpah movie, *The Getaway*. Steve McQueen and Ali McGraw are trying to escape with money stolen from a bank. They try to avoid both the police and the other bad guys who want the money. In the process of escaping, McQueen and McGraw destroy at least three cars and a hotel elevator, shoot holes in the hotel walls, and do other miscellaneous damage. The total cost of the damage they inflict would be over $50,000 in today's dollars. But that damage costs them nothing. The fact that they are destroying people's wealth is irrelevant to them because their actions don't destroy *their* wealth. They simply don't care that they've destroyed someone else's property.

What these characters did in the movie and what real-life criminals often do is much like what governments do: They destroy wealth in the attempt to pursue their own narrow ends. Take the U.S. government. At times, the government has actually bought up farm crops and destroyed them in order to pursue the narrow goal of increasing farmers' incomes. Agricultural economists have shown that such actions cause billions of dollars worth of destruction. But you don't even need to do a sophisticated economic analysis to reach the same conclusion; all you have to do is recognize that the government destroyed crops that would have some value to whoever would have been willing to buy them. That destroyed value doesn't go to farmers, to taxpayers, to anyone. It just goes. Similarly, when policemen break down doors and rifle through people's possessions to find illegal drugs, they cause a lot of damage, McQueen-McGraw style, that they don't care about.

Economists are usually awful at coming up with descriptive names for economic concepts. But they have a good name for this destruction: deadweight loss. It's just like McQueen and McGraw destroying someone else's car while trying to escape. And, just as the criminals didn't care much about whether they destroyed other people's wealth during their getaway, neither the farmers who lobbied for the government programs nor the politicians who passed them into law took much account of the costs of these programs to consumers and taxpayers.

There are literally thousands more cases of deadweight loss caused by government. Here are two. In the 1970s, the U.S. government decided to restrict imports of steel from other countries in order to save jobs of U.S. steelworkers. No one—not the government officials who pushed for and implemented this program and not the steel company managers and workers who lobbied for it—asked how the program might harm buyers of steel. Why would they care? After all, the wealth destroyed was not theirs. After the program was implemented, economists estimated that the restriction on steel imports cost consumers $750,000 for every job saved.[4] And not just $750,000 once, but $750,000 a year. At the time, a typical steelworker earned about $40,000 a year in pay and benefits. So the government was destroying $750,000 in wealth to create something worth $40,000. But even this exaggerates the gain to steelworkers. The real gain to a steelworker from having his job saved is the difference between what he makes as a steelworker and what he would earn in his next-best alternative. If a steelworker could have worked elsewhere for, say, $25,000 a year, then his gain from the restriction on imports was not $40,000, but $15,000. The net reduction in wealth for that one job saved, therefore, was $735,000 a year.

One final example. The government often prevents people from using their own property in peaceful ways. To take a small example, even though you paid for your mailbox, you can't legally have someone from UPS, Federal Express, or your local newspaper company put anything in your mailbox. The government does this, of course, for the narrow goal of protecting its own monopoly on mail delivery. But that mailbox is now worth somewhat less to you than it would be if there were no such law. Such destruction commonly occurs when government is involved because government is, by law, not accountable for much of the damage it does. Such destruction is much less widespread in the private sector when there's private property because no one, other than a criminal, has much incentive to inflict damage, and all others are pretty much accountable for the damage they do. For example, in the private sector, there's simply no demand for people to disrupt the choices you make. You certainly won't demand it, and the kind of people (other than those who represent the government) who would be willing to do so for a price are called criminals. There is one main difference between government and criminals, but it's not what you might think: Because governments can destroy wealth legally, they destroy orders of magnitude more wealth than criminals do.

Here's another way of thinking about government: government as the mean parent who never listens and never notices that we've gotten bigger and more mature. There are many things we would like to do in life but can't do because the government says we can't, whether it's driving without seatbelts, smoking marijuana, or buying low-cost insurance that doesn't cover pregnancy. (Federal law requires that employer-provided health insurance cover maternity benefits.) The government says the reason we can't make these decisions is that we wouldn't make good decisions. Therefore, it treats us as children—and very young children at that. We have had government needling us and interfering with and threatening us for the whole of our lives, starting, for most of us, from the time we hit kindergarten, letting up some when we graduate from high school, and then eating away at us day to day for the rest of our lives. So we become oblivious to it—it just seems like the way things are. But a recent *Candid Camera* skit reminded me of how really outrageous the government is. In the skit, a waitress told people who ordered a dish on the menu that they couldn't have it because it wasn't good for them. Instead, she'd bring what *she* thought was good for them. People got very incensed about it. Many of them defended their right to order what they wished and got up angrily to walk out. It's the most animated I've ever seen real, everyday people in defending their rights. Virtually everyone in the episode felt the same way: "How dare this waitress tell me what I can order, what kinds of goods I can ingest in my body, and how to spend my money on food!"

But guess what. Government acts like that waitress all the time. Government often intervenes in annoying ways that are none of their business. It prevents us from buying cheap oranges that might look a little blemished, but are perfectly safe. It also is currently trying to rig the rules so that almost the only kind of cheese we'll be able to eat is processed American cheese. As my late friend Roy Childs pointed out, government is incredibly petty, threatening us with fines and even prison sentences for doing things just a little different from the way some anonymous government official wants it. Government routinely makes even bigger decisions for us, from how we save for our retirement, to what kinds of changes we can make to our houses, to what kinds of prescription drugs we may take. Government, by and large, is full of strangers who often have little expertise in the areas they regulate and have virtually no knowledge of *your* particular goals, interests, capabilities, or concerns. Nor do most government officials even care about these things. Government is like the waitress, but with this crucial difference: The waitress was an actress, and her "victims" could easily leave the restaurant; the government is all too real and insists on controlling us as long as we stay in the country.

Baron de Montesquieu, in a book that was widely read by the framers of the U.S. Constitution, said it well when he wrote, "Often has it happened that ministers of a restless disposition, have imagined that the wants of the state were those of their own little and ignoble souls."[5] In that quote, "ministers" refers not to the clergy, but to high government officials. Actually, Montesquieu was too charitable to government officials. Congress imposes on us a horrid forced "pension" program called Social Security, but Congressmen don't kid themselves that they want it. They give themselves a special, much-sweeter retirement program that can pay them pensions in excess of $100,000 a year. Guess who pays for it.

President Kennedy never tried to get the U.S. government to quit enforcing the embargo against Cuba, but that didn't stop him from doing what many Americans wanted to do but couldn't: smoke illegal Cuban cigars. Senator Richard Shelby from Alabama says that he favors a drug war in which even nonviolent drug offenders can be sent to prison for life, but that didn't stop him from getting his drug-smuggling son off the hook for a $500 fine. I could go on and on. Congress, and government officials generally, want a lot of the things we want: They just don't want to let us have them, and they're willing to put us in prison for trying to get them.

One small surprise I got my first time in Washington was that government workers, as consumers, were just as demanding as anyone else. I shouldn't have been surprised. Government officials, in their private lives, want the same things we do. That's why the private sector in Washington works so well, and in fact works much better than anything in the government sector. The best directions I have ever found to museums in Washington were not in the expensive brochures that the government produces with taxpayers' money; instead, they were on the back of an ad for a pizza place. Cabs in Washington are relatively unregulated, with none of the large barriers to operating a cab that exist in New York and other cities and that keep cab fares high. The reason: the regulators (Congress) are the consumers, and while they may kid *others* in saying that regulation helps consumers, they don't kid *themselves*.

People who visit Washington often comment about how beautiful some of the old buildings and sculptures are, and I agree. But there's one beautiful sculpture in front of the old Federal Trade Commission building that has a telling message. It shows a man restraining a horse that would otherwise go out of control. The man stands for the government and the horse stands for business. That sculpture sums up how government officials think, not only of themselves in relation to business, but also of themselves in relation to us. Many of them think that if they don't restrain us, we will simply get out of control. In a literal sense, they're right: We'll get out of *their* control. But the people who are truly out of control are the government officials.

I've learned three other main things from my time in Washington and from 30 years of studying government policy. The first is the incredible power of the "tragedy of the commons," which I talked about in Chapters 5 and 10, to explain why the government works so badly. A widespread view today is that if there's some issue that a whole lot of people are concerned about, the best way to deal with it is to let the government decide and spend tax money implementing its decisions. Many people argue against the one-size-fits-all approach that results, and they're right, but this is only part of the problem. The much bigger problem is that the funds the government takes from us are now a commons, and we respond by fighting each other—using our elected representatives—for "our share." Not surprisingly, the commons get overused and abused. Consider this scenario: Say a million of us have gardens; instead of spending our money to maintain our gardens, we are forced to give that money to the government so that it can decide how the money should be spent on our gardens. Ridiculous, right? We know that most of our gardens would be less well maintained and that the tax cost to many of us would be higher than the cost of simply maintaining our own gardens. But, somehow, many of us think differently when it comes to health care or education or any of the hundreds of other things that government does.

The second thing I've learned is just how much government has grown. I saw that first-hand when I worked in the OEOB the first time. Being curious, I inquired around and found out that at the beginning of the twentieth century, almost the whole of the federal government, other than the Post Office, was housed in the OEOB, the White House next door, and the U.S. Treasury on the other side. In fact, my office, going by the beautiful old doorknob, was occupied 60 years earlier by some very high official in the U.S. Navy, maybe even by Franklin Roosevelt when he was assistant secretary of the Navy. In the twentieth century, the federal government grew from about 3 percent of GDP to over 20 percent of GDP, and in that time GDP grew by about 20 times, which means that the federal government grew by about 120 times. You might think that government would grow at some times and shrink at others, but, actually, it tends to grow either faster or slower, but never shrink. The one exception is that it shrinks after wars, but never close to its prewar size.

When I was in Washington, I came to understand why that's so. The main reason can be summed up in one word: incentives. Let's say you come to Washington as a politician or a bureaucrat determined to get rid of this or that spending program or regulation. Or let's say that you don't come with that goal, but you see many destructive programs around you. So, you decide to push to end or trim the program or regulation. Immediately, you get lots of opposition from those who benefit from the program. Even bad programs have beneficiaries—recipients of subsidies, companies whom a regulation is protecting from competition, or the bureaucracy that is managing the subsidy or enforcing the regulation, to name a few. As an example of this last, when Reagan proposed reducing federal subsidies to state employment services in 1982, all of the letters his government received opposing the cuts were from employees of those state agencies. Unfortunately, in your quest to end the program, you get very little support from the people who would benefit, typically taxpayers or consumers, because the benefit per person is so small. In the case mentioned above, for example, the Reagan administration received not one letter from a taxpayer saying, "Go ahead and cut the employment service subsidy." When no one makes noise in your favor, and all the noise is against you, you tend to lose.

That's why government doesn't shrink. The reason it grows is similar. Politicians and bureaucrats are looking around for things to do that are popular. Interest groups push for their special little favor, and the politician or bureaucrat can be popular with them by pushing for it. Often the interest group, again, is the bureaucracy that would administer the subsidy or enforce the regulation. Unless you go into government fiercely determined to cut the government program, you will tend to give in. The fiercely determined ones, like me, tend to leave after a few years; the others stay. To give you an idea how strong this incentive to have the government "do something" is, consider the following.

In about 1986, I visited Washington to see various economists I knew in the Reagan administration. One economist I visited was someone whom I agreed with on over 90 percent of the issues. A few months earlier, college basketball star Len Bias had overdosed on cocaine right after being drafted by the Boston Celtics, and Ronald Reagan was so upset by this that he announced harsher measures to fight the drug war. Economists tend to be skeptical because such measures generally make the problem worse, forcing drugs further underground, pushing their prices higher, thus leading to more crime by people to support their habit, and so on. The economist I visited was someone I would have expected to oppose the drug war, based on earlier opinions she had expressed to me. Instead, she strongly favored the drug war and Reagan's actions. She shared with me a memo she had written, in which she made a case for the drug war based on what economists call "market failure." The main such failure she highlighted in her memo was the loss of productivity of people who abuse drugs. But economists, including her, usually believe that people are paid an amount roughly equal to the value of what they produce. Therefore, someone who loses productivity because of drugs is paid less than otherwise and thus bears the cost of this lost productivity; there is no market failure. I made this argument to her and, because she was a seasoned economist, she knew very well the data supporting it. But she didn't answer with data. Her answer, rather, was that this was a way that she, as an economist, could help her boss, President Reagan, justify his measures. Her tone was one of desperation, as if she was so tired of saying "no" to every proposal for increased government regulation that she just wanted to be able to say "yes." So, even someone with strong professional training that had led her to an informed skepticism about government programs felt a strong incentive, even in the face of her own knowledge and understanding, to support augmenting an already-destructive government program.

The third thing I've learned is that the alleged trade-off between freedom and security is usually nonexistent. I often hear people, even those on my side of the political fence, say that if you're willing to take risks, you're more likely to want free markets and economic freedom generally, but that if you value security, you're more likely to favor government programs at the expense of economic freedom. The underlying view is that government reduces risk and increases security. But, in countless ways, government actually replaces smaller risks with bigger ones.

Take regulation by the Food and Drug Administration (FDA). FDA regulation reduces our freedom to decide which drugs we will consume, and manufacturers' freedom to decide which drugs to develop and produce. In return, we are assured of safer and more-effective drugs. There's the apparent trade-off between freedom and security. But, in fact, FDA regulation makes things riskier by ensuring that many potential drugs will not be developed. How? The FDA's regulations add years of testing to the development process, so that a drug discovered today probably will not be on the market for 10 or more years. A drug has recently been discovered that might actually reverse Alzheimer's disease. Think of what a boon that would be to Ronald and Nancy Reagan. But Ronald Reagan will never be allowed to take it, courtesy of the FDA. The high testing costs drive up the overall cost of drug development so that the average cost of developing a new drug is now estimated at close to half a billion dollars. Drug company executives, knowing this, tend to focus their efforts on drugs that are likely to have a huge market so that they can recoup their up-front costs. This makes new drugs for rare diseases rare themselves because developing them simply isn't worth it. One economist who has studied the issue estimates that by keeping new effective drugs away from people who could use them, FDA regulation causes at least 50,000 premature deaths annually.[6]

You might think that we're still getting some security from FDA regulation because the drugs that do pass the rigorous tests are safer than otherwise. But this is a benefit we would get in the marketplace even if the FDA took away none of our freedom. Imagine that we end the FDA's monopoly power over new drugs, turning it from a regulatory agency into a certification agency. The FDA could even insist that if it hasn't certified a drug, the pill bottle must contain a warning in large letters: "The FDA has not approved this drug for human use." Then, if we all believe that the FDA is an incredibly good certifier, and that anything they don't certify is unsafe, we could all refuse to take any drugs not certified by the FDA. In that case, we would have gained freedom and lost no security.

But that case is completely unrealistic. We already read magazines and consult friends before we buy cars. Why wouldn't we get information before buying drugs? In fact, a majority of us now use drugs even though the FDA has not found them efficacious for our particular use. That is, doctors prescribe them for "off-label" uses that the FDA has not approved them for. Doctors, and the various journals, other doctors, and other certifiers they consult, are our certifiers. Similarly, without the FDA monopoly over new drugs, many of us, and many of our doctors, would trust other certification agencies, whether the European Medicines Evaluation Agency or various private certifiers such as the U.S. Pharmacopoeia, American Hospital Formulary Service Drug Information, or *The New England Journal of Medicine*. Whenever we ignore the FDA's view and instead trust other certifiers, we are saying by our actions that we think we're better off with multiple sources of information.

THE BIG LOTTERY

The fact is that big government is a big lottery in which, as in all lotteries, you get a bad deal. The winnings of all the contestants are less than the amount they pay in ticket prices. It's ironic that so many people who want government to ban or restrict lotteries are themselves advocates of big government, which is the biggest lottery of all. There is a fundamental difference between the "big government lottery" and the more typical game of chance. In the typical game of chance, the players choose to play; in the big government lottery, by contrast, everyone is forced to play. Benjamin Franklin once said that people who are willing to trade liberty for security deserve neither. They'll also get neither.

ENDNOTES

1. *Washington Post,* October 10, 1975, A-1.

2. E.S. Savas, "Public vs. Private Refuse Collection: A Critical Review of the Evidence," *Urban Analysis* 6, 1979, pp. 1–13.

3. Roger S. Ahlbrandt, Jr., "Efficiency in the Provision of Fire Services," *Public Choice* 18, Fall 1973, pp. 1–15.

4. Gary C. Hufbauer, Diane T. Berliner, and Kimberly A. Elliott, *Trade Protection in the United States: 31 Case Studies,* 1986.

5. Montesquieu, *The Spirit of Laws*, Vol. 1, Bk. 13, ch. 1, p. 255, 1751.

6. Daniel B. Klein, "Economists Against the FDA," *Ideas on Liberty,* September 2000, pp. 18–21.

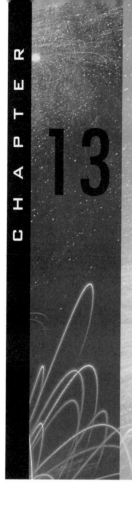

13

MAYBE WE CAN'T END DEATH, BUT LET'S TAKE A SHOT AT TAXES

[T]he great contests for freedom in this country were from the earliest times chiefly upon the question of Taxing.

—EDMUND BURKE[1]

[President] Clinton said that [James] Carville was the only one of them making top-tax-bracket money, and he would be the one paying the tax increase....Clinton bent Carville over his big Oval Office desk to pick his pocket.... About 20 of them posed around the desk with Clinton's hand in Carville's back pocket, the populist president fleecing the rich....

Clinton finally released the wallet from Carville's back pocket. Some $80 in cash was inside. The president took it out and started throwing the $20 bills around the Oval Office, symbolically redistributing the wealth.

—BOB WOODWARD
THE AGENDA: INSIDE THE CLINTON WHITE HOUSE, 1994

I was financially independent from age 16 on—independent not in the euphemistic sense of "rich," but in the literal sense of being on my own financially. When I started college at that age, my father gave me all the money he had saved for my college education—enough to pay all my expenses at the University of Winnipeg for a little over a year—and I combined that with scholarship money, my savings, and my own earnings from summer jobs to get through two years. At the end of the second year of my three-year degree, I was down to my last $50. So I hitchhiked to Thompson, a city in northern Canada that was the center of Manitoba's nickel-mining activity. My plan was to find a job in or around a mine at a fairly decent wage rate, work every possible hour of overtime, and come home with enough money to cover all my expenses for my last year of college. It worked. I got a job as a "helper" to a diamond driller at about $3.00 an hour (over $15.00 an hour in 2001 dollars) and worked lots of overtime. Out of what I earned, the government took a big cut.

The next winter, it was time to file my first T-1 income tax form, Canada's version of the U.S. 1040. It was actually a fairly simple form. I started working my way through it, but every time I tried, I got so angry I had to stop. In filling it out, I felt that I was begging the government to give me back most of the money it had taken from me. I had earned that money. They hadn't. I ended up having my brother fill out the form for me, and I signed it. I wanted the money back, but I just couldn't bring myself to play the government's game to get it back.

I was reminded of that time when I read a news article about Venus Williams in September 2000. Miss Williams had just won the U.S. Open at the tender age of 19 and had received a check for $800,000. President Clinton called to congratulate her, and Miss Williams recounted that conversation to an *L.A. Times* reporter.

> He said, "You really worked hard." I said, "See, I did work hard and I want to keep this for me. I'm a good citizen. Can you lower my taxes, please?"[2]

Clinton then had the gall to say there wasn't much he could do about it, although maybe he could get a lower rate for athletes.

Wasn't much he could do about it? That's not what he thought in 1993, when the tax increase he proposed, signed, and bragged about was implemented—a tax increase that cost Miss Williams more than $80,000 of her $800,000 win. The president can do a lot about taxes. If he had decided to seek repeal of his 1993 tax increase, he would have had enough Republican votes to pull it off, and he could have cut taxes retroactively also, just as he imposed them retroactively. I know this may sound shocking, but Clinton lied. Maybe Miss Williams knew some of this history, and maybe that's why she went on to ask him whether he was asking her to read his lips.

What a shock it is when you make money relatively early in life and have a big, anonymous organization come along and take it from you without your consent. I'm sure that's what Venus Williams felt, and she probably felt it even more when she started making a substantial income at 16.

When I complained about the taxes to adults around me, the most common response I got was that I shouldn't complain because those taxes were going to pay for my college education. I immediately granted the point, but said that I would be glad to give up government subsidies of my education, and of everything else, to avoid taxation. But no one was offering me that choice.

When a commission met at the University of Winnipeg to decide whether to increase subsidies for university education, I, 18 years old at the time and just about to go off to Thompson to work in the mine, submitted a statement to the commission. In it, I advocated completely ending all subsidies to college students, both in cash and in subsidies to colleges. I based my case, in large part, on an article written by UCLA economist Armen Alchian, which I still regard as one of the ten most insightful articles on economics I have ever read.[3] In it, Alchian pointed out that aid to higher education is a subsidy from the relatively poor to the relatively rich because all taxpayers pay state taxes, and almost all beneficiaries are wealthy in the sense that their future income is much higher than the income of those who don't attend college. So, I had done something to talk the government out of subsidizing me.

As I gained experience, I learned that the income tax was only one of many taxes that various governments impose. I also learned, partly from observation and partly from studying public finance—the discipline in economics in which you analyze tax policies carefully—just how much of our behavior is influenced by taxes. There are the obvious ones. We tend to buy bigger houses and finance them more with debt, for example, because we can deduct the mortgage interest. Most of us in the United States get health insurance from our employer because it's a way that employers can pay employees with tax-free income. One of the classic cases in England was the tax on windows. The government, having noticed that people with bigger windows tended to be wealthier, therefore decided to tax windows. The result: many people covered up their windows, and people building new houses built them with fewer windows. When I told this story to some of my students, most of whom were military officers who had traveled widely, they recalled that in some countries in Europe, houses don't have closets; instead, people buy portable closets for their homes. The reason is that governments in those countries tax houses according to the number of rooms—and a closet counts as a separate room. In another European country, noted one student, houses are like bowling lanes—long and narrow. When he had inquired about why, he found out that taxes on houses are based on the amount of street frontage. Another student told of a country in Asia in which few people ever complete their houses and, instead, live in houses that look as if they are perpetually under construction. The reason: the government sets a higher tax on completed houses than on uncompleted ones.

Income taxation gives the U.S. couple coming off the glow of their honeymoon a nasty surprise. Why? Because in the United States, married couples are taxed on their combined income rather than as separate individuals. Combine this with the fact that tax rates are graduated—that is, as your income rises, you are put in a higher and higher tax bracket—and you'll understand why it's called the "marriage penalty." Even if you got married on the last day of the year, you would pay income tax as a couple for that whole year. One result is that people who become conscious of the tax system often avoid the penalty by waiting until the New Year to get married.

Economist Richard Stroup wrote an article in the *Wall Street Journal* telling how the marriage penalty had caused him and his wife-to-be, Jane Shaw, to wait until New Year's day. That's the funny part. The less funny part is that some people choose to live together rather than get married in order to avoid the marriage penalty.

The income tax system also gives us an incentive to shift income from one tax year to another. A standard practice that many self-employed people use is to persuade clients to hold off paying them in the last few weeks of the year and, instead, to pay them early in January; that way, they defer taxes until the next year. Partners in law firms often do this to the extreme, taking payment for their whole income earned in the previous year on January 1 of the next year. Interestingly, Hillary Clinton, who followed this standard practice when she was at the Rose law firm in Arkansas, broke with tradition in December 1992, while her husband was President-elect. That year, rather than waiting until January 1 to take her income, she took it in December, making herself liable for taxes a year earlier.[4] Why did she do this? There are two possible reasons, either of which is sufficient. First, her husband's very low income as governor ensured that much of her high annual income in 1992 would be taxed at low rates. But she knew that he would be paid $200,000 as president, which would mean that if she waited until January 1, 1993, all her income would be taxed at higher rates. This first reason alone would be sufficient to make her wait. But there was probably a second reason. She probably had inside information about the hefty increase in tax rates that her husband planned to impose on high-income people and she probably also figured that he would make the tax increase retroactive to January 1, 1993. That is exactly what Bill Clinton did. By taking her income in 1992, Hillary Clinton had some of it taxed at a rate of 31 percent. If, instead, she had taken it in 1993, it would all have been taxed at rates ranging from 31 percent to the hefty 39.6 percent that her husband imposed.

Every tax distorts our behavior by leading us to find ways to reduce our tax burden. High gasoline taxes in Europe cause people to drive lighter and, therefore, less safe cars. When the top tax rate on investment income in Britain was 98 percent, it hardly paid to invest except in extremely profitable projects. So, for example, someone considering investing $100,000 at a rate of return of 20 percent would plan to earn $20,000 a year, of which he would keep a measly $400. If, instead, he used that one hundred grand to buy a Rolls-Royce, his annual capital cost, not including depreciation on the Rolls, would have been only $400. No wonder so many people in Britain drove Rolls-Royces. Incidentally, the Beatles learned about high tax rates in the mid-1960s when they started making serious income. No doubt they were in the top tax bracket for both their "earned" income (that rate was "only" 83 percent) and their income from investments. Not surprisingly, the Beatles took out their frustration in their song "Taxman," and even gave a close-to-accurate statement of the rates. Recall their lines, which the taxman is speaking:

Let me tell you how it will be,
One for you, nineteen for me.

If you get 1 and the taxman gets 19, that implies a tax rate of 95 percent. Why not 98 percent? My guess is that the Beatles figured out that "nineteen for me" had a better ring than "forty-nine for me," the number implied by a 98 percent tax rate. The high tax rates caused them, in the short run, to write their song, and in the longer run, to leave Britain.

The quote from Edmund Burke that opens this chapter is even more general: Some of the major historical events involving freedom were about resistance to taxation. That's what Lady Godiva's nude ride on horseback, the Magna Carta, William Tell's shooting an apple on his son's head, the Fourth Amendment to the U.S. Constitution, and Henry David Thoreau's "Essay on Civil Disobedience" have in common.

Lady Godiva. In thirteenth-century England, the countess Godiva tried to persuade her husband to refund the heavy taxes he imposed on the people of Coventry. Thinking he would shut her up, the count promised to do so if she would ride nude through the town. Guess what? The taxes were remitted and Lady Godiva's brave ride is still reenacted in pageants in Coventry.[5]

Magna Carta. Trying to scrape together ransom money to pay the kidnappers of his brother Richard the Lionhearted, King John raised existing taxes and tried to impose a new one. England's barons didn't like this and confronted him on the plains of Runnymede, forcing him to sign the Magna Carta. Its key provision was "No scutage [a tax collected from knights in lieu of service] or aid, save the customary feudal ones, shall be levied except by common consent of the realm." In other words, John could not impose new or higher taxes without the consent of the people paying them.[6] Wouldn't it be nice if the U.S. government followed the principles behind the Magna Carta?

William Tell. During their thirteenth-century struggle against taxes imposed by the Austrian government, Swiss tax resisters had, as one of their leaders, William Tell. He refused to acknowledge the Austrian Hapsburgs' authority to collect taxes. As punishment, he was ordered to shoot an apple from his son's head with a crossbow. This incident ignited a successful tax revolt, which lasted decades and ultimately succeeded. The united Swiss infantry, though outnumbered almost ten to one, defeated the Austrian military in the battle of Mortgarten Pass. In Switzerland today, the government is not allowed to increase taxes without explicit permission, via a referendum, of the voters.[7]

Fourth Amendment. The Fourth Amendment to the U.S. Constitution states,

> The right of the people to be secure in their persons, houses, papers, and effects, against unreasonable searches and seizures shall not be violated, and no warrants shall issue, but upon probable cause, supported by oath

or affirmation, and particularly describing the place to be searched, and the persons or things to be seized.

You might think, if you had studied Supreme Court cases for only the last 40 years, that the sole purpose of this amendment was to make it harder for police to arrest murderers, rapists, and burglars. You would be wrong. The founding fathers put the Fourth Amendment into the Bill of Rights because of their bad experience with "writs of assistance." British customs officers used these in the Thirteen Colonies to search for smuggled goods. If they had a writ, they did not need a court order allowing a search. The founding fathers wanted to restrict the federal government from searching the premises and records of suspected tax evaders without a warrant showing probable cause. The founding fathers failed, incidentally. Employees of the Internal Revenue Service can now easily swoop down on banks, check people's bank records, and even seize their bank accounts, without even a warrant, let alone probable cause.[8]

Henry David Thoreau. One of the most famous American essays ever written is Henry David Thoreau's "Essay on Civil Disobedience." In this essay, which he wrote after going to jail, Thoreau argued that under certain circumstances it is right to break oppressive laws. But what law did he have in mind? And what was he in jail for? The most common answer you get today is that he went to jail for resisting taxes because the tax revenues were going to pay for the Mexican-American war. That would have been a good enough reason for me. But it wasn't Thoreau's reason. The tax that Thoreau refused to pay was the poll tax. And he didn't refuse to pay it because of the intended uses of the revenue, which included spending on government schools. He refused to pay it because of the principle it represented. Thoreau wrote:

> It is for no particular item in the tax-bill that I refuse to pay it. I simply wish to refuse allegiance to the State, to withdraw and stand aloof from it effectually.[9]

THE ESSENCE OF TAXATION

Why did all these people—Lady Godiva, the barons of England, William Tell, the founding fathers, and Henry David Thoreau—oppose taxes? Because they understood that taxation is, in essence, legalized theft. When a government taxes you, it takes something you own without your consent. That's exactly what a thief does. The main difference is that the thief is breaking the law, whereas the government is (usually) taking your money legally. Interestingly, even liberal economist Joseph Stiglitz, at one time the chairman of President Clinton's Council of Economic Advisers, has come awfully close to calling taxation theft. Stiglitz wrote,

> This forced transfer [taxation] has been likened to theft, with one major difference: while both are involuntary transfers, transfers through the government wear the mantle of legality and respectability conferred upon them by the political process. In some countries and at some times, the distinction becomes, at best, blurred.[10]

Isn't there another major difference? Doesn't the thief take your money for his own purposes, while the government takes the money to use on things that benefit you? Not always. Governments often spend huge amounts of money on things that don't benefit those who pay taxes. For example, I pay property taxes, sales taxes, and income taxes in the state of California. Much of this tax revenue goes to government schools in California, even though I pay to send my daughter to a parent-financed school. I don't get any benefit from those tax revenues. Second, the key is not whether the government spends money on you. Imagine that a thief takes your money at gunpoint, uses your money to buy a steak, and then brings the steak to your house and gives it to you. Would you say that he didn't steal from you? I don't think so. He stole because he took your money and then made a choice about what would be best for you, rather than letting you decide how to spend your money.

Many people understand the essence of taxation, and my evidence for that is the number of euphemisms people use to cover up their understanding. When Franklin Roosevelt introduced the payroll tax to fund Social Security, he never referred to it as a payroll tax. He called it a "contribution," and even got his language put into law. That's why on your pay statement, you see the acronym FICA to describe the huge tax the feds take from your pay. FICA stands for Federal Insurance Contributions Act. When politicians advocate raising your taxes, they virtually never say that they want to force you to pay more; instead, they say that they're "asking" people to pay more. If that's what "asking" is, I'd hate to see what "telling" looks like. In late 1999, a school bond issue to raise property taxes passed in my town. One advocate of the bond issue, trying to explain why people voted for it, stated that "people were more willing to open their wallets."[11] But that language is seriously misleading. When people open their wallets, they are buying something voluntarily or donating something. The essence of taxation is that some people are voting to have other people's wallets (often along with their own) forcibly opened. So, a more accurate statement of why people voted for the tax increase would have been that people were more willing to open (pick?) other people's pockets. Note the difference in language. What looked like generosity in the misleading language of the tax advocates looks, when stated accurately, like some people using pretty serious force against others.

SHOULD WE HAVE TAXES AT ALL?

The concept of taxation as theft would appear to be enough of an argument for ending taxation. If that were the case, this chapter would end here. But I find myself torn. On the one hand, taxation is clearly theft. On the other hand, if the government can't tax us to pay for, say, defense, I fear that another government somewhere in the world will take over and treat us worse than our government does. During the Cold War, economist David Friedman wrote that he preferred to pay taxes to Washington than to Moscow because the rates are lower.[12] Some libertarians have argued that we, the people, could defend ourselves from foreign governments better and more cheaply than our government can. I don't necessarily think they are wrong, but I'm not sure they're right. What seems clear is that the federal government could defend the United States for under $200 billion, or less than 2 percent of GDP. That would imply a tax rate, if all income were taxed, of about 3 percent. (Why 3 percent rather than 2 percent? Because national income, not GDP, is what would be taxed, and national income is typically about 75 percent of GDP. Two percent of GDP, therefore, is the same as about 3 percent of national income.) I don't want to risk what may be the greatest civilization in human history to avoid a 3 percent tax. Certainly the United States is less threatened now by foreign nations than it was during the Cold War. Nevertheless, 3 percent of GDP is a small tax to pay to avoid a low-probability but catastrophic risk.

So, the rest of the chapter is premised on the idea that the federal government would need an amount of tax revenue equal to about 2 percent of GDP. This, incidentally, is just below the 2.5 to 3 percent that the federal government took through most of the nineteenth century.

How to Kill a Frog

They say that if you throw a frog in a pot of boiling water, that frog will jump out, but if you put a frog in a pot of lukewarm water and gradually heat it, the frog will boil to death. We taxpayers are like that frog. Imagine that we have today the situation that we had before 1913: no personal income taxes, no Social Security taxes, no corporate income taxes, and no death taxes. Imagine, also, that this has been true for the previous 40 years. Then, suddenly, the government decides to levy taxes at the rate it currently imposes—income tax rates ranging from 15 to 39.6 percent, Social Security and Medicare tax rates of 15.3 percent on the "first" $80,000 or so of your income, corporate tax rates of 34 percent, and tax rates on your estate at death ranging from 35 to 55 percent of the value of your estate over about $700,000. You would suddenly face the fact that the government, in one fell swoop, was trying to take about one-third of your income. Do you think that you and your fellow citizens would sit there and take it? Probably not. But the reason we put up with it is that it happened gradually, over 80 years.

There is one crucial difference between boiling a frog and raising taxes on taxpayers. When you boil a frog, you don't try to reassure the frog that he isn't going to be as cooked as the other frogs. But when government increases taxes, it usually targets small groups, meanwhile telling the others that they will be unaffected, and then gradually increasing their taxes, as well. When the Congress first debated the income tax, its proponents claimed—and might have even believed—that it would apply only to the very-high-income people in the United States. Indeed, the tax system started out that way. Moreover, the congressmen who favored the Sixteenth Amendment to the Constitution, which made income taxes legal, promised that the top rate would never exceed 10 percent.[13] I can just imagine some congressman back then saying, "Read my lips. No tax rate above 10 percent." The bottom rate was set at 1 percent on incomes up to $20,000, which would translate into about $300,000 today.[14] The top rate of 7 percent kicked in at $500,000, which is over $6 million today. In other words, income taxes on almost everyone were nonexistent and were very low even on the highest-income people.

But a brief three years later, even before America was at war, the top rate was set at 15 percent. The year after that, 1917, the top rate was pegged at 67 percent and it hit a whopping 77 percent in 1918. So much for the pledge to keep the top tax rate below 10 percent. Meanwhile, the bottom rate was raised from 1 percent to 6 percent in 1918.

Treasury Secretary Andrew Mellon slashed tax rates at all levels throughout the 1920s, which was a major cause of the 1920s economic boom. By the end of the 1920s, the top rate stood at 24 percent on incomes above $100,000 and the bottom rate was well below 1 percent on incomes up to $4,000.

But Herbert Hoover, in the midst of the Great Depression, more than doubled the top rate to 63 percent and increased the bottom rate by more than nine times to 4 percent. He did this in spite of the fact that raising tax rates during a depression lengthens the depression. Franklin Roosevelt carried on Hoover's policy throughout the 1930s and increased tax rates further. By 1940, he had raised the top tax rate to 81.1 percent on incomes over $5 million. During World War II, Roosevelt raised income tax rates substantially at all income levels. By the end of the war, the bottom tax rate had hit a hefty 23 percent on the first $2,000 of taxable income, and the top tax rate was a whopping 94 percent on taxable income over $200,000. The federal government also introduced withholding during the war. Why? So that the millions of new taxpayers would pay on the installment plan and be less aware of how much of their money the government was taking from them. (Remember the frog.) The so-called "class tax" had become the "mass tax." The end of the war brought a very small tax cut, which was reversed during the Korean war. After the Korean war ended, the bottom rate was 20 percent on income up to $4,000 and the top rate was 91 percent on income above $400,000.

In the early 1960s, President Kennedy proposed an across-the-board cut in tax rates that was passed in 1964, shortly after he was assassinated. His cut brought the top rate down from 91 percent to 70 percent on incomes above $200,000 and the bottom rate to 14 percent on incomes up to $1,000. Although he cut tax rates at every level, the thresholds were also cut so that the top rate kicked in at $200,000 versus $400,000 in the previous law and the bottom rate applied for income up to only $1,000—versus $4,000 in the old law. Nevertheless, this was a substantial tax cut.

Then something happened that few people anticipated: high inflation. Starting in the mid-1960s, inflation, which had averaged only 1.8 percent a year for the previous 15 years, started to increase and then rose further in the 1970s. Between 1965 and 1980, inflation averaged 6.6 percent a year, over three times its previous level. This led to something called "bracket creep." Even if your pay simply kept pace with the increase in the cost of living, your after-tax income actually fell because inflation put you into higher and higher tax brackets. Small tax cuts in the 1970s did little to reverse this trend. The federal income tax combined with high inflation to become an incredible revenue machine for the federal government, taking increasing percentages of income from people at all income levels. Between 1965 and 1980, the tax bracket for a family with one-half of the median income rose from 14 percent to 18 percent, for a family with the median income rose from 17 percent to 24 percent, and for a family with double the median income rose from 22 percent to 43 percent.[15] Thus tax rates that had been designed in the early 1960s to take a substantial portion of income from the highest-income people ended up applying to people with middle incomes, and tax rates that had been designed for people with middle incomes ended up being paid by people with low incomes. And the beauty of it all— from the federal government's point of view, that is—was that the government was getting this revenue without Congress having to pass a single piece of legislation.

Alan Blinder, a liberal economist at Princeton, became a member of President Clinton's Council of Economic Advisers and then vice-chair of the Federal Reserve Board before returning to Princeton. In 1988, Blinder wrote that this effect of inflation on taxes will, unless you are an economist or accountant, "leave you yawning."[16] In my review of his book,[17] I told the story of my secretary, Chrissy Morganello, at the University of Rochester in the late 1970s, when inflation reached high single digits. She noticed that even after getting a hefty pay raise one year, she could buy less than she'd been able to the previous year. This didn't "leave her yawning" at all; it made her angry.

Many other Americans got angry, too. When Reagan became president in 1981, he tapped into this anger and focused it by advocating two measures, both of which passed in his 1981 tax law. One was a phased-in decrease in tax rates at all income levels, so that the bottom rate fell from 14 percent to 11 percent by 1984, and the top rate fell to 50 percent by 1982. He also indexed tax brackets to the consumer price index so that inflation alone could never again put someone in a higher tax bracket. The government's tax revenue rose during this time, from $599.3 billion in 1981 to $769.2 billion in 1986, an increase of 28.3 percent. Adjusted for inflation, revenue increased by 6.4 percent. But because Reagan and Congress increased spending by 48.4 percent (23 percent when adjusted for inflation), we had high budget deficits.

Then, in 1986, Reagan and Congress again cut tax rates on personal income and eliminated a few deductions to bring the top rate to 28 percent and the bottom rate to 15 percent. President Bush reversed this in 1990, setting a top rate of 31 percent, a move that broke his 1988 "Read my lips, no new taxes" pledge and thereby probably cost him the 1992 election. His replacement was a little-known outsider named Bill Clinton, who had promised to cut tax rates for the middle class. Clinton broke this promise, instead adding two new tax brackets—36 percent and 39.6 percent. The frog is cooked.

THE HARM DONE BY TAXES

Tax rates on almost all working Americans are fairly high. Most Americans are in the 15 percent bracket; that is, they pay 15 cents in federal income taxes out of every additional dollar of income. Combine that with the 3 or 4 cents they pay to the state government,[18] unless they live in one of the 7 states with no income tax (free advertising—Alaska, Florida, Nevada, South Dakota, Texas, Washington, and Wyoming). On top of that, Americans pay, in Social Security and Medicare payroll taxes, 7.65 percent of every dollar earned, and it could be argued that they implicitly pay, in the form of lower wages, the 7.65 percent paid by the employer. Thus, even modest-income people are in an overall marginal tax bracket ranging from 26 to 33 percent. Middle-income people in a 28 percent bracket are typically in a state tax bracket of 4 to 6 percent which, combined with Social Security and Medicare, puts them in an overall marginal tax bracket of 40 to 50 percent. And high-income people in states with income taxes are in a combined tax bracket of about 50 percent (39.6 percent for the federal income tax plus a 0 percent marginal rate for Social Security—see Chapter 14—plus 2.9 percent for Medicare, plus about 6 to 8 percent for state income taxes).

These high tax rates cause a great deal of deadweight loss, in two ways. The first kind of deadweight loss, which economists don't emphasize but should, is the loss caused by spending tax revenue wastefully. When government has access to revenue, it has no difficulty finding things to spend it on. The most recent Congress, which met in 1999 and 2000, illustrated that. Both Republicans and Democrats were quite "generous" (if that word can describe how some people spend other people's money) with our tax dollars because, for the first time in over 30 years, they had substantial surpluses to work with. And when government spends our money on things, there's a strong basis for believing that those things are worth less than the items *we* would have bought with our money. Even if, for example, the government buys a truck using taxes from you that you would have used to buy the same truck, the government will typically value the truck less than you would have; it sits around, is not taken as good care of, is used for some low-value purpose, and so on. Governments have little or no incentive to spend money carefully because *it's not their money*. Anyone who has worked for a government agency or been close to government decisions on spending can supply countless examples. In fact, if you want to know how well or badly government works, one of the best ways is to ask a government employee. Just make sure that you have the person's trust and that he or she knows that you won't quote him or her. The difference between the value of the money to the taxpayer and the value of the money to the recipients of government benefits (assuming the first exceeds the second) is a form of deadweight loss.

The second kind of deadweight loss, which economists *do* emphasize, grows out of the fact that every tax causes people to alter their behavior in some way. The tax system "distorts" behavior, causing people to do things to reduce the amount of tax they pay; this distorted behavior leads to a deadweight loss, a loss to the taxpayer that is a gain to no one. Economists have proved that the deadweight loss from a tax is proportional to the square of the tax rate. Thus, doubling a gasoline tax from 10 to 20 cents doesn't double the deadweight loss from the tax; it quadruples it. Similarly, doubling someone's marginal tax rate from, say, 15 percent to 30 percent quadruples the deadweight loss. Martin Feldstein, a Harvard economist who is president of the National Bureau of Economic Research (NBER) in Cambridge, Massachusetts, and Daniel Feenberg, an employee of NBER, estimated that President

Clinton's increase in marginal tax rates for high-income people created almost two dollars of deadweight loss for every dollar collected by the federal government.[19]

What To Do, What To Do

The main thing we need to do is cut taxes drastically, especially at the federal level. Various conservatives and libertarians have argued about whether we should have a flat-rate tax—that is, charge the same tax rate on all incomes above some level—or whether we should abolish the income tax and move to a sales tax. My own preference is never to add another tax. The reason: a new tax intended to replace an old one may instead be added on to a reduced version of the old tax. If that happened, we would end up with both an income tax and a sales tax. In 2000, the Australian government reduced income taxes and substituted a sales tax. I predict that, within a few years, the combined revenue from both will be higher as a percent of GDP than the revenue from the old high income tax alone.

Instead of adding a sales tax, it makes sense to hack away at the current income tax, cutting marginal rates at every income level. Proponents of big government tend to oppose such tax cuts. The reason they give is that such tax cuts generate disproportionately higher benefits for high-income people than for low-income people. That's true for one simple reason: High-income people pay most of the taxes. The top 1 percent that former vice-president Gore attacked in the 2000 election campaign, for example, earned 18.5 percent of total adjusted gross income in 1998 (and had incomes of $269,496 or higher) and paid 34.8 percent of total federal individual income taxes. The top 5 percent that same year made 32.9 percent of all adjusted gross income (and had incomes of $114,729 or more) and paid 53.8 percent of total federal individual income taxes.[20] Clearly, a cut in all tax rates would benefit higher-income earners disproportionately because they pay a disproportionately high share of taxes.

Although you might think that an across-the-board tax cut would be hard to sell to middle-income and low-income people, that's probably not true. The problem is that those who want across-the-board cuts in tax rates have, with rare exceptions, never stated clearly that those who get most of the benefits of such a tax cut are now paying most of the taxes. Most Americans, if they heard that, would probably consider an across-the-board tax cut fair. I base my statement on a stunning poll by pollster Everett Ladd in 1995.[21] The poll asked what percent of their income a family of four making $200,000 should pay in all taxes to all levels of government—income taxes, social security taxes, sales taxes, property taxes, and so on. The median response of virtually all income and demographic groups was that the maximum should not exceed 25 percent. That hypothetical family, incidentally, now pays about 39 percent. Because income taxes paid to the federal government are only part of the taxes that the $200,000 family pays, getting that family to an overall average tax rate of 25 percent would require that their income tax rates be cut *by more than half*.

Moreover, to say that high-income earners would benefit disproportionately from a cut in income tax rates is not the same as saying that low-income people would lose. Virtually all low-income and middle-income people would gain too, partly because of a lower tax burden. But there are two other reasons why these groups, especially low-income people, would gain. First, higher-income people would work harder because they would keep more of their earnings; second, lower marginal tax rates would give everyone an incentive to save more, thus adding to the capital stock. Capital and highly skilled workers are typically what economists call "complements" of low-skilled workers; that is, the more capital and high-skilled workers there are for low-skilled workers to work with, the more productive, and thus higher-paid, low-skilled workers become. President Clinton's chief economist, Joseph Stiglitz, summarized this negative effect on low-income people: "[I]f as a result of the income tax, skilled workers supply less labor and investment is discouraged, unskilled laborers' productivity and, hence, their wage, will decline."[22] Of course, the opposite would be true for tax cuts: Cutting tax rates on high-income people would increase the wages of low-wage workers.

The Earned Income Tax Credit should also be modified. The EITC, started by President Ford in 1975, expanded slightly by presidents Reagan and Bush in the 1980s and 1990s, and expanded substantially by President Clinton between 1993 and 1996, is a combination of a tax cut and a subsidy given to low-income people with children. The EITC, given to millions of people earning less than $30,000 a year, offsets all of their income tax for many people and also pays subsidies to many others. The program covered about 18 million taxpayers in 1997 and cost about $25 billion, because President Clinton raised the maximum credit from $1,511 to $3,556 in 1997.[23] This $25 billion is substantially more than the federal government spent on welfare.

The EITC causes two incentive problems. First, people who pay no tax may favor, and vote for, bigger government because they don't see themselves paying for it. Just as many non-wealthy people supported an income tax on "the rich" in the early twentieth century, many low-income people who don't pay income tax now have less resistance to increased government spending. Second, low-income people who earn an additional dollar after some modest threshold lose some of their tax credit, making their implicit marginal tax rate very high. Take, for example, a low-income family with two children in which the husband worked and made $11,650 in 1997. If the wife then took a job, the tax credit fell by 21 cents for every dollar she earned. With federal and state income taxes and Social Security and Medicare taxes, the marginal tax rate on this low-income family approached 50 percent. The wife had little incentive, therefore, to take a job, even if her children were in school. People in such situations, because they are less inclined to earn additional income, find it harder to save and, therefore, are more dependent on government for their old-age pensions and medical care.

The EITC is bad tax policy, if the alternative is an across-the-board tax cut, because it favors one group at the expense of others. If we were starting from our previous tax system, I would not have implemented an EITC, but would instead have cut tax rates across the board. However, we now have the EITC. As a believer in freedom, I don't think it's right to take away the freedom from federal income taxes that many low-income people with children now have. But we should limit the EITC. At most, the EITC should reduce someone's income tax liability to zero but should not give anyone a subsidy.

Given how low taxes should be, virtually every tax that the government levies should be cut dramatically, whether the taxes are individual income taxes, corporate income taxes, taxes on telephone calls, or sales taxes. If we wish to reduce the size and intrusiveness of the government, one of our best strategies is to push always and everywhere for tax cuts. If you can't reduce the income tax because people say it favors the rich, then reduce sales taxes or property taxes or gasoline taxes.

Certain taxes, though, are even more unjust than others and should be given priority for elimination. One of these is the estate tax. When you die, the federal government levies taxes at rates ranging from 37 to 55 percent of the value of your estate in excess of $675,000. Because it's paid at death, many of its opponents call it, accurately, a death tax. Why is the death tax so unjust? Because it's levied on people who have already paid taxes on what they have accumulated. The money in their estate was taxed at least once. If the estate contains earnings from savings, then the earnings were taxed at least twice, once when they were earned as income and once when the interest and dividends on the savings were earned. If the earnings on savings were received from corporations, then the assets in the estate were taxed at least three times: first, when the person earned the money that he or she saved; second, when the corporation he or she invested in paid taxes on corporate earnings; and third, when he or she paid taxes on dividends from the corporation. Taxing the person yet a fourth time is absurd.

The tax on capital gains is another particularly unjust tax because it does not take account of the increase in asset prices that is caused by inflation. There's a simple solution that doesn't involve ending the capital gains tax, and that is to allow people to index their asset prices so that they are paying capital gains taxes on real capital gains only and not on phantom capital gains. Opponents of indexing have claimed that indexing is "too complicated." I doubt that, but if people do find it too complicated, there's an easy fix: Allow people to index, but don't require it. Then those who find it too complicated can continue to pay outrageously high tax rates on capital gains. The other 99 percent of us will take out our calculators and bear a little complexity to keep our money out of the government's hands.

One thing we know from centuries of history is that if the government has revenue to spend, it will spend it. One of my former students, Jim Black, now a successful lawyer in San Francisco, once pointed out that the big objection to taxes is how the government spends it. If, he explained, the government spent the tax money it took from you exactly as you would have spent it, and if we can assume zero collection costs, it wouldn't matter what taxes the government set on us. But the problem with taxes is that someone else decides how your money gets spent. Therefore, except to fund defense and a few other minor-expenditure items that are important and might not be provided without government provision, there is no justification for major taxes.

I haven't dealt in any detail with the biggest tax that most people pay. For all but the highest income people, the biggest tax is not on income, but for Social Security. Let's look at that.

ENDNOTES

1. From Edmund Burke, speech to the British House of Commons, March 22, 1775, *Burke Selected Works*, vol. 1, *Thoughts on the Present Discontents, Two Speeches on America*, ed., E.J. Payne (Oxford, 1881), pp. 178–89.

2. J. A. Adande, "Venus' Open Title a Hand-Me-Down," *Los Angeles Times,* September 10, 2000, D-1.

3. Armen Alchian, "The Economic and Social Impact of Free Tuition," *New Individualist Review,* 1968, Vol. 5, No. 1, pp. 42–52, reprinted in Armen Alchian, *Economic Forces at Work,* Indianapolis: Liberty Fund, 1977.

4. Charles R. Babcock, "Clintons Pay $70,228 in Tax on Income of $290,697 Last Year," *Washington Post*, April 16, 1993, A13.

5. Charles Adams, *For Good and Evil: The Impact of Taxes on the Course of Civilization,* London: Madison Books, 1993, p. 153.

6. Adams, *For Good and Evil*, pp. 156–158.

7. Adams, *For Good and Evil*, p. 179.

8. Adams, *For Good and Evil*, p. 296.

9. From Henry D. Thoreau, *Walden and Resistance to Civil Government,* ed. William Rossi, New York: W.W. Norton, 1992, p. 241.

10. Joseph E. Stiglitz, *Economics of the Public Sector*, 2nd ed., New York: W.W. Norton, 1988, p. 385.

11. Alex Friedrich, "Why Bonds Passed," *Monterey Herald,* November 4, 1999, A1.

12. David Friedman, *The Machinery of Freedom,* New York: Harper and Row, 1973, p. 197.

13. Robert E. Hall and Alvin Rabushka, *The Flat Tax,* Stanford, California: Hoover Press, 1985, p. 20.

14. The tax rates and taxable incomes cited are from Joseph A. Pechman, *Federal Tax Policy*, 5th ed., Washington: Brookings Institution, 1987, p. 313.

15. *Economic Report of the President,* February 1982, p. 120.

16. Alan S. Blinder, *Hard Heads, Soft Hearts,* Reading, Massachusetts: Addison-Wesley, 1987, p. 47.

17. David R. Henderson, "A Liberal Economist's Case," *Fortune,* November 9, 1987, p. 188.

18. For data on state income tax brackets, check *http://www.taxfoundation.org/individualincometaxrates.html.*

19. Martin Feldstein and Daniel Feenberg, "The Effect of Increased Tax Rates on Taxable Income and Economic Efficiency: A Preliminary Analysis of the 1993 Tax Rate Increases," National Bureau of Economic Research, Working Paper 5370, November 1995, p. 21.

20. These data, taken from the IRS's Statistics of Income, are reported in Patrick Fleenor, "Distribution of the Federal

Individual Income Tax," Special Report No. 101, November 2000, Tax Foundation, Washington, D.C. *(www.taxfoundation.org)*.

21. The poll's results are reported in Rachel Wildavsky, "How Fair Are Our Taxes?," *Reader's Digest*, February 1996, pp. 57–61.

22. Joseph E. Stiglitz, *Economics of the Public Sector*, 2nd ed., New York: W.W. Norton & Co., 1988, p. 493.

23. These facts and most of the other facts given here on the EITC are taken from Nada Eissa and Hilary Williamson Hoynes, "The Earned Income Tax Credit and the Labor Supply of Married Couples," National Bureau of Economic Research, Working Paper No. 6856, December 1998.

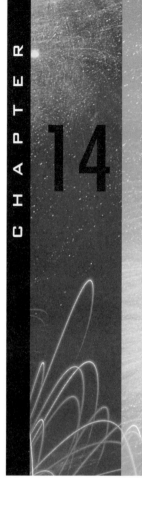

14

THE SOCIAL SECURITY CRISIS: WHY IT HAPPENED AND WHAT WE CAN DO

I say we scrap the current [Social Security] system and replace it with a system wherein you add your name to the bottom of a list, and then you send some money to the person at the top of the list, and then you . . . . Oh, wait, that IS our current system.

—DAVE BARRY[1]

In 1991, one of my students, Stephen Banus, wrote to the Social Security Administration requesting information about the Social Security taxes he had paid and the benefits he could expect to receive. In the form letter he got back, Gwendolyn King, the commissioner of Social Security wrote,

> I want to assure you that Social Security is built on a sound financial foundation. Social Security benefits will be there when you need them.

A prudent man and a good planner, Banus sent a similar request in 1995. This time, the message in the form letter was different. The commissioner of Social Security, Shirley Chater, wrote,

> The latest report of the Social Security Board of Trustees says the Social Security system can pay benefits for about 35 more years. This means there's time for Congress to make the changes needed to safeguard the program's financial future.

In just four years, the commissioner had scaled back the blanket assurance that the benefits would be there "when you need them" to "about 35 more years." What happened between 1991 and 1995?

Actually, nothing much happened in those four years except that the Social Security Commissioner in 1995 was perhaps less dishonest than her counterpart in 1991. The fact is that Social Security was never on a "sound financial foundation." Contrary to the Social Security Administration's official propaganda, there is no real trust fund. Roughly 80 percent of the payroll taxes collected from current workers today are sent out to current retirees, with only a brief stayover in Washington. The government spends the rest of the money on other items. The so-called trust fund contains bonds that the government has created. These bonds are simply IOUs from one branch of government to another. Chris Jehn, an associate director of the Office of Management and Budget compares these bonds to notes that you write every year and put in a box for your child's college education. The note says, "I owe $5,000 to my daughter's college fund." After 18 years of such saving, when your child turns 18, you open the box and out comes, not $90,000, but 18 worthless pieces of paper.

Those who retired in the early 1940s got huge benefits in return for paying low payroll taxes for only a few years. But as the system has "matured," so that current retirees have been paying Social Security taxes for virtually their whole working lives, these retirees have received a much lower return.

A private citizen who set up such a financial chain letter would go to prison. In fact, he did. His name was Charles Ponzi, and he was arrested in 1920 for promising investors that they could double their money in 90 days and using the proceeds from later participants to keep his commitments to earlier ones. Thus was born the term "Ponzi scheme."

There are two main differences between Ponzi's original scam and the Social Security system. The first difference is that Social Security is run by government and, whatever its constitutionality and its questionable ethics, is legal. The second difference follows from the first: Whereas Ponzi had to rely on suckers, the government can and does use force. It's true that the government refers to the Social Security payroll taxes—a hefty 10.6 percent (an extra 1.8 percent is for disability insurance and a further 2.9 percent, levied on all income from work, is for Medicare) of every worker's earnings up to $80,400 in 2001—as "contributions." But just try not "contributing." That's what Valentine Byler, an Amish farmer in New Wilmington, Pennsylvania, did in 1961. His religion taught that its members should care for each other and he tried to act on his religious beliefs by not paying Social Security taxes. The Internal Revenue Service responded by seizing three of his horses and selling them to collect $308.96 in unpaid taxes.[2]

The Social Security Administration's new line is that the fund is solvent until 2037. What the government officials who say that really mean is that by 2037, the last of the special federal government bonds that the Social Security Administration has bought and kept in the Social Security "Trust" Fund will be sold off to the U.S. Treasury. This "sale" of bonds is simply a transfer between the government's left and right hands. To free up the cash to pay for these bonds, the Treasury will have to float new bonds, increase taxes, or cut other spending.

The more relevant date, therefore, is when the government's benefit payments start to exceed its income from payroll taxes and from interest on these bonds—because that's when the bonds will first be sold and the government will have to come up with extra cash. That date, the Social Security Administration now projects, will be 2024, about two-thirds of the way through the retirement of the baby boomers.

In the late 1990s, the government's own actuaries estimated that, to maintain promised benefits, the tax rate would have to rise over the next decades from its current level of 12.4 percent to more than 18 percent.[3] At an 18 percent rate, Social Security taxes would be about 7.5 percent of overall GDP. But total federal revenues from all sources, not just from the Social Security payroll tax, have stayed within a narrow range of 18 to 20 percent of GDP since the early 1950s. If this historical constant held, then the Social Security program alone would take about 40 percent of the total tax revenues collected by the federal government, leaving the remaining 60 percent to pay for Medicare, interest on the debt, defense, and everything else the federal government does. That doesn't seem likely, which means that the odds of raising the Social Security tax rate substantially are, fortunately, fairly small. At some point in the future, therefore, benefits will have to be less than promised.

FLAWED FROM THE START

How did we get into this mess? It started in 1935, when President Franklin D. Roosevelt, together with Congress, explicitly designed Social Security as an intergenerational "chain letter." That, more than any other single feature, virtually guaranteed a big mess for future generations. Interestingly, when the proposal was debated, its chain-letter aspect was little discussed. Politicians in neither the Democratic nor the Republican party seemed upset about that crucial aspect of the plan. At the time, some of its proponents thought of the Social Security tax as a way of extending the income tax to lower-earning people. W. R. Williamson, an actuarial consultant to the first Social Security Board, stated that Social Security extends Federal income taxes "in a democratic fashion" to the lower-income brackets.[4]

Roosevelt and Congress also rejected the Clark amendment, named after Missouri Senator Bennett Champ Clark, which would have exempted employers and employees who had government-approved pension plans. Although the Senate backed this amendment by a vote of 51 to 35, it was later removed. Had that exemption been in the law, many fewer people would have been in the Social Security program and, in fact, with the growth of private pensions, the fraction of the workforce in Social Security would probably have shrunk over the years.

Roosevelt strongly believed in a payroll tax as the way to finance the program. Calling the taxes "contributions," which the federal government did from the start, would make people think of Social Security as an annuity that they had paid for and that they therefore had a right to. That's also why Roosevelt wanted to use a special payroll tax rather than general revenues. If people paid a payroll tax earmarked for Social Security, reasoned FDR, they would think themselves entitled to benefits from the program. FDR stated,

> [T]hose taxes were never a problem of economics. They are politics all the way through. We put those payroll contributions there so as to give the contributors a legal, moral, and political right to collect their pensions....With those taxes in there, no damn politician can ever scrap my Social Security program.[5]

Roosevelt was saying, in effect, that once the entitlement mentality had taken hold, it would be very difficult ever to cut or eliminate Social Security. He was right. What he didn't say—but what the chain-letter financing implied—was that the other reason Social Security would be entrenched was that older people would press politicians for continued benefits, which would necessitate continued taxes on working people, who, when they retired, would push for further taxes on the next generation, and on and on forever. In short, FDR implemented a system of passed-on intergenerational abuse that is still with us today.

Presidents Johnson and Nixon made the problem worse. Between 1967 and 1972, Congress and the President raised Social Security benefits by 72 percent (37 percent after adjusting for inflation). When Wilbur Cohen, Johnson's Secretary of Health, Education, and Welfare, proposed a 10 percent hike in Social Security benefits, Johnson replied, "Come on, Wilbur, you can do better than that!"[6] President Nixon added to the problem by getting into a bidding war with Wilbur Mills, a powerful congressman who was jockeying for the 1972 Democratic presidential nomination. The net result was a 20 percent increase in benefits.

MIT economist Paul Samuelson added some of the intellectual backing for these policies. "The beauty about social insurance is that it is *actuarially* [italics Samuelson's] unsound." Samuelson's point was that if real incomes were growing quickly, each generation could get more out of Social Security than it paid in. While its critics attacked Social

Security as a Ponzi scheme, Samuelson beat them to the punch in 1967 by *blessing* it as one. "A growing nation," wrote Samuelson, "is the greatest Ponzi game ever contrived."[7]

We are now paying through the nose for that "beautiful" Ponzi game. If we include the portion paid by the employer, over 62 percent of families now pay more in payroll taxes (most of which is for Social Security) than they pay in federal income taxes.[8]

The initial payroll tax rate when the program first began was 2 percent on the first $3,000 of income, split equally between employer and employee. In the year 2001, the tax rate for Social Security was 10.6 percent on income up to $80,400 and zero after. This increase in income taxes is not simply an adjustment for inflation. Three thousand dollars in 1938, adjusted for inflation, is less than $38,000 today, or only about half the base income that is taxed today. The maximum tax, employer and employee combined, is $8,077 today versus $60 when the program first started. Had the tax been increased just for inflation, but no more, it would be only about $735 today. See Table 14.1.

TABLE 14.1 Maximum Tax for Social Security (excluding Disability Insurance)

CALENDAR YEAR	MAXIMUM TAX	MAXIMUM TAX IN 2000$
1939	$60	$735
1950	$90	$636
1955	$168	$1,066
1960	$264	$1,518
1965	$324	$1,750
1970	$569	$2,496
1975	$1,234	$3,902
1980	$2,341	$4,835
1985	$4,118	$6,512
1990	$5,746	$7,483
1995	$6,438	$7,187
1997	$6,932	$7,348
2001	$8,522	$8,274 (estimated)

SOURCE: *Tax rates and tax base from* Social Security Board of Trustees Report, *various issues; inflation adjustment from* Economic Report of the President, *various issues.*

PONZI VERSUS STOCKS

Many critics of Social Security have claimed that the current elderly are getting a windfall from the system, but that the younger you are, the worse a deal you will get. They're half right. The younger you are, the worse your deal. But many of the current elderly are also hurt. The reason is that the return from Social Security compares very unfavorably to the returns available in the stock market.

In a 1987 article in the *National Tax Journal,* Stanford economists Michael Boskin (later to be chairman of the first President Bush's Council of Economic Advisers), Douglas Puffert, and John Shoven, and Boston University economist Laurence Kotlikoff presented data on the rate of return earned from Social Security taxes.[9] The real rates of return varied from *minus* 0.79 percent to 6.34 percent and depended crucially on the person's age (older is better), income level (low income is better than high income), and marital status (being married with one spouse not working is better than either being single or being married with both spouses working). Interestingly, even the person who did the best—someone born in 1915, the sole wage earner for a married couple, earning only $10,000 a year in 1985 dollars—received a return of 6.34 percent. Every other category of income earner they considered, including those slightly younger or with a slightly higher income, earned a lower return from Social Security taxes.

In a more recent study,[10] Harvard economist Martin Feldstein and Dartmouth economist Andrew Samwick found that the average rate of return on taxes paid will be as shown in Table 14.2.

TABLE: 14.2 Average Real Rate of Return on Social Security Taxes Paid

YEAR OF BIRTH	Pre-1915	1915	1930	1945	1960	1975	1990
REAL RATE OF RETURN	7.0%	4.21%	2.52%	1.67%	1.39%	1.39%	1.43

SOURCE: Feldstein and Samwick, "The Transition Path in Privatizing Social Security," *National Bureau of Economic Research, Working Paper # 5761, September 1996.*

Compare these rates of return with what you could have earned with an indexed portfolio of stocks. According to Ibbotson Associates, a Chicago-based firm that computes stock market returns, the average rate of return on stocks between 1926 (before the 1929 crash) and 1997 was 11.0 percent, or 7.7 percent when adjusted for inflation.

For shorter periods, of course, the rate of return has been higher and lower than this, but for no 30-year period has the real rate of return ever been below 4 percent. So a rate-of-return comparison shows private investment in stocks to be superior to the government system for people who invest for 30 years or more. Of course, you can find 5-year periods and even 10-year periods during which you would have done considerably worse. According to Ibbotson Associates, the worst 10-year period was October 1, 1964 to September 30, 1974, when the annual inflation-adjusted rate of return in stocks was -4.3 percent.[11] The moral of the story is that you shouldn't put all your savings in stocks if you plan to draw on the funds in 10 years or so.

Another equally valid way to compare makes the contrast starker: Look at the effect that Social Security taxes and benefits have on your wealth. Economists do the computation in three steps. First, they compute the present value of Social Security taxes paid by you and your employer—the value at retirement age of all the previous taxes paid, assuming that they earn compound interest. Second, they estimate the present value of Social Security benefits—the value at retirement age of a stream of future income—using the same rate of return they use for the taxes. Finally, they subtract the present value of taxes from the present value of benefits.

The crucial variable for such a calculation is the interest rate. A pessimistic real rate to use is 4 percent. Why? Because, as noted above, you could have earned over 4 percent with a portfolio of stocks for the worst 30-year period for stocks. Shawn Duffy, a student at the Naval Postgraduate School, using an inflation-adjusted rate of return of 4 percent, found that someone born in 1929 who paid the maximum Social Security tax his or her whole working life and who retired in 1994, would have been $120,000 better off with a private savings plan instead of Social Security. Someone who worked at the average wage his or her whole life would have been $54,000 better off without Social Security. And even a 1994 retiree who earned the minimum wage for the whole of his or her working life, supposedly the quintessential Social-Security-windfall king, would have been about $9,000 better off with a private savings plan.[12] With a more realistic 6 percent real rate of return, Social Security caused the maximum-earning 1994 retiree to lose $262,000 in wealth, caused the average earner to lose $160,000, and caused the minimum-wage earner to lose $66,000.

It's true that the earliest recipients of Social Security did very well. That's because they had paid into the system for only a few years, but received substantial benefits for many years. Miss Ida Mae Fuller, for example, the first recipient of Social Security, received, by the time of her death at age 100, $20,000 in benefits in return for $22 in taxes paid. But now that all future and most current beneficiaries have paid taxes over a working lifetime (when this happens, economists who study Social Security call the system "mature"), there is no windfall for current and future retirees.

THE INJUSTICE OF SOCIAL SECURITY

Imagine that someone takes a certain percent of your income every year and promises to give it back with some accumulated interest when you reach 65. There's only one problem: You don't think you're going to reach age 65 because you're now 29 and you have AIDS. You desperately need that money now to pay for medical bills, rent, and meals, but that person won't let you have it.

I have just described how the Social Security system works. No matter how desperately you need that money now, the government won't let you have it. If you applied to a Social Security office for a form to exempt you, the employees there would refuse to give it to you because no such form exists. There is no exit. You are locked in, and as far as the federal government is concerned, your desires, needs, and interests literally do not matter.

The AIDS example is extreme. There are millions of less extreme cases, cases of people with bad health who are unlikely to live to collect much in benefits. One such group is cigarette smokers, whose life expectancy is years less than the life expectancy of nonsmokers. Though smokers can expect to collect fewer years of Social Security benefits than nonsmokers will, they don't pay a lower tax rate on their earnings. Another large group of people who can expect to live substantially shorter lives is black men. In 1996, according to the insurance Web page *www.insure.com,* a 40-year-old black man could expect to live until age 71, compared to 76 for a white 40-year-old man. In other words, the black man could expect to collect Social Security for about 5 years (the age for receipt of full benefits will be 66 by the time he retires) versus 10 years for the white man.

Another injustice arises from the way the Social Security system treats workers in state and local government, who are the only people left who can be exempt from Social Security. When retired state or local government employees spend 10 or more years in jobs covered by Social Security, they still qualify for Social Security benefits. I do not advocate that Social Security be extended to them at the start of their working lives—the solution, when you have a deep hole, is not to throw people in it. I simply point out that state and local government workers have an unfair advantage over the rest of us.

SOCIAL SECURITY IS NOT GUARANTEED NO MATTER HOW MUCH YOU'VE PAID

In July 1956, Ephram Nestor, a Bulgarian immigrant who had lived in the United States since 1913, was deported from the United States for having been a Communist 17 years earlier. Between December 1936 and January 1955, Nestor and his employers had paid Social Security taxes. In 1954, Congress passed a law providing that any person deported because of past Communist membership would be cut off from Social Security benefits. Nestor sued—ironically, given his Communist past—on the grounds that his rights were being denied. (Communist governments regularly trampled on people's rights and murdered millions of innocent people.) The Supreme Court, in *Nestor v. Flemming,* found, equally ironically given their presumed anti-Communism, that Congress could do what it wished, and if that meant cutting off people who had paid into a fund that they had mistakenly thought guaranteed them a pension, that was just too bad. Of course, the Supreme Court dressed it up in fancier language than I'm using, but the tone was remarkably similar. Here's one of the Court's key sentences:

> To engraft upon the Social Security system a concept of "accrued property rights" would deprive it of the flexibility and boldness in adjustment to ever-changing conditions which it demands and which Congress probably had in mind when it expressly reserved the right to alter, amend or repeal any provision of the act.

In other words, too bad.

ABOLISH SOCIAL SECURITY IN SLOW MOTION

The first step is to recognize that we have been lied to. There is no trust fund, Social Security is a Ponzi scheme, and it's a lousy deal for almost everyone. Therefore, the best solution to these problems is to abolish Social Security. That way, we could be free to decide when, how much, and in what form to save. We don't have that freedom now.

Those of us who decide to invest in stocks linked to such broad indexes as the Standard & Poors' 500 or the Russell 2000 are likely, over time, to accumulate a multiple of what we would get from Social Security. Those who want to invest in bonds because they fear the ups and downs of the stock market could do so. Those who want to invest by buying a rental property could do so. Those who wish to save only a little for retirement and to work through their sixties and seventies could do so. The great virtue of freedom is that it would allow each of us to make decisions about how we want to spend our money.

It's true that the vast majority of us aren't experts on how to invest our money. But we can hire experts, which is what we do when we invest in mutual funds. Moreover, there is one issue on which each of us has incredible expertise that no one else shares: Each of us knows what we want.

Absent Social Security, would people save for their own retirement? Many people are skeptical because those on the verge of retirement save so little: In 1991, for example, the median financial assets of households with heads aged 55 to 64 were only $8,300, and the median net worth, including the value of the home, for all households headed by someone under age 65 was only $28,000.[13] What these skeptics don't realize, though, is that Social Security is one of the main reasons why so many people don't save. As Martin Feldstein has pointed out, someone with average earnings over his whole lifetime who retires at age 65 with a "dependent" spouse receives benefits equal to 63 percent of his earnings the year before retirement.[14] Since such a person's Social Security benefits are not taxed, this is equivalent to about 80 percent of pre-retirement net-of-tax income. If you think Social Security will provide for your retirement, why bother saving?

Most Americans alive today would be better off if we didn't have Social Security. But how do we get from here to there? There are many possible transitions that could benefit almost everyone. Here's a rough sketch of one such transition. It is in two parts. The first part consists of steps that should be taken even if the goal is just to *preserve* Social Security and avoid steep tax increases on younger generations. The second part is composed of measures to abolish Social Security in slow motion.

First, simply to preserve Social Security without increasing taxes, the three steps needed are to (1) increase the retirement age, (2) change the benefits formula, and (3) change the indexing of benefits. The current age for receiving full Social Security benefits is 65, but that number was set in the 1930s. Back then, 65-year-old men could expect to live an extra 12 years, and 65-year-old women could expect to live 13 more years. Today those numbers are 15 and 19 respectively, and work for virtually everyone is much less physically demanding than it was then. The age for full receipt of Social Security benefits is already slated to rise to 66 in 2009 and 67 in 2027. But this could be raised in stages to 70 by, say, 2017, giving people ample time to adjust their plans. Along with this increase, the early retirement age for partial benefits could be raised from 62 to, say, 66.

Raising the retirement age, of course, further hurts smokers, black men, and other people who tend to die earlier. Therefore, a related reform should be an option under which anyone who wants it can receive the equivalent of, say, six years of benefits as a lump sum. That way, those who expect to die early would not be left high and dry, as the government leaves them today if they have no dependents.

The benefit formula could also be altered. Built into the benefit formula are steady increases in real benefits as long as real wages rise. The average annual benefit per retiree in 1995, for example, was $7,510. According to Feldstein and Samwick, if there were no change in the system, the average annual benefit (in 1995 dollars) will be $8,790 in 2016 and $9,290 in 2023.[15] Instead, benefits could be frozen in real terms so that the average benefit in 2023 is no higher than it is today.

Finally, Social Security benefits are indexed to the Consumer Price Index. The Boskin Commission, appointed by the federal government to study the CPI,[16] found that the CPI overstated inflation by about one percentage point a year. Reforms implemented in response to the Boskin Commission's report have cut this overstatement to about half a percent a year. The government could start now to index to the CPI minus this half percentage point. If it did so, then this reform, combined with the reform to CPI calculations that has already taken place, would cause benefits to grow less quickly. These changes taken together—raising the retirement age to 70, indexing benefits to a truer measure of inflation, and freezing real benefits—would eliminate the funding crisis and would probably allow some modest decreases in the Social Security tax rate today. Then people should be allowed—allowed, not forced—to save the difference between the old payroll tax and the new lower payroll tax in an Individual Retirement Account.

Even with all those changes, though, we would still be left with a government-run compulsory Ponzi scheme. But government is not our parent; it simply has no business telling us how much we must save for our old age. It has even less business pooling our "savings" (taxes) with other people's taxes and then deciding how much we get back, based loosely on how much we paid in (don't earn too much), our income when retired (don't save too much), our marital status (marry someone who didn't pay Social Security taxes), and our age (live long). Therefore, we should end Social Security gradually.

Why end it gradually rather than immediately? Because Social Security is a chain letter that makes many current and future retirees depend on being able to tax younger generations in order to get something back for their taxes. That, as Franklin Roosevelt rightly figured, is what makes the transition problem so tough. The only way to end the program is to start *sometime*. The government could start by telling everyone under a certain age, say 30, that he or she will not collect Social Security. Then cut the payroll tax rates of people under 30 to, say, 5 percent (split between employer and employee) of their incomes. Allow these younger people to save the 5.6-percentage-point difference (between the old 10.6 percent tax and the new 5 percent tax) in an Individual Retirement Account.

If polling data are to be believed, 70 percent of Generation X thinks that Social Security will not be there when they retire. That means that 70 percent already think they're paying taxes for nothing in return. The bad news is that my proposal merely confirms their suspicion; the good news is that it cuts their tax rate as a bonus. Social Security would then be virtually abolished in about 60 years.

Such a transition is not ideal for young workers, who would do better if they could invest the whole 10.6 percent. So, if I had been advising Franklin Roosevelt in 1935, I would have said, "Franklin, don't do this." Unfortunately, in 2001, we're trying to plan our way out of the mess that this Machiavellian man created. Under this transition, people under 30 would continue to pay into a system from which they would get nothing. It sounds unfair that people under age 30 would be paying for nothing—and it *is* unfair. But it's not worse in principle than making them continue to pay a higher payroll tax into a system from which they can earn a very low—or even negative—rate of return. Moreover, those who took the amount by which their payroll tax was cut and invested in stock-index funds would likely end up better off than if the current system went on unchecked.

Consider, for example, a worker who decides, at age 20, to invest all of his or her 5.6 percent in stocks, does so until age 67, and reinvests dividends along the way. Then, if the stock fund yielded a real return of 7 percent, he or she would end up with annual retirement income equal to 122 percent of his or her pre-retirement income, versus the much smaller 42 percent that is promised under current law, and the even smaller 29 percent that is payable with the current Social Security tax rate.[17] That same worker, if he or she invested in a 50/50 mix of stocks and bonds yielding a return of 5 percent, would end up with retirement income equal to 56 percent of pre-retirement income, which is still well above what he or she can get from Social Security.[18]

I would add one other reform. I would allow anyone who is at least 45 years old and who has paid Social Security taxes for at least 10 years to immediately leave the Social Security system. A person who left would never be allowed back in and would give up all claim to past taxes paid and future benefits; but he or she would no longer pay Social Security taxes. I haven't actuarially costed out this proposal. I don't even know how it would affect me. But here's one thing I do know: If this choice were offered to me, I would take it in a New York minute. I wouldn't bother to compute the amount I would lose from no longer qualifying for Social Security and the amount I stand to gain from never again paying Social Security taxes. Why would I, a rational, numerate, analytic economist, not make these calculations? Because I value freedom highly, and I would give up a lot not to have the federal government treat me like a helpless, irresponsible waif. (But if you wait and give me the choice when I'm say, 55 or older, I'll do a much more careful calculation.) I might be extreme in this respect, but I'd bet a few million other people are like me. With us out of the system, the federal government loses our tax revenues for the next 20 years—but it doesn't need them as much during this period because it will collect payroll taxes in excess of benefit payouts. Then, when the government faces a financial crunch during the 2020s and 2030s, it will not have to pay us benefits.

ONE POSSIBLY BAD, AND TWO DEFINITELY BAD, PROPOSALS FOR SOCIAL SECURITY REFORM

Some economists and politicians who have studied the long-run problems with Social Security have advocated two other ways to change the system. One change is privatization, whereby the government lets people out of a substantial portion of the payroll taxes they pay and forces them to save the difference in a personal savings account. There are two differences between privatization and my proposal for abolition. First, under virtually all of the privatization proposals, people would be *forced* to save. So such proposals do little for those who wish to spend their money through their lifetime and to work beyond normal retirement, or for those who are ill now and want to use their money for health care. The government is still left dictating to people how much, and when, they should save. If a 40-year-old would rather spend that money on a trip to California or to Europe, for example, he or she cannot. The government says he or she must save and is willing to enforce that at gunpoint. The second problem is that most such proposals would cut the payroll tax by a larger amount than under my proposal, and because they don't change the retirement age or adjust the benefits formula or the over-indexing of Social Security, they would leave the system with a large shortfall between payroll taxes collected and benefits paid out to current recipients.

Some people have suggested that the federal government sell its land and other assets as a way of making up the shortfall. Asset sales are an excellent idea, but their power should not be overstated. Pete Peterson, chairman of the Blackstone Group, a private investment bank, estimated that the federal government's assets, as of September 1995, were worth $2.3 trillion, compared to unfunded liabilities for Medicare and Social Security totaling $15.3 trillion.[19]

Other privatization advocates, especially economists, have considered the huge shortfalls in the future and have detailed how the transition would be handled. Here's where privatization gets nasty because, in all these proposals, taxes would increase dramatically and very soon.

Take, for example, Kotlikoff's proposed Personal Security System. He would end the portion of the current payroll tax that is used to fund old-age benefits.[20] This is not a bad idea, but to finance the transition, Kotlikoff would impose a national sales tax at a rate of close to 10 percent. The rate would fall to about 2 percent, claim Kotlikoff and Harvard economist Jeffrey Sachs, within 40 years.[21] When's the last time you've heard of a sales tax rate falling that much? In U.S. history, sales tax rates have almost always gone in one direction, and that direction is up.

Five pro-privatization members of President Clinton's advisory council on Social Security voted for a plan formulated by Carolyn Weaver of the American Enterprise Institute and Sylvester Schieber of Watson Wyatt Worldwide that would increase taxes. They would divert 10 percentage points of the payroll tax, half of which would finance a flat benefit paid to all retiring workers and half of which would go into a personal security account. To make up the shortfall, Weaver and Schieber advocate an additional payroll tax of 1.5 percentage points that would last 70 years, and additional federal debt of $1.2 trillion.[22]

Privatization advocates worry that if nothing is done now, taxes will rise even more in the future. But if nothing is done now, then benefits will be cut later because there is simply no way that the U.S. government can get away with imposing payroll tax rates of 18 percent. In fact, one of the main supporters of the current system, former Social Security Commissioner Robert Ball, has said that he fears a taxpayer revolt against current payroll tax rates.[23]

The irony is that many believers in freedom who would otherwise lead that revolt are instead advocating their own tax increase. They would replace the possibility of a major tax increase later with the certainty of a tax increase today. Would-be privatizers should instead draw a line in the sand and say, "No more tax increases." Then those who want the current system would have to deal. Social Security is a mess. But as Martin Feldstein has said, when you're in a hole, at least quit digging.

The second bad proposal, which many people have advocated recently, is to have the government invest in stocks. The problem is that the government's Social Security tax revenues are so huge that within 10 years or so, the federal government would own a substantial fraction of U.S. stocks. What government controls it has great difficulty leaving alone. The federal government would almost certainly use its power to dictate business policy for many of the firms in which it held substantial ownership. Also, the government could use its funds to make bad investments. This is what Pennsylvania's government employees' pension plan did in the 1970s when it financed a Volkswagen plant that closed just a decade later.

The third bad proposal, made by Pete Peterson and others, is to impose an "affluence test" for receipt of Social Security, Medicare, and other benefits. If your income exceeds $40,000, according to Peterson's proposal, you would lose 10 percent of your federal benefits for every additional $10,000 of income you make.[24] So, a family making $50,000 and receiving $12,000 in federal benefits would lose $1,200. A family making $100,000 and receiving $12,000 in benefits would lose 60 percent of that $12,000, or $7,200.

Aside from the difficulty of enforcing such a plan ("Mr. Smith, we just learned that your income last year was $10,000 higher than the previous year; please send us a check for $1,500, which is 10 percent of the cost of your hip replacement."), there is a fundamental moral objection. The affluence test would penalize people who make the same income as others their whole life, but who save more and earn a return on these savings. Someone who never saved, but instead spent money on restaurant meals, nice cars, or trips to Europe would benefit more than someone who gave up some of life's luxuries to build a nest egg. The tax system—with taxes on dividends, interest, and capital gains—already discriminates against savers. An "affluence" test would increase this discrimination.

You might argue that events outside people's control, such as high medical bills or large inheritances, are the cause of much of the disparity in wealth of people nearing retirement. But according to economists Steven Venti and David Wise, such uncontrollable life events have little impact on people's wealth at retirement. Instead, most of the differences in people's wealth in their later years are due to one simple factor: the percentage of their income that they chose to save.[25] The affluence test is also economically objectionable: It would deter retirement saving, which is, after all, one of the main ways that people save.

CONCLUSION

The government cannot be trusted with our pensions. Government officials have little incentive to care for us as well as we would care for ourselves. They are particularly bad when it comes to long-term planning because they rarely look beyond the next election. And when they do look far ahead, as Roosevelt did, it can be more for mischief than for good. Johnson and Nixon increased Social Security benefits dramatically, even though this meant that taxes would have to increase dramatically in the 1970s and 1980s. They didn't seem to care a whit about that. Because the Social Security system is unsustainable in its current form, simply to keep the system in existence without further tax increases requires that the government gradually raise the retirement age to about 70, apply more accurate inflation indexing to benefits, and reduce the real growth in benefits that is currently scheduled to occur. But that would still leave us with an expensive Ponzi scheme that is always threatening to get worse. It would also leave us with a system that arbitrarily and unjustly takes wealth from black men, smokers, high-income people, people with AIDS, and single people, and gives to white men, nonsmokers, low-income people, and married couples with one partner not working. It also would keep the government in the position of making our pension choices for us.

Therefore, the Social Security system should be abolished. This can be done so as to allow retirees and those within 30 years of retirement still to get benefits, while freeing younger people to save for their own retirement and be better off than they would have been under the current system. Our pensions should not be based on a scheme that, when carried out by private parties, causes them to be sent to jail.

ENDNOTES

1. From Dave Barry, "Election could come down to who kisses most orifice," *Miami Herald*, September 24, 2000.

2. This story is told in Martha Derthick, *Policymaking for Social Security,* Washington, D.C.: Brookings Institution, 1979, p. 5, who in turn got it from *Congressional Record,* June 26, 1961, pp. 11307–08.

3. Martin Feldstein and Andrew Samwick, "Two Percent Personal Retirement Accounts: Their Potential Effects on Social Security Tax Rates and National Saving," National Bureau of Economic Research, Working Paper No. 6540, April 1998, p. 1.

4. "26,000 in Brooklyn Defy Security Law," *New York Times,* November 29, 1936, p. 37.

5. From Arthur M. Schlesinger, Jr., *The Age of Roosevelt,* vol. 2, *The Coming of the New Deal* (Houghton Mifflin, 1959), pp. 309–310, referenced in Martha Derthick, *Policymaking for Social Security,* Washington, D.C.: Brookings Institution, 1979, p. 230.

6. This story is told in Peter G. Peterson, *Will America Grow Up Before It Grows Old?,* New York: Random House, 1996, pp. 93–99.

7. Samuelson quotes are from *Newsweek,* February 13, 1967, and are quoted in Derthick, p. 254.

8. Andrew Mitrusi and James Poterba, "The Distribution of Payroll and Income Tax Burdens, 1979-1999, National Bureau of Economic Research, Working Paper No. 7707, May 2000, p. 24.

9. Boskin, Michael, Laurence Kotlikoff, Douglas Puffert, and John Shoven, "Social Security: A Financial Appraisal Across and Within Generations," *National Tax Journal* 40, 1987, pp. 19–34.

10. Martin Feldstein and Andrew Samwick, "The Transition Path in Privatizing Social Security," National Bureau of Economic Research, Working Paper # 5761, September 1996, p. 20.

11. I thank Heather Fabian, public affairs manager at Ibbotson Associates, for providing the computations.

12. Shawn P. Duffy, *Social Security: A Present Value Analysis of Old Age Survivors Insurance (OASI) Taxes and Benefits,* Naval Postgraduate School, Masters Thesis, December 1995.

13. Martin Feldstein, "The Missing Piece in Policy Analysis: Social Security Reform," National Bureau of Economic Research, Working Paper #5413, January 1996, p. 13.

14. Feldstein, "Missing Piece," p. 13.

15. Feldstein and Samwick, "Transition Path," p. 22, Table 2.

16. "Toward a More Accurate Measure of the Cost of Living," Final Report to the Senate Finance Committee from the Advisory Commission To Study The Consumer Price Index, December 4, 1996, p. ii.

17. Derived from Stephen J. Entin, "Private Saving vs. Social Security: Many Happier Returns," *IRET Congressional Advisory,* September 4, 1996, No. 56, Institute for Research on the Economics of Taxation.

18. Entin, p. 4.

19. Peterson, *Will America Grow Up?,* p. 18.

20. Laurence J. Kotlikoff, "Privatizing Social Security at Home and Abroad," *American Economic Review,* May 1996, Vol. 86, No. 2, p. 368.

21. Kotlikoff and Sachs, "It's High Time to Privatize," *Brookings Review,* Summer 1997, p. 22.

22. Bob Davis, "Senior Project," *Wall Street Journal,* July 9, 1996, p. A14.

23. Bob Davis, "Senior Project," p. 1.

24. Peterson, *Will America Grow Up?,* p. 167.

25. Steven Venti and David Wise, "Choice, Chance, and Wealth Dispersion at Retirement," National Bureau of Economic Research, Working Paper No. 7521, February 2000.

FREE
AND HEALTHY
AT HALF
THE COST

A 70-year-old man on Medicare, the government-run health insurance program for people over 65, entered a hospital with a ruptured abdominal aortic aneurysm. He made it through the night and spent three-and-a-half months in the hospital. During that time, he was in the intensive care unit for two months, and nine consultants looked at his case. He lived. During his lengthy recovery, no one—not the patient, his friends, or his family—had talked about the cost. The total for his hospital stay, paid by Medicare, was $275,000. The patient's doctor wanted him to wear his false teeth to eat, but the man had lost so much weight that they didn't fit. So the doctor called in a dentist. The evening after the dentist's visit, the doctor asked the patient if the dentist could help him. The man responded: "Oh, sure he can, but it's going to cost me 75 bucks! That's a lot of money for me. I'm not going to have it done!"[1]

This story sums up in a dramatic way much of what I learned from 1982 to 1984 when I was the health economist with President Reagan's Council of Economic Advisers under Martin Feldstein. The main thing I learned was this: Health care costs so darn much because we pay so darn little for it. If we get our health care from Medicare or Medicaid (government-run health insurance for poor people and, increasingly, for people who are above the poverty line), then our health care is paid for by taxpayers. So we have almost no incentive to care about how much it costs. If we get our health care from employer-provided insurance, as most Americans do, we act as if someone else—the insurance company—is paying for most of what we use. Again, we have little incentive to care about cost. Most of what we spend on health care is other people's money. We never spend other people's money as carefully as we spend our own.

One way we overspend is with unnecessary tests. Doctors often run expensive tests to look for highly improbable illnesses because the patients pay so little for the tests. During a White House hearing on health care, for example, Al Gore, then vice-president, related that after his daughter swallowed a feather, the emergency room doctor wanted to X-ray his daughter's throat. Gore was right to conclude that there's something wrong with a system in which expensive tests are administered with so little evidence to justify them. But he was wrong to conclude that it was the doctor's fault. After all, Gore, not the doctor, was the one who took his daughter to the hospital, knowing full well that the odds of harm from a swallowed feather must be low. Gore acted as many of us would have in the same circumstance: Faced with a low out-of-pocket price for an emergency room visit that was unlikely to have much value, he chose to make the visit.[2] Health insurance insulated him, just as it did the 70-year-old man on Medicare, from the cost of his decisions. Gore, like most of the rest of us, was spending other people's money.

In the mid-1970s, the federal government spent $80 million to have the RAND Corporation run a five-year health insurance experiment, surely one of the most expensive social-science experiments in history. For a few years, thousands of families in the experiment were given one of four health insurance plans. All plans had a zero deductible: In other words, there was no initial amount paid entirely by the patient. The main difference between the plans was the copayment rate, that is, the percent of health expenses paid by the family. The copayment percentages were 0, 25, 50, or 95. Thus, if a family had a 0 percent copayment rate, the insurance provider paid all bills; if the family's copayment rate was 95 percent, the insurance provider paid only 5 percent of the bills. Under all the plans, if a family's out-of-pocket expenses reached $1,000, what insurers call the stop-loss limit, the insurance paid for all additional expenses. The 95 percent copayment rate for one plan, combined with the $1,000 stop-loss limit, essentially made that plan into a catastrophic plan with a $1,000 deductible. Here's the RAND experiment's main finding: The higher a family's copayment rate, the less often members of that family went to a doctor and the less often they incurred medical expenses generally. Specifically, those with a 0 percent copayment rate spent 46 percent more on health care than those with a 95 percent copayment rate. Bottom line: People consume more health care when they're spending other people's money. Interestingly, the RAND experiment found no substantial improvement in health outcomes among the families with low copayment rates, who spent more on medical care.[3]

One important implication of the RAND experiment, as Joseph Newhouse, one of the economists involved in it, pointed out in 1992, is that if everyone in the United States switched to a catastrophic health insurance policy with a high family deductible, our health care spending would fall by about 30 percent.[4] That would free up about 4 percent of GDP for us to spend on other things that we value more. How high would the deductible have to be? One thousand dollars in the mid-1970s translates into about $3,000 today. With that deductible, instead of spending about 14 percent of our GDP on medical care, as we do now, we would spend only about 10 percent. This is a stunning implication. It means that simply by buying health insurance with high deductibles, we could get rid of the least valuable expenditures on health care and spend about the same percent of GDP that Canadians spend, without price controls and without the regular waiting lists that Canadians must endure.

TAX AVOIDANCE 101

So why do we have such low deductibles? The main reason is that the government gives us a tax break for doing so. Our employer-provided health insurance system is the unintended consequence of government regulation and taxation. During World War II, the federal government had imposed general wage controls on the economy. Thus, an employer who wanted to pay employees higher wages than the controls allowed had to get the government's permission. In a dynamic economy, especially one in which the government is financing wartime spending by printing money, employers often need to raise wages in order to keep more-productive employees. Thus, employers needed some legal way to pay employees more. The wage controls prevented employers from raising wages, but did not restrict what they could do with benefits. An obvious benefit to provide was health insurance, and that's what many employers began to do.

Another advantage of giving employees health insurance was that, although the payments were deductible as expenses from the employer's taxable income, they did not count as taxable income to employees. So, even after the wage controls of World War II ended, employers and employees found it mutually beneficial to keep health insurance as part of employee compensation. The Internal Revenue Service caught on and tried to tax the benefits as if they were taxable income. But, responding to employers' and employees' protests, Congress passed a law enshrining the tax-free status of health insurance.[5]

The tax avoidance benefit of health insurance is higher at higher marginal tax rates. If the marginal tax rate is only 20 percent, so that you pay 20 cents in taxes for each additional dollar you earn, then an employee can avoid 20 cents of taxes if his or her employer pays one dollar less in salary or wages and one dollar more in tax-free health insurance. But if the marginal tax rate is 40 percent, shifting that same dollar helps avoid 40 cents of taxes. Throughout the 1950s, 1960s, and 1970s, with one major interruption for the Johnson-Kennedy tax cut of 1964, marginal tax rates rose, making it increasingly attractive for employers to shift compensation from taxable money payments to nontaxable health insurance. Tax rates rose for three main reasons. First, and most important, inflation put people in higher tax brackets because tax brackets were not adjusted for inflation. Second, throughout the post-Korean War period, more and more state governments introduced state income taxes, and most state governments increased income tax rates for a given income level. For example, in 1954, 31 states plus the District of Columbia taxed income from salaries and wages, and their typical tax rate on a middle-income family was about 2 percent.[6] By 1981, 41 states plus the District of Columbia had a tax on income from wages and salaries, and the typical marginal tax rate for a middle-income family was about 4 percent.[7] The third reason that marginal tax rates rose was that the federal government substantially raised the tax rate for Social Security and Medicare. In 1954, the Social Security tax rate was only 4 percent.[8] By 1981, the payroll tax rate was up to 13.3 percent and is now 15.3 percent.

Consider an employer and employee trying to decide on an extra dollar in taxable wages or an extra dollar of health insurance. The employee is earning, say, $40,000. If this employee has a spouse making $25,000, the family is likely to be in a 28 percent federal tax bracket. The Social Security tax rate (for employer and employee combined) is 12.4 percent. The Medicare tax rate (employer plus employee) is 2.9 percent. The employee's family is likely to be in about a 5 percent marginal state income tax bracket. The marginal tax rate of this employee, who is by no means unusual, is thus 28 percent + 12.4 percent + 2.9 percent + 3.6 percent,[9] or a whopping 46.9

percent. Thus, almost half of an additional dollar of cash compensation goes to various governments, and the employee can avoid giving this half to the government by taking additional compensation in health insurance rather than in cash. Thus, as long as the employee values an extra dollar in health insurance at more than about 53.1 cents,[10] he or she is better off taking it in that form. That, point out health economists, is one main reason that employers have paid for insurance policies with low deductibles. The employee is better off charging a $50 doctor's bill to the insurance company, even if the insurance company spends $20 to process it, and having the employer pay the extra $70 in a higher premium to cover the bill and the processing cost. The alternative, having the employer pay an extra $70 in cash, yields the employee only about $42 and costs the employer $75.36—$70 plus $5.36, the employer's portion of the Social Security and Medicare tax on $70.

That is how the tax law has led employers to provide employees with low-deductible health insurance. As a result, employees who spend on health care are spending mainly other people's money. This is not to say that they are free-riding. They are not. Much of the money they spend on health insurance is the money they would have otherwise received as higher wages and salaries. Nevertheless, once it is spent on insurance, it becomes other people's money.

HIGH DEDUCTIBLES

In the mid-1990s, I gave many speeches on health care. I pointed out that with high deductibles causing people to spend their own money, people would put much more thought into the amount of health care they'd buy and, shockingly, might even start asking doctors' offices how much they charge.

At one of my talks, a man in the audience told us his story. Because he was self-employed, he got only a small tax break on his health insurance. Therefore, he decided to buy an insurance policy with an annual deductible of $10,000. While on the policy, he broke his arm and paid to have it fixed; the bill was well below $10,000. When he showed up for his first appointment after the surgery, his doctor told him that he should come in for about 30 physical therapy appointments in the next few months. He asked the doctor how much each appointment would cost and the doctor answered, "Eighty dollars." The man replied, "I don't have insurance. Could I get a lower price, or is there any cheaper way of doing this?" "You don't have insurance?" replied the doctor. "Okay, here let me show you what the therapist does, and you can just do it yourself."

GOVERNMENT VERSUS PRIVATE SPENDING

We often hear that it doesn't matter whether you look at government spending or private spending on health care because both have risen rapidly in the last few decades. Actually, it matters a lot. Between 1970 and 1999, government spending on Medicare and Medicaid grew from $12.3 billion to $403.0 billion. Adjusted for inflation, this is an increase of 663 percent. During those same years, private spending grew from $46.7 billion to $662.1 billion. Adjusted for inflation, this is a 230 percent increase, or only about one third of the growth in government spending.[11] When the Medicare law was passed in 1965, the House Ways and Means Committee forecasted that by 1990, annual spending for hospital care under Medicare would be $9.6 billion.[12] In fact, it turned out to be $67 billion.[13]

These numbers show that the explosion of costs in health care is mainly an explosion of *government* costs. This has always made me wonder about the idea that the way to get health care costs under control is to give more power to government. Moreover, the increase in demand for health care due to increases in government spending has also driven up the price of health care. Part of the increase in costs for the private sector, therefore, is due to increases in government spending on health care.

THE TWO-TIER BRICK WALL

As the Council's health economist, I attended many policy forums on health care in Washington. Over and over, I would run into the same group of about 30 to 40 health policy analysts, all in jobs with think tanks, Congressional offices, or lobbies. There seemed to be two kinds of speakers and speeches, the hopeless and the visionary. The hopeless kind laid out the depressing data about spending increases in various government health care programs, and would lament the fact that we couldn't do anything about it. The "visionary" speakers would lay out some of the same problems with health care and then propose draconian solutions. One favored solution was "global health care budgets" for various areas of the country, under which health care spending would be limited by law and, once you reached the spending limit, the government would spend no more. Sometimes, the speaker would point out that the danger of running out of budget would cause the decision makers to ration health care; other times, someone in the audience would make the point, and the speaker would agree. Occasional remarks of other health policy analysts made me think they liked the idea of government rationing.

I wish I could say that I bravely challenged the hopeless and the visionary speakers by suggesting another alternative: getting rid of Medicare and Medicaid. That would have made sense: At the time, the programs were only about 17 years old, and some relatively recent history showed that both old people and poor people had managed to get health care before Medicare and Medicaid came along. But I made this suggestion only occasionally. More often, I suggested implementing modest cost-sharing, requiring people on Medicaid, for example, to pay $3 for a doctor visit or $50 per day in a hospital. My idea was not that the government would collect huge revenue from this cost-sharing, but that it could save huge revenue because people would have some reason, other than their loss of time, to treat medical care as if it had a cost. It just didn't make sense to price a costly thing like health care as if it was worth nothing. Whenever I suggested either abolishing Medicare and Medicaid, and almost every time I suggested implementing cost-sharing, I invariably got one response, one sentence, a discussion ender: "But that would create a two-tier health care system," that is, one system for the rich and one for the poor. Maybe I should have argued with that, but I didn't; I could see that the Washington health care policy establishment was wedded to the idea of a huge role for government in health care and would not be easily swayed. Occasionally, when someone made the two-tier point but seemed open to discussing it, I would say something like the following:

> It doesn't create a two-tier health care system; it creates a thousand-tier system, just as we have a thousand-tier auto system, food system, housing system, and almost every other kind of system. Even people with the same income and wealth often spend very different amounts on cars and food. The same would be true of health care. Also, just as lower-income people sometimes buy expensive cars and higher-income people sometimes buy cheap cars, the same would be true of health care.

Typically, the person's comeback was that health care is unlike any other good because it's a life-and-death issue, and the kind of car you buy is not. I pointed out that most health care is not a life-and-death issue—failing to take care of your acne, or your back pain, or your eyesight will not typically kill you. I also pointed out that, because the larger cars are safer and more expensive, purchases of cars *are* occasionally life-and-death decisions. But we don't respond by having government buy people cars. Finally, I noted that one reason we buy so much health care is that the price to us is artificially low; if we paid the full price for health care, we would make better life-style decisions on exercise, smoking, and foods and would need less health care.

In the rare case where the person I argued with agreed with all these points, he or she would still want the government to subsidize poor people who literally could not afford a life-saving surgery. My answer in that case was that if particular people couldn't afford such surgeries, our society has ways of taking care of them without using government coercion. Such ways include charity care by doctors and hospitals, which has an honorable tradition in the United States, and contributions by friends, families, and neighbors. (Since those discussions, I have been involved in two community fund raisers for people who lacked health insurance and needed critical, expensive health care.) When I made that suggestion, the person typically had one or both of the following objections: We can't depend on people's charitable feelings because people aren't benevolent enough (see Chapter 11 for my answer to that argument); and it's demeaning to poor people to have to depend on other people's benevolence. My answer was—and still is—that it's not demeaning to ask people for help. It's true that some people will feel demeaned by asking for help. But the issue we're discussing is government subsidies, which the government finances by forcing people to pay taxes. There is no justification for using force against innocent people to prevent other people from having "uncomfortable" feelings.

THE UPS AND DOWNS
OF TECHNOLOGICAL PROGRESS

In the 1930s, Frank Knight, an eminent economist at the University of Chicago, asked a medical colleague if he knew when doctors had reached the point where they cured more than they killed. The doctor pondered a minute and said, "Any day now." We've come a long way since then, and technology has brought us there. As Burton A. Weisbrod, a health economist at Northwestern University, wrote in the early 1990s: "Fifty years ago, physicians were little more than diagnosticians."[14] All they could do back then was identify an illness and predict the likely outcome. Now they can actually *do* something. There are many effective medical procedures: kidney dialysis, chemotherapy, bone marrow transplants, organ transplants, polio vaccines, arthroscopic surgery, CT scans, and nuclear magnetic resonators.

Such technological change seems good, right? It helps save and extend lives. It is good. Here's the problem: Technological progress is a major source of the large increases in Medicare spending. Technological progress usually brings down costs, and that's true in medicine also. But technological progress also makes certain procedures possible that couldn't have been contemplated before. These new possibilities lead to spending increases. Spending increases are not bad, per se. The fall in air-fares caused by deregulation has led to so much more travel that overall spending on air travel has risen dramatically. However, people who spend on airfares are almost always spending their own money or the money of employers or others who voluntarily pay. But when medical care advances technologically, much of the money spent on the elderly comes from the taxpayers, who have no say about how it is spent. Given how little progress we in the Reagan administration made in cutting the growth of Medicare, let alone abolishing it, I found myself secretly wishing that technological progress in medical care would slow down. I found other health policy analysts who admitted they had the same thought. That was a horrible thought, because slowing down technological progress would mean that people would die who wouldn't have had to die as soon.

Health-policy analysts still worry about technological progress, as evidence by the following, from a 1990 article in *Newsweek*:

> The first specimens [of artificial hearts] aren't expected for another 10 or 20 years. But some critics are already worrying that they'll work—and that the nation's overextended health-care programs will lose a precious $2.5 billion to $5 billion a year providing them for a relatively few dying patients.[15]

Worrying that they'll work? In other words, the critics were worried that technological improvements would extend the lives of a small number of people. Presumably, their concern was the same as mine: that much of this progress would be paid for by taxpayers rather than by the people who benefited from the progress.

IS THERE A RIGHT TO HEALTH CARE?

The reason we get in such a bind is that many people believe, and many of our laws are based on, the idea that health care is a right. During various discussions I had in Washington in the early 1980s, health care analysts self-righteously claimed that health care is a right, and few people challenged them. Once we assume health care is a right, then someone, presumably the government, needs to enforce that right. They'll do it by taxing some to pay for others' care. With all our medical care paid for by others, we would have no incentive, other than the cost of our time, to hold back on the amount we use, and there would be no upper limit to the amount that could be spent on it. Following that assumption through to its logical conclusion could lead to spending on health care a much higher percent of GDP than we do now, maybe even all of GDP. Then we would begrudge each other our health care. Thus, the assumption that health care is a right would lead to a war of all against all. Well before that point, we would ask the government to step in and ration care. That, in a nutshell, is what has happened in countries that have socialized medicine.

But health care is not a right. As my friend Charles Hooper has put it, "Health care is a transaction." How can you have a right to a transaction? Health care doesn't exist freely in nature, like air, but must be produced by people like you and me working at their jobs. A right is a claim on someone. Who is that unlucky person whose job just happened to be on the other end of my transaction and why does he or she have to give me something of value just because I'm there?

Real rights are protections from actions against you. You have a right to life. That creates a claim on me, not to support your life, but simply to refrain from killing you. The only way you can have a right to a transaction is if someone else has an obligation to transact on the other side or to pay for your transaction. So, for example, if you have the right to enter the hospital when you're sick, then either the hospital has an obligation to take you or other people have an obligation to pay for your hospital stay. But where did this obligation come from? Did the hospital get its obligation just by being in business? Did other people get their obligation simply by making money that someone thinks should be taxed?

Few people who claim that health care is a right of Americans that should be enforced by the U.S. government also claim that it's a right for everyone in the world. They don't want the U.S. government taxing people, for example, to provide high-quality health care to one billion people in India. Doing so would quickly bankrupt the United States. Thus, the alleged right to health care becomes not a right at all, but a privilege that comes from being American or, at least, from living in America. Moreover, when various U.S. judges decree that even people who have immigrated to this country, legally or illegally, have a right to taxpayer-funded health care and education, many resident taxpayers now have a strong incentive to oppose immigration, legal or otherwise. This results in beefed-up border patrols, incredibly intrusive W-9 forms to make sure no one's working here illegally, and barbed-wire fences. Much of this is due to the attempt to legislate the phony right to health care.

Fortunately, if we drop all the regulations and government programs based on the view that health care is a right, and if we drop all the other regulations based on the view that the act of *supplying* health care is a privilege, then we would have better health care at about half the cost. Incidentally, no health economist I know of disagrees that the current system drives up health care spending artificially and, by restricting supply, drives up prices. Also, even though many health economists may disagree with particular parts of the massive deregulation and liberation of health care that I propose, none that I know of would disagree that, on net, my reforms would reduce costs and prices and increase efficiency in health care.

Why, then, don't we see health care economists advocating such reforms? Actually, we do. Virtually everything I propose in health policy is something I learned from some other health economist. But one other thing I learned within a few months of becoming a health economist in Washington is that most of the health economists in Washington, and many others around the country, had given up on ever getting what they saw as rational reforms. But I haven't given up.

YOUR RIGHT TO SPEND

The other idea that needs to be challenged is that the government should be able to prevent us from buying the medical care we want. Elderly people are often willing to pay more than the Medicare-allowed fee for doctors' services because they know that doing so will encourage the doctor to take them as patients rather than turn them down. But a doctor who tries to charge more than the Medicare-set fee can be found guilty of a serious crime and be made to pay a large fine. It's ironic that many of those who believe most fervently in the "right to medical care" also strongly believe that government should prevent people from purchasing medical care at terms agreeable to doctor and patient. You would think that the right to health care would mean, at a minimum, that the government should not prevent you from spending your own money on health care. Yet, there is an underlying logic to both positions. The logic is that many people who advocate a right to health care don't really mean it. What they really want is to have government run the health care system, make choices for people, and prevent people from having a way out. In other words, it's not about rights at all, but about power. And the advocates of these phony rights want the government to have lots of power.

Some years after I left Canada, I got my first inkling that what many people really want is government power. In Canada, the government had nationalized health insurance and prevented doctors and hospitals from providing medical care to willing payers. When I heard someone advocate the Canadian system, in which "every Canadian is guaranteed health care by law," I pointed out that they aren't really guaranteed health care. It's true that, by law, they are *supposed* to get health care. But it's also true that the government sets the system up to create persistent shortages. When my father was hospitalized for 10 days in the 1990s, he was billed $20—$2 a day for a TV rental. All of his hospital care, both from doctors and from the hospital, was priced at zero. Such a pricing scheme is a setup for a shortage, which is what the Canadian system is riddled with. This is a shortage in the economic sense: People want more than is provided and, therefore, the government rations health care—by forcing people to wait for treatment.

When I flew to Canada a few years ago to visit my father, a fellow passenger told me he was returning to Canada after a vacation and would soon have surgery for lung cancer. The wait, he explained, was weeks long and he had to do something while waiting. The Fraser Institute, a think tank in Vancouver, publishes annually an estimate of the number of weeks or months patients must wait in various parts of the country for heart surgery, mastectomies, and various other procedures. In 1999, for example, the median waiting time between referral by a general practitioner and an appointment with a specialist was 3.7 weeks. The median time between the appointment and treatment was 8.4 weeks.[16] Because doctors are not allowed to charge patients for procedures deemed "medically necessary," it often doesn't pay to provide services, no matter how much the patients want them. A Canadian newspaper[17] reported that in Toronto in 1991, dogs could get CT scans for $300 with less than 24 hours notice, whereas people had to wait up to three months for the same CT scanner. Why couldn't people get scans as easily? Because, explained the news story, only the provincial health service could legally pay for a human CT scan. Get it? The dogs' owners are allowed to get a CT scan within 24 hours because the government doesn't care about dogs. Humans are not allowed to pay anything and, as a result, wait months because the government "cares" about them. In the movie *Cool Hand Luke,* when the sadistic warden explains to Luke that he is punishing him for his own good, Luke replies that he wishes the warden weren't so good to him. Many Canadians probably wish their government weren't so "good" to them.

Similarly, because of socialized medicine, many young Canadian women get to experience the pleasures of natural childbirth. An Ontario doctor who administers an epidural is paid only about $100 for it, versus about $1,000 in the United States. At that price, it is often not worthwhile for an anesthesiologist to stick around at, say, 3:00 a.m., when a delivering mother would like him there.[18] No matter how much a woman may want an epidural, she is not legally allowed to pay for it.

You might expect that, given this way of running things, some Canadians would die for lack of prompt care. Some do. Take the case of Joel Bondi, a 2-year-old boy from London, Ontario, who badly needed heart surgery that was postponed again and again. His condition deteriorated to the point that his parents, being good parents, contacted Heartbeat Windsor, which scheduled him for surgery in Detroit. When the media picked up on the story, Canadian officials, worried about bad publicity for their system of socialized medicine, promised to put Joel at the top of the waiting list. His parents agreed. After a four-hour ambulance ride, he arrived at a hospital in Toronto—but no bed was available. So the family spent the night in a hotel. The next day, Joel Bondi died.[19]

Interestingly, the people in power understand well that socialism has rationed care and lowered its quality. When the late Quebec premier Robert Bourassa wanted his skin cancer treated, he did not think Canada's socialized medicine was good enough for him. Instead, he went directly to the National Cancer Institute in Washington for treatment.[20]

It's hard to say that the Canadian government guarantees health care, at least in the usual sense of the word "guarantee." In fact, what the government really guarantees is that if you get health care, you won't be allowed to pay for it, and it is this guarantee that makes you have to wait to get it. The government also guarantees something else: If health care providers try to set up their own clinics and charge willing patients for medical care, the government will shut them down. When I tell this to advocates of the Canadian-style health care system, some are often unwilling to part with their belief in socialized medicine. I find this strange because I believe them when they say that their motive for advocating socialized medicine is to have everyone covered. Yet, many advocates of socialized medicine seem to prefer that everyone be forced into a rationing system rather than have the government provide some basic minimum and let patients and providers who want to opt out of the system do so. So, what started out as a belief in a right to health care ended up as a belief in preventing people from getting health care. Thus my conclusion that it's not about rights at all, but about power.

We saw this same logic unfold in the debate on health care brought on by the Clinton proposals in 1993. While the Clintons seemed to believe strongly that health care was a right, their proposals would have prevented people from buying health care. The essence of their plan was government monopolies, price controls, and government-enforced limits on health-care spending. Virginia Postrel, editor of *Reason* magazine at the time, summed it up best:

> [T]he heart of the plan is not expensive indulgences. It is, rather, an attack on choice and competition. In page after mind-numbing page of bureaucratic detail, the plan closes every conceivable avenue of escape, plugs every possible source of diversity, eliminates every incentive for innovation. It threatens new drugs with price controls, forbids hospitals and universities to train more than a constricted number of specialists, requires urban health plans to serve rural areas, and makes paying extra for care a crime.[21]

The good news is that both Congress and most Americans rejected the Clinton plan. The bad news is that Clinton settled for introducing it in little bits. As economist Charlotte Twight noted in a profoundly insightful article,[22] the Health Insurance Portability and Accountability Act, passed in 1996, contains provisions that criminalize some aspects of the practice of medicine and jeopardize the privacy of doctor-patient relations through a compulsory nationwide electronic database. Fines of up to $10,000 can be levied on physicians who simply order tests from a lab at no personal profit. If doctors bill Medicare for preventive services that are not recognized by Medicare, the doctor is deemed to have engaged in a criminal offense and is branded a fraud. The absence of intent to cheat Medicare doesn't matter. According to Dr. Philip Alper, the Health Care Financing Administration (HCFA), which oversees Medicare, is being accused of instructing medical labs to set up programs to spy on physicians and to report "suspicious" test-ordering patterns. Labs that cooperate are told that they can expect the HCFA to go easier on them when it is their own turn to be audited.[23]

MAKE MONEY OFF MY SICKNESS...PLEASE

In May 2000, Senator Paul Wellstone said of pharmaceutical companies, "We have an industry that makes exorbitant profits off sickness, misery, and illness of people, and that is obscene." In a literal sense, the first part of his sentence is right: Health care providers do make money off our sickness, just as the food industry makes money off our hunger. But the food industry doesn't make money by keeping us hungry; it makes money by feeding us. Similarly, the health care firms make money, not by keeping us sick, but by making us *well*.

One day in the fall of 1995, I got very sick quickly. I was unable to keep liquids in my body and I lost almost 10 pounds in less than 24 hours. My wife took me to the Community Hospital of the Monterey Peninsula, which we locals call CHOMP. There, I rested in a nice, quiet, private room in a clean, wonderfully comfortable bed, while an intravenous device pumped about 8 pounds of fluid into my body. I slept 22 of the next 24 hours. The bill for one day, slightly over $2,000, was mostly covered by my health insurance. But I would have gladly paid the whole amount out of my own pocket. My doctor later told me that every cell in my body had been damaged and that, had I not gone to the hospital that evening, I might have died. For the next few months, whenever I drove by that hospital, I cheered. Sometimes, when I was alone, I blew that hospital a silent kiss. The men and women working there didn't know me and didn't even care much about me, but spent their best energy making me well and, maybe, saving my life. However much they like helping people heal, they would not have been there if someone hadn't paid them. They made money off my sickness. Bless them.

And thank goodness there are countless other strangers all around the world working late at night in labs, trying and trying again to find drugs that will cure sicknesses that I, or those I care about, will probably have in the future. What motivates many of them, besides their belief in their work, is that a drug company is paying them. What motivates the drug company is the large revenue it can earn by developing drugs that cure diseases and save lives. Think about your family. I bet you can think of family members who were seriously ill who could have avoided illness had these innovations existed earlier. It's true of my family. My father had polio in both legs in 1944. My sister had polio in 1952. Unfortunately for them, the drug company Parke-Davis was unable to produce high-quality Salk vaccine until February 1954.[24] Now we take for granted that we won't get polio—and that's thanks to a drug company that wanted to make money for its shareholders and thanks to some scientists who wanted to make money for themselves and their families. I sure as hell *do* want people making money finding cures for my sicknesses.

Think about it another way. When you really want something, the way to show it is by being willing to pay a lot to get it. The alternative, not being willing to pay much for what you say you really want, reminds me of the old joke about the man who needs surgery and finds out who the best surgeon is for his particular condition. The surgeon's services, of course, are in high demand. When the man shows up at the surgeon's office, the surgeon tells him he can do the operation.

"How much will it cost?" asks the man.

"Twenty-five thousand dollars," replies the surgeon.

"I can't afford $25,000," answers the man.

"I understand," replies the surgeon. "In such cases, I charge $15,000."

"I can't afford $15,000," answers the man.

"Okay," says the surgeon. "I'll do you a favor, which I do only occasionally for people who have little money. I'll do it for $5,000."

"I can't afford $5,000," answers the man.

The surgeon, exasperated, asks, "Well what can you afford?"

"I can't afford to pay anything," answers the man.

"I don't understand," says the surgeon. "You know I'm the best in the business and you must have known that my prices reflect that. Why didn't you go to another surgeon instead of coming to see me?"

"That's easy," said the man, "when it comes to my health, money is no object."

The view that it's wrong for people to make money from curing our sickness is not only wrong-headed and, if followed, destructive; it's also profoundly immoral. How could it be right for you to get a life-saving treatment but wrong for the person providing it to be paid? And how could it be right for wine producers and ice-cream producers to make money but wrong for healers to make money? Is a good wine more important than a cure for AIDS or cancer? The view that health care should be free of the profit motive reflects either a simple failure to think through the consequences of that view or, in some cases, profoundly perverted values.

Having said that, let me add that it is often reasonable to object if people make money off our sickness by rigging the system to prevent competition. One main reason doctors make so much money, for example, is that state governments impose licensing requirements that prevent motivated, qualified people from becoming doctors. At the Naval Postgraduate School, where I teach, many of the officers I meet who are in the Medical Service Corps are people who wanted to be doctors but couldn't make the cut. Of course, you could argue that they wouldn't have been good doctors. My own view is that most of the ones I've met would have been fantastic doctors. But there's a market solution that we follow for economists and for many other occupations: We let consumers make their own choice. No government agency says you have to have a Ph.D. in economics to be an economist. A Ph.D. is neither a necessary, nor a sufficient, condition for being a good economist. Some of the worst economists I know—worst in the sense of having no basic understanding of how markets work—have Ph.D.s in economics, many of them from leading schools. Conversely, three of the economists whom I would put in the top 500 (out of over 50,000 economists in the United States) never earned a Masters degree, let alone a Ph.D., in economics.[25] Had the government required people to get licenses to be economists, the odds are high that we would have seen few or none of the many contributions that these men have made.

Similarly, licensing keeps many qualified and creative people out of the medical profession, slowing down innovation and driving up the prices charged by doctors. We should end licensing and move instead to a system of certification. Pop quiz: What two letters on much electrical equipment I use make me feel confident that I won't electrocute myself? UL, short for Underwriters' Laboratory. Underwriters' Laboratory is a completely private organization that, for a fee, tests and certifies the safety of various items. The fact that they charge a fee to the manufacturers whose products they certify creates an inherent conflict of interest. But UL is aware of that and, to offset this incentive, has representatives of insurance companies on its board. The insurance companies have a strong incentive to make sure that UL doesn't certify as safe something that isn't because unsafe products cost insurance companies money. Similarly, with or without government certification, if we eliminate licensing barriers from the medical professions, we would start to see private certification agencies certify the qualifications of medical professionals.

In fact, there are groups in place ready to become private certifiers: They're called managed care organizations (MCOs). Most MCOs don't actively judge the quality of doctors; they don't have to because state government agencies do that. But with the government out of that business, MCOs would have an incentive to take its place. In fact, one of the earliest and most well-known MCOs, Kaiser Permanente, has been certifying doctors for years. Kaiser hires doctors and puts them on salary, which means that it implicitly certifies doctors. Milton Friedman predicted in his 1962 classic, *Capitalism and Freedom,* that with private certification, medical teams would form that are, in his words, "department stores of medicine."[26] Just as department stores implicitly, and usually explicitly, guarantee the quality of the goods they sell, so would "department stores of medicine." This evolution is happening even with government licensing, making government certification irrelevant. The problem is that government licensing also restricts people from practicing and does so, not in response to a market test, but due to political power held by doctors.

The problems with government licensing will become more obvious over the next few years because state restrictions will slow down and sometimes prevent the medical progress that the Internet is creating. It is now possible for a patient in, say, Davenport, Iowa, to be diagnosed by a doctor in Baltimore, Maryland. However, state licensing agencies are getting in the way, insisting that a doctor who practices on the Web is really practicing in the state where his patient resides and must therefore meet that state's licensing standards.[27] But any private certifier is likely to be nationwide rather than statewide and, therefore, would not get in the way of such progress.

HOW THE FDA "SAVES" US
FROM LIFESAVING DRUGS

The other main area in which the government prevents competition in health care is in prescription drugs. The government prevents competition in two ways, the first of which I favor and the second of which I don't. First, the government grants patents to drug developers that give them a legal monopoly for 17 years. Without the prospect of a patent as its reward, a firm would not have nearly enough incentive to develop some of the wonder drugs that we hope to have in the future. The other way the government prevents competition and drives up the price of drugs is, however, unjustified, and has caused the unnecessary early death of tens of thousands of people. I refer to regulation by the Food and Drug Administration.

Almost any American born before the middle of the twentieth century remembers the story of thalidomide, a drug given in the late 1950s to help pregnant women with morning sickness. The drug had one horrible side effect: It caused some babies to be born with deformed limbs. Because of the thalidomide tragedy, the Food and Drug Administration was given new power, under the 1962 Kefauver amendments to the law, to regulate new drugs not just for safety, a power it had held since 1938, but also for efficacy. Notice something interesting: The thalidomide episode was used as a reason for efficacy standards, even though the problem with thalidomide was safety, not efficacy. No one claimed that thalidomide was inefficacious at helping with morning sickness; rather, it caused horrible consequences for babies.

This kind of occurrence—using a tragedy as an excuse for regulations that are not designed to prevent future such tragedies—has a precedent. I did my Ph.D. dissertation on federal government regulation of safety in underground coal mines and found the same thing happening there. In 1968, a major explosion in Farmington, West Virginia, killed 78 men—an explosion that would not have happened had existing federal safety standards been followed. As a result, the U.S. Congress passed a law in 1969 that added new regulations that would not have prevented the explosion. Yet, Congress used the explosion as the justification for the new law. The reason this happens is that various interest groups, not the least of which is the federal bureaucracy itself, want new regulation and are willing to use almost any argument to get it.

The efficacy regulations on drugs, economists have found in countless studies, have delayed the introduction of new drugs by years and added hundreds of millions of dollars to the cost of developing a typical new drug. Santa Clara University economics professor Daniel Klein surveyed all of the studies by economists that he could find on the effect of FDA regulation and found that all were critical of the extent of the FDA's monopoly power over new drugs.[28] In a study of 46 new drugs approved by the FDA in 1985 and 1986, for example, researchers at Tufts University's Center for Drug Development found that 33 were available, on average, 5.5 years earlier in foreign markets.[29] This delay is all courtesy of the FDA.

These delays are killing people. In December 1988, for example, the FDA approved Misoprostol, a drug that prevents gastric ulcers caused by aspirin and other nonsteroidal anti-inflammatory drugs. In some other countries, Misoprostol was available as early as 1985. Using the FDA's own estimates, Sam Kazman, an FDA expert at the Competitive Enterprise Institute, a public-interest lobby in Washington, concluded that Misoprostol would have saved 8,000 to 15,000 lives a year.[30] Thus, the FDA-caused delay cost over 20,000 and as many as 50,000 innocent lives. And that's just their delay on one out of hundreds of drugs.

The tragedy is that these regulations are not necessary. The FDA may have some expertise when it comes to drug safety and efficacy, but on the only issue that matters—your trade-offs between various risks—you are the expert, and the FDA's scientists are rank amateurs. Earlier in this chapter, I mentioned my friend Charles Hooper, who also happened to be one of my star undergraduate students and who is now a partner in the biotech consulting firm Objective Insights. Charley wrote:

> The choice a patient makes between therapies (with the help of his agent, the doctor) is based on many variables: efficacy, tolerability, side effects, riskiness, monetary cost, nonmonetary cost

(e.g., hassle), speed of action. These drug costs and benefits must be judged within the context of many personal values and trade-offs: the fear of death, the fear of surgery, the fear of the hospi-tal, potential pain, and the individual's health profile, financial status, value of time, value of health, and risk tolerance. For the FDA to decide what compounds pass this complex tradeoff is preposterous, given that the FDA can never frame the problem from the individual patient's perspective. One individual's best alternative could be another's worst. We have seen this with AIDS patients: "I don't care if I develop cancer and this costs me $20,000 a year because without it I'm dead in 6 months." If, instead of medical therapies, they were telling us what kind of washing machines to buy or where to go on vacation, we would consider it laughable. This is what von Mises [Ludwig von Mises, the noted Austrian economist who showed that information problems would prevent socialism from working] said. Centralized bureaucrats cannot make the proper decisions for individuals because they lack the requisite information.[31]

A recent instance of this was the FDA's July 2000 banning of the drug Propulsid, a heartburn remedy, after the FDA linked it to dangerous irregular heartbeats in 340 people, 80 of whom died. Sounds reasonable to ban it, right? It turns out, though, that for some people with cerebral palsy, Propulsid was a godsend. One patient, 22-year-old Rob O'Neill, began to moan in pain when digesting his food because the government forbade him from having Propulsid, the only drug that had worked to help him digest.[32] It's true that the FDA will still allow the drug to be sold to some patients, but the agency insists that they meet strict criteria and that they be placed in special scientific studies. Of course, that raises the cost to the patients and the drug companies, making it less worthwhile to provide the drug at all, and certainly less worthwhile to find new users for the drug. Peanuts kill people; those people typi-cally know who they are and can avoid peanuts. But we don't ban peanuts just because they can kill some people. If peanuts were a drug, the FDA probably would ban them.

The solution, both for safety and for lower-cost, more-available drugs, is to strip the FDA of its monopoly power over drugs and let any patient use any drug that a doctor is willing to prescribe. The FDA would then be a certifier of drugs, but not a regulator. Any drug not certified by the FDA would have to carry a warning label, similar to that on a cigarette package, saying: "WARNING: This drug has not been certified by the FDA."

Divide drug buyers into two groups: those who would like choices that the FDA won't allow them and those who want only what the FDA has certified. Those in the first group would now have new choices and would believe themselves to be better off. Those in the second group would turn down those new choices and would thus be unaffected.

Moreover, as I noted in Chapter 12, if the FDA were made just a certifier rather than a regulator, virtually all patients and doctors would begin to trust alternate sources of information. What sources? There are many. In Europe, the European Agency for the Evaluation of Medicinal Products (EMEA) competes with national agencies of various European countries, so that a drug company in a given country can decide whether to go through the country's agency or the EMEA. Currently, in the United States, doctors often rely on private certifiers, such as the American Hospital Formulary Service.

Unfortunately, not content to enforce its monopoly power over what new drugs get produced, the FDA also seeks to limit doctors' uses of legal drugs for uses not specified on the label. According to Donald R. Bennett, M.D., Ph.D., then director of the American Medical Association's Division of Drugs and Toxicology, 40 to 50 percent of all drugs are prescribed for off-label uses. Sixty to 70 percent of drugs used to treat cancer and 90 percent of drugs used in pediatrics are for off-label uses.[33] A branch of the FDA called the Division of Drug Marketing, Advertising, and Communications (DDMAC) routinely sends warning letters to drug companies that advertised off-label uses, even if the advertising was in the form of reprints of peer-reviewed medical journal articles sent to doctors. Drug companies routinely obey, even though the FDA has no legal power to impose such requirements, because they fear that the FDA will slow down their drug approvals, a life-and-death matter for a drug company[34]—and, as we've seen, for many patients. Interestingly, the FDA rarely, if ever, claims that the drugs are ineffective; all they claim is that the FDA hasn't certified them for the advertised uses. When I testified at FDA hearings on its marketing restrictions in 1995, much of my testimony[35] consisted of quotes from the FDA's own warning letters. Predictably, my testimony was much harder on the FDA than that of various drug companies, because I had so much less to lose.

After my testimony, a number of drug-company employees came up and thanked me for saying what they couldn't say. Some told me that they wanted to applaud but didn't dare. However, one drug-industry employee approached me, looking pale and drawn, with his company's chief lawyer beside him. He expressed his anger at me for quoting his criticisms of the FDA in my testimony. (I had quoted him in an earlier published piece after interviewing him and getting his permission to quote him.) He explained that their company had a major new drug up for approval with the FDA and that the agency could delay its approval and cost his company a lot of money. I apologized. It took a lawsuit by a public-interest law firm with no formal ties to the drug industry to get a court decision restraining the FDA. Unfortunately, the restraint doesn't mean much because the FDA stated in its appeal that it had never claimed the power to regulate. It doesn't have to, because, as mentioned earlier, companies that don't go along with its desires will find themselves penalized in other areas. We often hear that free speech is alive and well in the United States. But free speech means the freedom to speak without being thrown in jail, fined, or in some other way penalized by government. In the United States today, the federal government has severely limited free speech for drug-company employees. And the victims are people who go without valuable drugs.

A VISION FOR THE FUTURE

We are so used to the health care sector being high-priced and inefficient that it is hard for most of us to imagine any alternate way of running things. We tend to think that health care spending is like an earthquake that we can do nothing about.

That thought, I suspect, more than any other factor, motivates many people to throw up their hands and say, "Let's get rid of all this and substitute a government-run system like Canada's." But with serious health care reform, it would take only a few years to reverse the decades of government-caused problems.

A MEDIUM REFORM: HOW THE MARKET IS HANDLING THE COST PROBLEM

At some point, people will tire of overly expensive health care, and some of them will do something about it. That's what started to happen, without any government prodding, in the 1980s. Health maintenance organizations (HMOs), such as Kaiser-Permanente, had already existed. With HMOs, the insured person pays a fixed annual fee to the provider, who is also the insurer, and the provider chooses whether to send the patient to a specialist. Other insurance companies have adopted so-called managed care, under which the patient must get permission before being admitted to a hospital and sometimes before getting certain tests. Previously, no one said "no" to more health care spending. The doctors and other providers benefited from spending, as did the patients, and the insurance companies passively paid the bills. But finally, with HMOs and managed care organizations, someone had an incentive to say "no." Health economist David Dranove has pointed out that, in the early 1990s, most informed observers of the U.S. health care system expected health care spending, then at 14 percent of GDP, to be at 18 percent or more by 2000. In fact, it stayed at 14 percent, and Dranove finds that this was mainly due to savings from managed care. He points out that managed care is now saving people with private health insurance a cool $2,000 a year.[36]

Doctors often complain about having to call a young, anonymous, unknowledgeable person to get permission for certain procedures and tests. But the person answering the phone when the doctor calls isn't simply making up an answer: He or she looks it up in an expert-created system. We know that managed care organizations will make mistakes. But doctors do also, and the managed care organizations' advantage is that they generalize from tens of thousands of cases whereas even the most experienced doctors generalize from a few hundred.

A RADICAL REFORM: GET RID OF WHAT'S CAUSING THE PROBLEM

When politicians look at health care, they usually try to address the symptoms without understanding the underlying causes. The symptoms that are most complained about today are high health care costs, high insurance costs, and people going without insurance. I've laid out how Medicare, Medicaid, and the tax code lead to high health care costs and high insurance costs: People spend so much on health care because they personally pay for so little of it.

The way to solve the problem of people spending other people's money on health care is to get rid of the laws that are causing them to do so. Start with employer-provided health insurance.

To get employers to buy employee health insurance with higher deductibles, the government does not need to regulate. It simply needs to end the favorable tax treatment of health insurance. There are two ways to do this. One is for Congress to declare that, henceforth, employers' contributions to their employees' health insurance are taxable income. This would be politically unpopular—and a dangerous revenue-raiser for a power-hungry federal government—because both employers and employees would face a stiff tax. The other way is to make a certain amount of compensation, say $4,000 per employee per year, tax-free income that the employee can use to buy health insurance and/or put in a Medical Savings Account[37] that's similar to an Individual Retirement Account. If the employee were trying to choose between a catastrophic insurance policy with a premium of, say, $2,000 per year, and a low-deductible policy with a premium of $4,000, he could buy either. But he would be spending his *own* money and could know that if he didn't spend it now, he could let the earnings from it accumulate for future medical bills, or, ultimately, until retirement.

Think how this one relatively small change in the tax law would revolutionize and "incentivize" the health care market. Think of someone who has a $2,000 deductible and is trying to decide whether to go the doctor. This person knows that she will pay the whole amount out of her own pocket. Let's say she decides to go. Now, she has a good reason to find out in advance what she will be charged and to do some comparison shopping. Even if she doesn't find out the charge in advance, she will know the charge after the fact and will take that into account in deciding on future visits and on which doctors to visit. Say the doctor prescribes a drug. Suddenly she has a strong incentive to find out if a lower-price generic drug will do. Before, she didn't, because her saving was typically only about 15 percent of the difference in price. Now her saving is 100 percent of the price difference. Also, if she can wait for the drug, she might decide to buy it from a discount mail-order supplier rather than from the local pharmacy.

Most people can imagine doctors quoting prices—many of them already do—but few can imagine hospitals quoting prices in any way that's understandable. But if people were paying the price out of their own pocket, hospitals would quote firm prices. As health economist John Goodman has pointed out, hospitals and doctors do quote firm prices for cosmetic surgery, which patients pay for out of their own pockets. Even though many parties—physician, nurse, anesthetist, and the hospital—are involved, patients are often quoted a single package price in advance. Sums up Goodman, "Ordinary people, spending their own money, have been able to get advance price information that large employers, large insurance companies, and even federal and state governments generally have been unable to obtain for any other type of surgery."[38]

Medicare and Medicaid, like employer-provided health insurance, cause people to buy expensive health care as if it were cheap, thus driving up costs even when the benefits are small. Moreover, Medicare is giving the federal government an excuse to regulate doctors' fees, thus making it harder for many Medicare patients to get care. Finally, without significant reform, Medicare will eat up an increasing share of the federal budget and will require major payroll tax increases within a decade or two. The best reform is to end both. For most people today, ending Medicare and Medicaid is unthinkable. But that's mainly because we're used to both programs. It's simply not true that the elderly and the poor went without health care before 1965, when Medicare and Medicaid began. Medical care was cheaper then, in part because Medicare and Medicaid didn't exist and therefore were not around to drive up costs. Also, there has always been a strong tradition of charity care in this country: doctors and hospitals willingly cutting prices and often giving care for free to the needy, and the population in general contributing to hospitals. That tradition would revive once we all realized that the government-caused "I gave at the office" response no longer makes sense. It's hard to believe that the concern that so many people express about the elderly and the poor is phony. But that's what you would have to believe to buy the idea that, without government programs, the old and the poor would go without health care.

On grounds of simple justice, there is a strong case for ending Medicaid more quickly than Medicare. Medicaid is essentially a welfare program whose recipients pay, in taxes, few of the costs. Although Medicare is also a welfare program, most of its recipients paid for it through their working lives. A transition for Medicare would be to cash it out, by dividing the amount of last year's Medicare budget by the number of people eligible and giving each of them a check for this amount. They could then use this check, which would be about $5,000 a year,[39] to buy health insurance, health care, or anything else they wanted. Then this check could be cut by two percentage points a year so that the program would be ended in 50 years, and people currently in the program and those a few years away from retirement would have an easy transition. The rest of us would have ample time to save for our old-age medical costs.

Former President Clinton made the case for abolishing Medicaid, although he did not state it as such. In discussing his health care proposals, Clinton pointed out that someone on welfare receiving essentially free health insurance through Medicaid has little incentive to take a low-wage job that offers no health insurance. His "solution" was to mandate health insurance on the job, which would have reduced the wage even further and not necessarily made the job any more attractive than welfare and Medicaid. A real solution would be to end Medicaid.

Another government intrusion also makes health insurance expensive and causes many people to go without. That intrusion is government regulation of health insurance.

BEING UNINSURED IS USUALLY TEMPORARY

Many people believe that the 43 million uninsured people in the United States are the same people, year-in, year-out. That belief is false. Imagine you could take a photograph of those 43 million people, then take a photo of the 43 million people who are without health insurance five months later. What percent of the people in the first photo are also in the later photo? About 50 percent. In other words, fully half of the people who lack health insurance at a given time have health insurance just five months later. Why do they go without health insurance for such a short time? Because most jobs in the United States carry health insurance for those employees who want it, and many of the noninsured are people who are out of work. Because unemployment is short-term for most people who are unemployed in a given year—the median duration of unemployment today is about seven weeks[40]—going without health insurance is also short-term. Only 15 percent of those who lack health insurance at a given time are still without health insurance two years later.[41] In other words, of the 280 million people in the United States, only 6.5 million of them, or under 2.5 percent of the population, lack health insurance for two years or more. Going without health insurance, though, is not the same as going without health care. Virtually no one in the United States who needs health care goes without, except as a voluntary choice.

Two kinds of government regulation have been particularly harmful. First, many state governments, and the federal government, prohibit employers from providing a bare-bones, high-deductible, catastrophic insurance plan for their employees. How? By mandating various coverages. Many state governments require employee health plans to cover AIDS, alcoholism, drug abuse, acupuncture, and in vitro fertilization. Mandated coverages include heart transplants in Georgia, liver transplants in Illinois, hairpieces in Minnesota, marriage counseling in California, and sperm bank deposits in Massachusetts.[42]

The federal government has three main mandates for employer-provided insurance. The federal Pregnancy Discrimination Act of 1978 requires employer-provided health insurance to cover pregnancy. MIT economist Jonathan Gruber has found that the 1978 law is paid for mainly out of the wages of female employees who are in their childbearing years, which means that women who don't have children are implicitly subsidizing those who do.[43] Gruber also pointed out that between 1975 and 1981, the number of cesarean births per 1,000 population doubled.[44] Cesarean births are much more costly than vaginal births, but with a federal mandate, the patient doesn't directly bear the expense. In the 1990s, the federal government began to dictate that employer-provided health insurance cover a minimum of 48 hours of hospital care for women having vaginal birth. It also began to require more expensive mental health coverage. As a result, an employee who doesn't want such coverage and an employer who doesn't want to provide it are out of luck. Instead of being able to offer a bare-bones health insurance policy at a modest cost and, therefore, a modest reduction in wages, employers must offer an expensive program with an accompanying large cut in wages. The way out is not to offer health insurance benefits at all, and many employers of low-wage employees, for whom an expensive health insurance policy would mean a large percentage cut in wages, have opted not to insure their employees. Interestingly, the people lobbying for these regulations are not groups of employees who want more coverage, but various associations of health care providers—chiropractors, mental health professionals, and others—who would rather persuade a government official than a patient that their services are needed.

The second kind of regulation that prevents low-cost insurance is state regulation of insurance pricing. Two specific regulations, in particular, cause problems and, when combined, cause the price of insurance for families often to be more than $10,000 a year. The regulations I refer to are community rating and guaranteed issue. Under community rating, insurers are not allowed to vary their premiums according to gender, age, occupation, or any other characteristics that affect the probability that their customers will use medical care once insured. This is like requiring that auto insurance companies charge the same premiums to 21-year-old males as to 40-year-old males. Because the rates must cover all the insurers' costs, including the expected payout, the rates are a bad deal for the healthy and a good deal for the less healthy. As a result, healthy people are less likely to buy insurance, and less healthy people are more likely to buy insurance. The mix of the insured thus shifts toward the unhealthy, driving up premiums further, making it even less attractive for the healthy to buy insurance. The economic term for this effect is "adverse selection," so called because the mix of the insured is adverse to the insurance company. Interestingly, economists have written a great deal on how adverse selection is caused by asymmetric information, that is, by the potential buyer knowing more about his health status than the seller does. But this adverse selection is caused by government policy. These economists have, with virtual unanimity, believed that adverse selection due to asymmetric information is bad, which means that they have favored insurers pricing according to risk. Yet they have been less than outspoken in their criticism of community rating.

The other regulation, guaranteed issue, requires the insurance company to insure all comers. That regulation, on its own, does little harm as long as an insurance company is free to price the insurance according to the risk. So, for example, someone with AIDS who wants insurance will be able to get it, but only by paying an extremely high premium. The moral for an insurance buyer is that you shouldn't let guaranteed issue lull you into waiting until you're sick before you buy insurance.

But guaranteed issue combined with community rating has devastating consequences. If insurers must provide coverage to all comers and cannot price accordingly, then people will tend to wait until they get sick before they buy coverage. Insurance companies, knowing this, raise their rates, making it even less attractive for the healthy to buy insurance, causing many of them to drop out, and making rates even higher. In the seven states in which these regulations are combined—New Jersey, New York, Washington, Kentucky, Vermont, Maine, and New Hampshire—the result has been huge increases in premiums, hundreds of thousands of individuals dropping their coverage, and the drying up of the market for individual insurance policies. In New York, for example, insurance premiums increased by 50 percent or more.[45] The fact that many firms left the insurance market in New York and every other state where these "reforms" were tried means that these premium increases were not a big benefit to the insurance companies but, rather, the result of the higher riskiness of the patient pool. One insurance agent I spoke to speculated that politicians and other government officials who support these regulations not only understand these effects, but also like them. Why? Because they cause more people to go without insurance and thus create a demand for government-provided insurance. His speculation may be warranted.

If we did all this—change the tax code, eliminate Medicaid, phase out Medicare, remove the FDA's monopoly power over drugs and the doctors' monopoly power over medicine, and deregulate insurance—I predict that within a few years, health care would be more available, higher quality, and cheaper. A little freedom goes a long way—and a lot of freedom goes even farther.

Does all this seem hard to imagine? Perhaps, but then, who imagined 20 years ago that the Berlin Wall would fall? Who imagined that someone would be able to produce a laptop computer that has more computing power than the sum of the entire world's computing power in 1955? The main bar to progress in health care is our thinking—and acting on the thought—that progress cannot occur.

ENDNOTES

1. Story taken from James P. Weaver, "Pricing Health Care: The Best Care Other People's Money Can Buy," *Wall Street Journal,* November 19, 1992, p. A14.

2. See Christopher Byron, "Another Con Job: Clinton's Hustle on Health Care," *New York,* April 12, 1993, p. 14.

3. See Willard G. Manning, Joseph P. Newhouse, Naihua Duan, Emmett B. Keeler, Arleen Leibowitz, and M. Susan Marquis, "Health Insurance and the Demand for Medical Care: Evidence from a Randomized Experiment," *American Economic Review,* Vol. 77, No. 3, June 1987, pp. 252–277.

4. Joseph P. Newhouse, "Medical Care Costs: How Much Welfare Loss?" *Journal of Economic Perspectives,* Vol. 6, No. 3, Summer 1992, pp. 3–21.

5. See Milton Friedman, "The Folly of Buying Health Care at the Company Store," *Wall Street Journal,* February 3, 1993.

6. See *The World Almanac and Book of Facts for 1955,* ed. Harry Hansen, New York: New York World-Telegram and The Sun, 1955, pp. 636–637.

7. See *The World Almanac and Book of Facts, 1982,* New York: Newspaper Association, Inc., pp. 47–52.

8. It does not matter that the employer nominally pays half of this tax. What matters in computing the tax advantage from employer-provided health insurance is the combined taxes that the employer and employee can escape.

9. If the family itemizes its deductions on its federal tax form, it can deduct its state income taxes. Therefore, the family's 5 percent tax rate, after taking account of deductibility, is really 3.6 percent: $(1 - .28) * 5$ percent.

10. 100 minus 46.9.

11. Data on rates of expenditure growth are from Suzanne W. Letsch, Helen C. Lazenby, Katharine R. Levit, and Cathy A. Cowan, "National Health Expenditures, 1991," in *Health Care Financing Review,* Winter 1992, Volume 14, No. 2, p. 18. Updated data are taken from *www.hcfa.gov/stats*. Adjustments for inflation are made using the Consumer Price Index.

12. House Committee on Ways and Means, 98th Congress, 1st Session, July 30, 1965, Public Law 89-97, p. 33, cited in Peter J. Ferrara, "The Clinton/Gephardt Bill," Policy Backgrounder No. 133, Dallas: National Center for Policy Analysis, p. 14.

13. *1994 Annual Report of the Board of Trustees of the Federal Hospital Insurance Trust Funds,* Washington, D.C., April 11, 1994, cited in Peter J. Ferrara, "The Clinton/Gephardt Bill," Policy Backgrounder No. 133, Dallas: National Center for Policy Analysis, p. 14.

14. Burton A. Weisbrod, "The Health Care Quadrilemma: An Essay on Technological Change, Insurance, Quality of Care, and Cost Containment," *Journal of Economic Literature,* Vol. XXIX, pp. 523–552.

15. "Demise of a Miracle Heart," *Newsweek,* January 22, 1990, p. 53.

16. Martin Zelder, *Waiting Your Turn: Hospital Waiting Lists in Canada,* 10th ed., Vancouver: Fraser Institute, 2000, pp. 28–29.

17. See "Humans Wait in Pain, Dogs Don't," *The Daily Mercury,* Guelph, Ontario, June 14, 1991.

18. Danielle Crittenden, "Don't Give Birth Up Here," *Wall Street Journal,* March 31, 1994.

19. John A. Barnes, "Canadians Cross Border to Save Their Lives," *Wall Street Journal,* December 12, 1990.

20. Stuart M. Butler, "A Policy Maker's Guide to the Health Care Crisis, Part I: The Debate Over Reform," Heritage Foundation, February 12, 1992.

21. Reprinted with permission from the December 1983 issue of REASON Magazine © 2001 by the Reason Foundation, 3415 S. Sepulveda Blvd, Suite 400, Los Angeles, CA 90034. www.reason.com.

22. Charlotte Twight, "Medicare's Origin: The Economics and Politics of Dependency," *Cato Journal,* Vol. 16, No. 3, Winter 1997.

23. Dr. Philip R. Alper, "Free Doctors from Medicare's Shackles," *Wall Street Journal,* November 5, 1997.

24. See Richard Carter, *Breakthrough: The Saga of Jonas Salk,* New York: Trident Press, 1966, pp. 216–17.

25. They are Gordon Tullock, Alan Reynolds, and David Friedman. Tullock earned a law degree, took only one economics course in his life, wrote dozens of books and hundreds of scholarly articles in economics, and almost shared the 1986 Nobel prize in economics with his longtime collaborator James Buchanan. Reynolds finished his coursework for a Masters degree in economics but never wrote his thesis, and went on to become the chief economist for the Hudson Institute, a think tank in Indianapolis, Indiana. Milton Friedman's son, David Friedman, who earned his Ph.D. in physics, never took an economics course, but, as he once put it to me, had the most expensive economics education in the country, since he was taught by his father. David is now an economics professor at Santa Clara University and has written path-breaking books and articles in law and economics.

26. Milton Friedman, *Capitalism and Freedom,* Chicago: University of Chicago Press, 1962, p. 159.

27. See Bill Richards, "Hold the Phone: Doctors Can Diagnose Illnesses Long Distance, to the Dismay of Some," *Wall Street Journal,* January 17, 1996, p. A1.

28. Daniel Klein, "Economists Against the FDA," *Ideas on Liberty,* September 2000.

29. See K.I. Kaitin, B.W. Richard, and Louis Lasagna, "Trends in Drug Development: The 1985-86 New Drug Approvals," *Journal of Clinical Pharmacology* 27 (August 1987): 542-48.

30. Sam Kazman, "Deadly Overcaution: FDA's Drug Approval Process," *Journal of Regulation and Social Costs,* Vol. 1, No. 1, August 1990, pp. 42–43.

31. Charles Hooper, letter to David Henderson, September 18, 1995.

32. "Drug ban brings misery to patient," Associated Press, November 11, 2000.

33. The data and source are cited in Andrew A. Skolnick, "Pro-Free Enterprise Group Challenges FDA's Authority to Regulate Drug Companies' Speech," *Journal of the American Medical Association,* February 2, 1994.

34. See John Calfee, "The Leverage Principle in the FDA's Regulation of Information," in *Competitive Strategies in the Pharmaceutical Industry,* ed. R. B. Helms (Washington D.C.: American Enterprise Institute, 1996), pp. 306–21.

35. For my testimony, and for the policy analysis that preceded it, go to *www.davidrhenderson.com.*

36. David Dranove, *The Economic Evolution of American Health Care,* Princeton, New Jersey: Princeton University Press, 2000, p. 162.

37. See Goodman and Musgrave, *Patient Power.*

38. John C. Goodman, "Health Insurance," in David R. Henderson, ed., *The Fortune Encyclopedia of Economics,* p. 685.

39. The federal government spent about $197 billion on Medicare in 2000 (taken from *Economic Report of the President, 2001,* p. 370) for 39.8 million beneficiaries (taken from Marilyn Moon, *Growth in Medicare Spending: What Will Beneficiaries Pay?,* Urban Institute, January 1999.)

40. Hoyt Bleakley, Ann Ferris, and Jeffrey Fuhrer, "In a Booming Economy, Unemployment Has Remained Surprisingly High," *Regional Review,* Federal Reserve Board of Boston, 1999.

41. These data are taken from Katherine Swartz and Timothy D. McBride, "Spells Without Health Insurance: Distribution and Their Link to Point-in-Time Estimates of the Uninsured," *Inquiry,* Vol. 27, Fall 1990, pp. 281–88.

42. Facts taken from Goodman and Musgrave, *Patient Power,* pp. 324–325.

43. Jonathan Gruber, "The Efficiency of a Group-Specific Mandated Benefit: Evidence from Health Insurance Benefits for Maternity," National Bureau of Economic Research, Working Paper No. 4157, September 1992.

44. Gruber, p. 39.

45. Bureau of National Affairs, "New York State to Use Insurance Pool Funds to Avert Major Health Premium Increases," *Health Care Policy,* Vol. 6, No. 17, April 27, 1998.

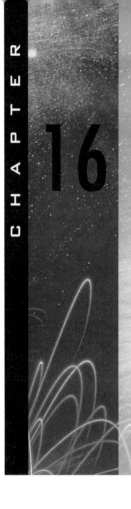

16

FREEDOM AND EDUCATION VERSUS "PUBLIC" SCHOOLS

Not long ago the education establishment promised that if we would only invest more in the nation's schools they would produce a nation of Einsteins and Edisons. Today, we'd be pleased if upon leaving school our children have heard of Einstein and Edison.

—GEORGE WILL

I resolved from an early age not to let school get in the way of my education.

—MARK TWAIN

n the following page is a space with ten lines. I guarantee you will get much more out of what follows if you take at least a few minutes to fill it out. Write down the 10 most important things you've learned in your life. These can be particular skills, important thoughts and ideas, whole areas of knowledge (e.g., math), or important facts. You might say that you would have to take days or weeks to figure out the answer. Go ahead and do that if you want to. But you're probably better off taking less than 10 minutes. Try writing down the first things that pop into your head. Ready? Begin.

THE TEN MOST IMPORTANT THINGS I'VE LEARNED IN MY LIFE

_____ .

_____ .

_____ .

_____ .

_____ .

_____ .

_____ .

_____ .

_____ .

_____ .

I decided to join you and make my own list:

1. How to walk.
2. How to speak.
3. How to read.
4. Math.
5. How to think through something logically.
6. Forgiveness.
7. Touch typing.
8. How to budget money and invest for the future.
9. How to drive.
10. Why free markets work so well.

Now, go through your list and write down, if you can remember it, how or from whom you learned those things. I've done that with my list.

I was able to walk and speak before I started school, and, although, I don't remember with perfect clarity, I think I was able to read. I learned math in school from teachers who were generally pretty good at it. In my last year of high school, though, we went through four math teachers, and my father, who was a public school teacher, taught me a pile of math at home, lying on his bed, smoking his cigar, while I gasped the fumes and grasped the concepts taught by a master. Some of my classes helped me to think logically, but the main thing that helped me was my burning desire to understand things, which often got me in trouble at school. I'm still learning forgiveness, but the biggest lessons that I remember were from my mother and father and from various people I've met over the years, especially my friend Bill Haga. I learned touch typing in school, although my mother had already taught me the basics out of a manual at home. I learned budgeting on my own because, given my parents' meager resources, I had to in order to save for special things. That reminds me: I left out one important thing I learned—how to make money. I learned that from necessity: If I wanted to buy anything that used up more than my weekly allowance, which ranged from 25 cents when I was young to one dollar when I was a teenager, I had to make money. A huge part of what I learned, simply by doing it, was to overcome my fear of applying for a job or selling golf balls to golfers. My parents taught me to drive, and my friend Blake McCutcheon added to my knowledge by teaching me to drive his standard-transmission Honda 65. I learned about free markets from my own outside reading and definitely not in a school.

In short, I learned only two of my ten most important things—math and typing—in school. And I received instruction in both those subjects at home, as well. I'm curious about your list. I would love for you to share it with me, along with your notes about whom you learned from. If you are willing to share it, please email it to me at *drhend@mbay.net*. My guess is that of the ten most important things you've learned in your life, you learned a similarly small number of them in school.

One of the biggest snow jobs that advocates of government schools have successfully pulled is to convince the public to think of "schools" and "learning" or "schools" and "education" synonymously. They are not synonymous. Schools don't have a monopoly on learning: They don't even have a large market share. Think about what schooling is: A lot of it is the three Rs—reading, writing, and arithmetic. Who is teaching it now to students who attend public schools? Often it's parents, siblings, friends, and Hooked-on-Phonics kinds of packages produced and sold in the free market. Then, beyond the three Rs, what is *ideally* taught is the excitement of learning, the possibility of satisfying one's curiosity. If you went to a government school, or if your children go to a government school, is "exciting" the first adjective, or even the fifth adjective, you would use to describe the experience?

My daughter Karen knows how to use the computer better than I do. And she learned none of it at school. She learned by trial and error, and she was motivated by the desire to contact her friends online, to shop online, to hear music online, and to design a screen that she enjoyed looking at. She's not unusual; millions of children have had the same experience. Karen learned to use the computer by pretty much teaching herself, and she did it because the prospect excited her. Thank goodness schools were slow to embrace the computer revolution; they probably would have messed that up too.

Or take something that happened very early in my daughter's time at public school. After she had been in first grade for a few weeks, Karen came home wanting to play something called "Chinese jump rope," and she needed our help to hold the rope. So we would ring one end around the leg of a chair and the other end around my leg. Then she would go through an elaborate series of moves, in a strict order, and to go to the next one, she had to complete the one prior. If she made a mistake, she had to go back a certain number of steps that seemed to vary with where she messed up. The rules were so complicated that in 10 or so times helping her, I didn't quite learn them. Yet she completely remembered the order. Being a proud Dad, I figured that my bright daughter was one of few who'd been able to master all these complicated steps at age 6. But when I asked her how many other girls in first grade knew this game as well as she did, she said matter-of-factly, "They all do." So here were all these girls who all knew the steps in a complex game, and they knew them because they cared about them. If they had been *required* to learn Chinese jump rope, they wouldn't have learned it nearly as well as they did.

That people learn so much outside of school classrooms explains a paradox. Observers have marveled at how well our economy does—that is, how well individual workers in the economy do—in spite of our lousy education system. That has made many wonder if the U.S. school system isn't as bad as it appears. But what it really shows is that the U.S. school system is only one of many inputs into people's learning. Many people who never learned the basics of reading, writing, and arithmetic in public school—and who either dropped out or were graduated anyway—learn it quickly when businesses teach it to them. This suggests that the schools are indeed doing a terrible job. It also suggests that one of the main resources that the government school system wastes, one that is rarely talked about, is children's time.

Schools don't have a monopoly on learning. But public schools do have a monopoly on children's time and on taxpayers' money—a monopoly enforced by law. It is enforced in two ways. First, the government uses force—by requiring us to pay taxes—to fund public schools. Well over 90 percent of the funds for public schools in the United States now come from local government taxes, state taxes, and federal taxes. If you doubt my statement that government uses force to fund public schools, try not paying your taxes and see what happens. This fact is why the word "public" in "public school" is a misnomer. McDonald's is open to the public, but is not funded by taxes. A more accurate term is "government school" or "tax-funded school."

This tax funding gives government schools an unfair price advantage in the competition for students. Government schools don't have to produce as good a product as the schools that depend on voluntary grants and tuition. Say you're currently sending your child to a tax-funded school, and you're not particularly satisfied with it. So you look around and find a Catholic school that charges $3,000 in tuition. For you to move your child to the Catholic school, you have to find the education there to be worth at least $3,000 more to you than the education at the tax-funded school is worth. $3,000 is a lot of money to most people. Therefore, the government school can compete effectively even by being substantially worse in the eyes of most parents. If you send your child to a private school, you're paying twice. For the public school you're not using, you pay through property taxes, state income taxes, and sales taxes, and for the private school you pay tuition. That creates a tough dilemma for most parents and is key to why government schools have close to a lock on the school market.

HORROR STORIES

The government's monopoly is what has allowed it to produce so bad a product for so long. There are lots of horror stories. One is of Stephen Jackson, a conscientious high-school student who had perfect attendance and studied two-and-a-half hours a night. As the valedictorian from Western High School, a government school in Washington, D.C., Jackson planned to go on to George Washington University, but was turned down flat. His Scholastic Aptitude Test (SAT) score was 600. On the verbal, it was 320, putting him in the lowest 13 percent of college-bound students, and in math it was 280, putting him in the lowest 2 percent. (The highest possible total score is 1,600. The lowest possible score is 400, which, according to Kevin Gonzalez, spokesman for the Educational Testing Service [ETS] in Princeton, one could get "simply by signing one's name, date of birth, and social security number, and then sleeping through the whole test.")[1] Joseph Ruth, dean of admissions at George Washington University, commented, "My feeling is that this kid has been conned. He's been deluded into thinking he's gotten an education."[2]

Or how about this description of Goudy Elementary School, written by Bonita Brodt, a *Chicago Tribune* reporter who spent significant time at the school. According to Brodt, this school was not the best of the Chicago public school system but "was by no means the worst."

> There was a M*A*S*H-like atmosphere about Goudy. All day long, voices crackled over the public-address system. The principal interrupted one afternoon to alert the whole school to the fact that a group of boys was running wild in the second-floor corridor. The clerk sent her voice into classrooms when she needed to know something, when she wanted to continue an argument after a teacher had stormed out of the office, or on paydays when she ordered some teachers to come to the office during class time to pick up their "negotiables," the school's euphemism for paychecks. (The word had been used since a teacher had complained that she did not feel secure when the word "paychecks" was said in the presence of the low-income students who attended Goudy.)[3]

When my wife and I sent our daughter to the local government school, we joined the Parents-Teachers Association (PTA). One year we had an objection to her physical education teacher's behavior. We talked about it with other parents and found some who were willing to go to the principal with us. After he gave us a noncommittal answer, we decided to attend the PTA meeting, which my wife did regularly anyway, to state our objection to this particular teacher and to get other parents energized. When I stood up and started talking about it, one of the teachers present said, "This is not the place to talk about that teacher's behavior. This is the PTA." It reminded me of the line in the famous movie, *Dr. Strangelove,* when General Turgison, played by George C. Scott, is fighting in the war room with the Russian ambassador. The president, Murken Muffly, tries to stop the fight with one clinching line: "Gentlemen, this is the war room." It was clear that this teacher thought of the PTA the way virtually all the teachers and parents thought of it. Despite the fact that my membership card stated that the PTA's purpose was to enhance our children's education—a statement that I read out loud to the gathering in response to the teacher's comment—everyone there knew that the PTA's real purpose was to raise money. The teachers were clear that they wanted no input on their teaching. We were a captive audience—actually, our children were a captive audience—and everyone knew that.

The next story comes from an educational tester who, for reasons you will quickly understand, is no longer an educational tester. His name was Charles Johnsen, and when he wrote this story in 1995, he was a Lutheran preacher and a computer chip designer in Aurora, Colorado. Twenty years earlier, Johnsen worked on a proposed test for a testing firm in Chicago that had a contract with the Chicago Board of Education. One of the questions on the test was about the "el," the word used locally for Chicago's system of elevated trains. Johnsen put a photocopy of an actual el schedule in the test and asked a question like the following: "CJ has a job interview at 9:00 a.m. The company is a block away from the State Street station. What is the last train CJ can take to get to the interview on time?" Then he listed five different train times from the schedule, only one of them right.

The results surprised him. Students in the suburban schools did well on the other items, but, in his words, "blew the item about the el big time." But the kids in the inner schools generally got the right answer on the el question even when, as was obvious from the rest of the test, they could barely read.

That was the first surprise. Then came his bigger surprise. His employer's software generated statistics about each test question. A "good" question did not discriminate between ignorance and knowledge, but instead discriminated between "good" students and "poor" students. No matter how important the question, if the obviously good students—the ones in the suburbs—got the answer wrong and the obviously bad students—the ones in the inner cities—got the answer right, the question was thrown out.[4] I think of this story whenever I hear people say that the SAT does not discriminate against black people.

Finally, two last stories, the first disturbing, the second downright frightening. The first one was what tipped the scales, causing my wife and me to commit to spending between 10 and 20 percent of our after-tax income on sending our daughter to a private school. When we had a mid-year parent/teacher meeting to discuss Karen's progress, we noted that she was earning A's in virtually everything, but we wondered what an A meant. Her teacher responded, "You worry too much about Karen. She always does well. I hardly have to pay any attention to her."

The second story comes from a 1994 Associated Press news article in the *St. Louis Post-Dispatch* that was supplied to me by Marhsall Fritz, head of the Separation of School and State Alliance:[5]

> CHICAGO (AP)—Clarence Notree barely had time to act when a gunman burst into the elementary school gym. As the bullets flew, the physical education teacher spread out his arms to shield the children and pushed them out a door to safety. He got shot in the wrist.

> His school and community lauded Notree as a hero, but the Chicago Board of Education insisted he wasn't entitled to Workers' Compensation. They said saving children's lives was not part of his job.

> Here is the board's exact language:

> Playground activity does not inherently contain a risk of being shot by some unknown assailant.

I doubt that anyone on the Board of Education would have advised Notree to run if his students were being shot at. But one of the many problems with government schools is that there's no one person in charge. Board members share responsibility, and shared responsibility often amounts to no responsibility. Thus was an evil result reached by people who were probably not evil.

Although most of people's stories about their unpleasant experiences at school are about government schools, private schools are not immune. One friend was once stuffed into a trash can by his "colleagues" at a Catholic school and is still trying to exorcise the shame demons that the nuns at his school implanted in him. Another friend attended the Upper Canada College, the premier English Canadian prep school for boys (the equivalent of Andover in the United States). He told me about a large boy who ripped my friend's pants off, held him in the air, and threatened to drop him on his head on the cement.

It's true that any institution that throws together a large number of young people under the control of a group of adults can be a breeding ground for cruelty. Still, I think there is a systematic difference between government schools and private schools. As educational analyst and activist Douglas Dewey said, one thing you never hear people say when they're talking about a government school is that it was "a loving environment." By contrast, Dewey, who is the executive vice-president of the Children's Scholarship Fund, a New York-based fund that gives scholarships to help low-income families send their children to private school, says that many of the scholarship recipients describe the private schools as being "like family." It would stand to reason that private schools are better than government schools. Private schools, even though almost all of them are nonprofit, are selling a service and must produce something that people are willing to pay for. Government schools, by contrast, face no similar market test.

Another related difference between government and private schools is the way they pay teachers. Pay at government schools is based on seniority and on formal education. In 1997–98, for example, the average government-school teacher received, for teaching nine months, a salary of over $39,385.[6] Adjusted for inflation, this would be about $44,000 in the year

2001. The average government-school teacher with over 20 years of teaching experience earned $43,796 in 1993–94, an amount that would translate to over $54,000 in the year 2001. Private schools, by contrast, tend to pay less. Another important difference has to do with pensions. Teachers in government schools typically get generous pensions, equal to a large percent of their highest few years of pay, that are adjusted to inflation. They typically qualify for these pensions sometime in their fifties. Pensions for private-school teachers, by contrast, are not nearly as high. Think about the incentives this pay scheme creates: The way to get the whole compensation as a government-school teacher is to be in the system for 30 years or more. The worst teachers my daughter had in government schools were the ones who were within five years or so of retirement. They had obviously lost interest some years ago and seemed to be just hanging on for the big reward. If I wanted to motivate people *not* to teach well, I would design the pay structure almost exactly the way the government schools have designed it.

When you think about it, most schools are pretty weird. Kids are thrown together with other kids roughly about the same age. In government schools, neither they nor their parents have any choice about who else attends. The kids are all expected to do math at, say, 8:30 (or, at the Pacific Grove Middle School near where I live, at 8:13). They are all expected to work at roughly the same pace. Although there used to be continuity in what is taught from year to year, so that where you started one year was where you left off the previous year, most of that continuity no longer exists. In kindergarten or first grade, many teachers try to teach reading by having children memorize what words look like, but never teaching them how to sound out words based on their consonants and vowels. This would make sense as a way of teaching only if the English language were a series of symbols, like Chinese. History textbooks are now written to satisfy this or that interest group, so that you could, for example, go through a history class without having much idea of who George Washington was, but having heard a lot about the important role of women in the American Revolution. Some of the school year is taken up with so-called drug education, which is really propaganda about how drugs are bad for you. The propaganda is often taught by policemen, whose expertise is usually about the law and not about the pharmacological effects of drugs. When kids get to a certain age, many schools now teach them how to put a condom on a banana. One 11-year-old girl in Atlanta was recently expelled for two days for bringing a Tweety Bird key chain to school, on the grounds that the chain was a "weapon."[7]

With all this, it would be a real surprise if schools worked by anyone's standards.

People often criticize government schools in the United States for teaching little and doing it in boring ways, yet many advocate increasing the amount of time that children are in school. This reminds me of the old joke about two people complaining about the food at a restaurant. "The food tastes awful," says one. The other replies, "And the portions are so small." Given the amount of oppression and simple boredom that goes on in government schools today, thank goodness the portions are so small. That at least frees up time for students to do some real learning and to have fun outside of school.

There *is* one part of public schools that works very well: after-school sports. In such programs, children learn skills, persistence, and teamwork, and they are highly motivated. Why is there such a stark difference between after-school sports programs and what goes on during the school day? The reason can be summed up in one word: compulsion. Every state government requires attendance at public school or in some other school setting for every child in some age range, usually beginning at age 6 and ending on the child's sixteenth or eighteenth birthday.[8] In California, for example, children are not free until age 18, unless they pass a special exam that they can take at age 16. But in no state that I know of does the government require children to participate in after-school sports. The difference is like night and day. Many of the children who are in classes day to day don't want to be there, and some of them make it difficult for the ones who do want to be there, whereas almost all of the students in after-school sports want to participate, and most coaches, if they sense that a child doesn't want to be there, will kick him or her off the team. As a result, after-school sports are one of the few success stories of government schools. They are successful whether judged by performance, skills learned, raw desire, or shaping of character. Interestingly, sports are one of the few activities of schools in which objective standards regularly apply. No one pretends that a student who didn't score a basket actually got one, and a referee and scorekeeper who colluded to fake a basket on the score sheet would be severely reprimanded. Not so for a math teacher who tells a student that he got a right answer because telling him the truth might hurt his (phony) self-esteem.

One of the most damaging effects that compulsion has on people is that it reduces motivation. Learning is the most natural thing in the world. We do it from the time we are a few days old. We start by learning that if we cry, one of our parents will come and change our diaper and feed us milk or hold and comfort us. We learn when we are a few months old that when we drop something, sometimes someone will pick it up and put it back on our high-chair tray. We learn when we are a year old, give or take a few months, how to walk. At each stage, we feel total delight as we master each step.

My daughter learned how to read before she entered kindergarten, and it wasn't because we set out to teach her. Instead, we would read one of her favorite books to her over and over, and after a while, she could go through the book and "read" it back almost perfectly, doing it from memory. Then, at around age 4, she wanted to read books to us that she wasn't quite as familiar with. When she would get to a word and want help, we would point to each letter and sound it out and then show her how to put the sounds together to get the whole word. We *never* corrected her mistakes unless the mistakes were crucial to her understanding of the story she was reading. At our first meeting with her government-school kindergarten teacher, about a month or so into the school year, the teacher told us how impressed she was with Karen's reading and asked us how she had learned it. We told her what I just told you. The teacher became suddenly agitated. "But if you didn't correct her," she said, "how was she to learn how to do it right?" I answered that pointing our every error to someone who is learning something can easily discourage the person and that's why we were careful not to do so. Furthermore, I said, "Look how well Karen reads; obviously, our method worked." But it was clear that this teacher, presumably a specialist in teaching, didn't see the potential harm in correcting someone's every little mistake.

I'm convinced that that is why so many millions of people associate learning with pain rather than with the pleasure that accompanied their first learning in life. In fact, I think the standard school setting turns the classroom into the intellectual haves and have-nots, creating a distinction where one doesn't exist. My second-grade teacher, Mrs. Orris, divided the class into the Eager Beavers and the Busy Bees. Within seconds of hearing who was in each group, everyone in the class, beavers and bees alike, knew that the Busy Bees were the "slow" learners and the second-class citizens. But, being a member of the Eager Beavers, I was strongly tempted—and I didn't resist the temptation—to think of myself as superior. For the remainder of my school career, and part of my college career, I carried that way of thinking with me. Those who did well in classroom settings, I thought, were intellectually superior to those who didn't. Along with it, I held the view that working-class people weren't intellectual, and I thought of myself as an intellectual. I could have easily gone through life with that view. But, thank goodness, something happened in the summer before my last year of college that changed my thinking on this dramatically.

At the start of that summer, I hitchhiked to Thompson, Manitoba, a mining community in northern Canada, to get a high-paying blue-collar job because I wanted to make enough money to pay for my last year of college. I ended up getting a job as a diamond driller's "helper" in an underground nickel mine at Soab Lake, 40 miles from Thompson. About 300 men worked in this mine and lived in the adjacent mining camp and, with two years of college under my belt, I was the most formally educated person in the entire group. I am a very social person and I wanted interaction and conversation. These, therefore, were the people I had to pick from. So within a few days, I was sitting around with these guys, ranging in age from 18 to

45, arguing about the upcoming provincial election, the wisdom of the socialist party's proposed government takeover of the auto insurance industry, and various other political issues. I learned quickly that many of these people had reasons for their views and could argue them, and that they weren't noticeably worse at making their case than most of the students or even many of the faculty at the University of Winnipeg. The main differences were that they were blunter and put on fewer airs, and that some wanted to line up hippies against the wall and shoot them. (Some of the U. of Winnipeg students agreed about the firing squads, but wanted the guns aimed at capitalists instead of hippies.) By the end of that summer, I had concluded that the population cannot be divided into an intellectual class and a nonintellectual class; instead, I concluded, everyone is to some extent an intellectual. The college professor is an intellectual who, it is hoped, applies his intellect to his teaching and research. The skillful auto mechanic is an intellectual who uses logic to eliminate various possible causes of an engine's failure in order to narrow it down to the actual cause. Everyone is an intellectual. Compulsory schooling has robbed millions of people of the knowledge of their intellectual birthright.

Back to compulsion. In 1999, I attended some presentations at the Hoover Institution given by 11 leading U.S. education scholars/school reformers.[9] They agreed that smaller class sizes and higher teacher pay are not the answer, basing their belief, no doubt, on copious evidence, showing little relation between such things and standard measures of educational achievement, that one of them, economist Eric Hanushek, had assembled. But many of them wanted to stiffen and make uniform the content of school curricula, have teachers give more homework, have statewide testing, and impose other requirements to make schools and teachers do a better job. During one of the question and answer periods, I posed the following question:

> One of my heroes when I was a teenager was Sammy Davis, Jr. In his autobiography, *Yes I Can,* he tells of going on the road with his father and uncle as a performer starting at age two-and-a-half. Sammy Davis, Jr. never went to school. But in

every state today, governments require attendance at school. They enforce that requirement by threatening noncomplying parents with prison sentences. My question for each of you is, if you were in charge back then, would you have been willing to send Mr. and Mrs. Davis to prison?

Three of them—Paul Petersen, Herb Wahlberg, and Williamson Evers—said they would not have been willing to send Sammy Davis, Jr.'s parents to prison. The other eight said that they would have sent his parents to prison. One of the eight, Dianne Ravitch, said, "For every Sammy Davis, Jr., there would be one thousand kids whose parents didn't care." The purpose of compulsory attendance, she implied, was to keep the parents in line.

Ravitch was expressing a widespread view that, without compulsion, a large percent of parents would not send their children to school. This view is, in fact, one of the main pillars supporting compulsory attendance laws. It is also false. The vast majority of parents, rich and poor, did send their children to schools well before the government required attendance or paid for it.

The most complete evidence about how widespread education was before government involvement comes from economic historian Edwin G. West. In his modern classic, *Education and the State,* West digs through the data on provision of education in the early to mid-nineteenth century in Britain, when incomes were very low, and before the government required children to go to school or paid for them to do it. The facts he presents are staggering.

West points out that early in the nineteenth century, the British government was quite upset about the number of working-class people who were reading political literature. The government, writes West, took "fiscal and legal action against the spread of newspapers, especially those critical of government."[10] Thomas Malthus, the famous economist who worried about population growth, was also worried about the widespread sales of Tom Paine's *The Rights of Man*. Indeed, writes West, Paine's book is now thought to have sold 1.5 million copies. Since the population of England at the time was only about 10 million, such widespread sales imply widespread reading ability.

But this just scratches the surface of West's data. Here are some further highlights:

- Of people put on trial for crimes between 1837 and 1839, 44.6 percent were able to read.[11] This would be a substantial underestimate of juvenile literacy at the time: first, because people charged with crimes are likely to be less educated than the population generally, and second, because the criminal data mix older with younger people.
- In the early nineteenth century, the poorest of the poor, so-called paupers, often lived in workhouses. Data on workhouse children living in Norfolk and Suffolk in 1838 show that 87 percent of children between ages 9 and 16 could read, and 53 percent could write.[12]
- Of 843 men employed in Northumberland and Durham's coalmine pits in 1840, 445 (53 percent) could read and write and 665 (79 percent) could read.[13] It was common in those days to teach children to read, but not to write.

Why was literacy so widespread? West answers this question also. Various private organizations, such as the Mechanics Institute, the Literary and Philosophical Societies, and the Sunday Schools, taught children to read. Also, much teaching occurred in people's homes.[14] But also, strange as this may sound today, people often got education for their children the in same old-fashioned way they got other things: They paid for it. West offers an 1813 quote from famous economist James Mill:

> From observation and inquiry assiduously directed to that object, we can ourselves speak decidedly as to the rapid progress which the love of education is making among the lower orders in England. Even around London, in a circle of fifty miles radius, which is far from the most instructed and virtuous part of the kingdom, there is hardly a village that has not something of a school; and not many children of either sex who are not taught more or less, reading and writing. We have met with families in which, for weeks together, not an article of sustenance but potatoes had been used; yet for every child the hard-earned sum was provided to send them to school.[15]

As England recovered from the huge cost of fighting the war against Napoleon and disposable income increased, the number of children in school increased from 675,000 in 1818 to 1,277,000 in 1833.[16] England's government began subsidizing education in 1833, with a small subsidy totaling 20,000 pounds for the whole country.[17] Thus, the number of children in school, 1.3 million out of a total population (children and adults) of about 14.5 million, is a measure of what was achieved on meager incomes with almost no subsidy.

There's similar, but more anecdotal, evidence for the United States. In 1818, 34 years before the first compulsory schooling laws, Noah Webster estimated that his Spelling Book had sold over 5 million copies.[18] In a country with a population under 20 million, it was clear that someone was buying these books. Alexis de Tocqueville, writing in his 1835 book *Democracy in America,* called Americans the best-educated people in history. Today, per capita income in the United States, adjusted for inflation, is over 12 times what it was in England in 1833.[19] Therefore, it would be easier now than it was in the past for families to pay for privately provided education.

Moreover, education, like many goods, is something we buy more of as our income increases. You might think that the high price of education would discourage people from buying much of it. But one main reason education is expensive is that government provides it. David Friedman, son of Milton Friedman and a first-rate economist in his own right, once formulated Friedman's First Law, which is that when government provides something it is approximately twice as expensive as when it's provided by competing, private producers. Economists have found rough confirmation of the law by comparing the cost of government and private provision of garbage collection, firefighting, and insurance claims. The average tuition at non-tax-funded schools in the United States in 1993–94 was $3,116; adjusted to 2001 dollars, that would be about $3,800. The cost per pupil for a government school was $7,896 in 1998–99, which would translate to about $8,700 today. Of course, the tuition at private schools is less than the costs because some of the cost is covered by donations. But you can see that Friedman's Law roughly holds up. Moreover, the Internet and the Web are poised to crush the cost of education by making high-quality learning available at low cost.

But if education worked so well before government came along, why did the government intervene? We tend to assume that governments intervene when markets don't work. But, more often, governments intervene because various people who influence them don't like the fact that markets work too well. Market education was working; it was allowing parents to have their children educated cheaply and efficiently, with no central direction. *This lack of central direction was the problem.* According to John Taylor Gatto, an education scholar who was the New York State Teacher of the Year in 1991, when the United States abandoned freedom of education in the nineteenth century, it explicitly adopted the Prussian system and for the same reasons Prussia adopted it: to teach obedience and limit learning. Gatto points out that the old one-room schoolhouse had vested "too much" responsibility in the children and therefore didn't fit the Prussian model. What did fit was to fragment whole ideas into subjects—math at 10:00, history at 10:30, and so on. "The whole system," writes Gatto, "was built on the premise that isolation from first-hand information and fragmentation of the abstract information presented by teachers would result in obedient and subordinate graduates, properly respectful of arbitrary orders."[20] Here is what Gatto says of the famous philosopher John Dewey, a fan of the Prussian system:

> Dewey said that the great mistake of traditional pedagogy has been to make reading and writing constitute the bulk of early schoolwork. He advocated that the phonics method of teaching reading be abandoned and replaced by the whole-word method, not because the latter was more efficient (he admitted it was less efficient), but because reading hard books produces independent thinkers, thinkers who cannot be socialized very easily.[21]

Think about that the next time you see your child, or hear about another child, struggling while trying to learn the whole-word method.

Each of us parents has the right and the responsibility to teach our children the virtues that we hold dear. Teaching virtues doesn't mean just sitting them down and telling them what the important virtues are. Virtues are taught by example. If, for example, our children hear us lie to our employer, our neighbors, or our spouse, then merely telling them that lying is wrong is unlikely to have much impact. If we are liars, then our children are likely to become liars, too; the only thing we achieve by telling them that lying is wrong is to create liars who tell their children that lying is wrong. If we tell our children not to use drugs, but they observe us taking our daily fix of alcohol, nicotine, and caffeine, then our teenagers, who seem hard-wired to spot hypocrisy a mile away, will see through our antidrug message.

Teaching virtue doesn't stop just because we're away from home. We want our virtues taught, or at least adhered to, even when we are not present. If I hire a baby sitter who brags to my daughter about how she stole from a store, then my daughter is seeing a bad example, and I want that example to stop. How do I do that? One way is to talk to the sitter and get her to see what is wrong with theft. That might work, but the key word is "might." The other way to make sure that my daughter is around people who share my values is to fire the baby sitter and to hire someone who thinks theft is wrong. That's what most of us do.

What happens when we send our children to school? Just as with the baby sitter, we want our schools to teach the virtues that we value. That is entirely natural and proper. Our responsibility as parents doesn't end at the end of our driveways. There's a well-known Latin term for what we expect of our schools: in loco parentis. It means that we expect the schools to act as parents for our children when our children are at school: The schools are our children's parents in that locality. And acting as parents means not just protecting our children's physical safety, as did the unappreciated Clarence Notree, who saved his students from a gunman. It means also teaching them, by word and deed, the virtues that we value.

What do I mean by the virtues that "we" value? Different ones of us value different virtues. Sometimes our values simply differ but do not conflict. While I might want my daughter to be taught a lot of English composition, you might want your son to be taught a lot of math. Teaching math doesn't conflict with teaching English composition, at least not in the usual sense of the word "conflict." But there is still a tough tradeoff. You and I might not both be able to get our way simply because there are only so many hours in the school day.

Sometimes there will be conflicts—*real* conflicts. You might want your eighth-grade child to be taught about safe sex, as if there is such a thing. I might think that that begs the question of whether my son should even have sex at age 14, and that such questions are better handled at home or in the church, synagogue, or mosque. This is a conflict in the usual sense of the word. Or we might both agree that we want our children taught that stealing is wrong. But inquiring minds want to know why. Your basis might be that it's wrong because the Bible says so. My basis might be that it's wrong based on some utilitarian criterion. This is a conflict also. Who's right? Obviously, you think that you're right and I think that I'm right. That's what differences in values mean. I'm not advocating relativism. If I value a virtue, I really do believe in that virtue, and therefore I believe that what contradicts it is wrong.

How do we get around either kind of conflict? One way is for you to get together with people who agree with you and force your values down my throat. The other way is for me, with my allies, to force my values down your throat.

That is exactly what has happened throughout the history of government-run schools in the United States. I'm not talking just about the most recent conflicts between Darwinism and creationism in the science curriculum, or between phonics and the whole-word method in reading. The history of government schools in the United States is a history of conflict. Early on, the Protestants dominated government schools and used their domination to knock the Catholicism out of Catholic kids. Indeed, some education scholars have documented that the rise of government schooling in the United States was, in part, an attempt by Protestants to dominate Catholics.

What's clear is that the current system of tax-funded schooling cannot work. If we say that taxes can't be used to support religion, a perfectly legitimate viewpoint in a country that has the First Amendment to its Constitution, then we can't have government schools teaching that the reason theft is wrong is that it contradicts Biblical teaching. But if teachers then teach that theft is wrong for utilitarian reasons and completely leave out theistic reasons, they are implicitly taking the position that the Bible is irrelevant. That contradicts the First Amendment rights of theistic parents.

There must be a better way to live in a society in which parents' rights to teach their values to their children are respected. Look at religion. There are violent conflicts around the world between various religious groups. But although Americans do have strong differences in their religious beliefs, these conflicts rarely lead to violence. Why? Because we have the right to send our children, or not send them, to a particular church, mosque, or synagogue. Isn't it interesting that in the United States, a founding principle of which is freedom of religion, we have very few religious conflicts, whereas other societies, where particular religions are enforced by law, there is much more conflict?

Hmmm. Maybe the same approach would work with schools. Maybe we could end the deep, unresolved, and unresolvable conflict about what is taught in schools by letting parents choose schools for their children.

There are two kinds of school choice: self-financed choice and tax-financed choice. Real choice is like choosing a car or shoes. You investigate your choices, buy whatever fits within your preferences and your budget, and, with your own money, pay for it. Tax-subsidized choice is like food stamps. You fill your shopping cart, take your merchandise to the checkout stand, and, with your food stamps, have anonymous taxpayers pay for it. Unfortunately, the "tax-subsidized choice" people, the advocates of charter schools and/or vouchers, are currently dominating on the choice side. I say that, having been a card-carrying member of their side. I was card-carrying in the sense that I wrote three articles advocating vouchers, a short one in the University of Western Ontario's student newspaper in the fall of 1971, a much longer essay for the Hoover Institution, "The Case for School Choice," in 1993, and another short one for *Insight* in about 1994. The reason I held to this view for so long, from 1968, when I read Milton Friedman's case for vouchers in his *Capitalism and Freedom,* until sometime in 1995, was that the only people I ever ran into who argued against vouchers based their arguments on a distrust of markets, competition, and parents. Because I have strong trust in markets, competition, and parents, I never found their arguments persuasive. But the best anti-voucher argument I've heard is based on a distrust of government. Government vouchers would almost certainly be accompanied by heavy regulation, which would dramatically reduce the independence of private schools. You could still argue that the other 90 percent of students would be better off because now schools would compete for their business. I think it's a reasonable argument. I just don't think that governments will allow much competition when they're paying. Economist Estelle James, in a study done for the World Bank,[22] looked at various other countries that have voucher-like funding. In these countries, once a parent has chosen a private school, a certain amount of government funding follows, which is the essence of vouchers. The governments of Holland, Belgium, France, Luxembourg, Denmark, Norway, and New Zealand fund more than 75 percent of the costs of private schools in those countries. James found that highly subsidized private schools are also highly regulated—on teacher credentials, teaching hours, and hiring and firing. The governments also often limit the methods schools may use to choose students.

Although I'm opposed to vouchers, I'm not sure I'm right.[23] I would feel more comfortable, though, if more advocates of vouchers were seriously confronting these pitfalls and not wishing them away.

We should become modern abolitionists, like the abolitionists of the nineteenth century who demanded the end of slavery, and for similar reasons. Abolition brings an end to the government's role in schools, which means four things: the end of compulsory attendance; the end of government control of content; the end of government control of who teaches; and the end of the government's practice of taxing some people to pay for other people's children to go to school. With the end of government's role, learning would flourish. I can't tell you how. No one can. I can tell you what I think is unlikely: classes every day in big buildings from 8:30 to 3:00, or, in the case of our local government middle school, from 8:13 to 2:40. The beauty and the power of freedom is that different people use their freedom differently to produce all kinds of results, results that they themselves, and certainly the rest of us, can't predict. I can make some educated guesses though.

If freedom of education were restored, I would expect to see formal schooling occur more often on a part-time basis, giving children time to explore, with their parents or other mentors, the world around them, including the world of work. Many successful adults report that one of the most valuable learning experiences was their part-time jobs when they were teenagers, or, in some cases, preteens. One of my best work experiences, for example, was hunting for golf balls on the local course and selling them to golfers. I learned about the relation between effort and reward. I learned, by trial and error, where to find the maximum number of golf balls in a given amount of time. I learned some minimal negotiating skills. I also learned about exchange rates because the golf course was in Canada and many of the golfers were Americans. During years when the Canadian dollar was worth a few pennies more than the U.S. dollar, I insisted on those few pennies when they paid in me in U.S. funds. (In years that the U.S. dollar was worth slightly more and they asked if I would accept U.S. funds, I said, "Sure.") And I learned all this between ages 8 and 13. I would bet that many parents would let their children use some of their freed-up time to take part-time jobs. Some children would even take apprenticeships. If you wanted to make movies, for example, think about how much you could learn, at age 15, by being a gofer on a movie set.

For educational freedom to come about, though, the government must get out or at least cut back. So, here are some interim political goals to pursue:

1. Any time you can vote against school taxes, do so.
2. Push to narrow the age range in which the government uses compulsion, making it, say, age 6 to 14 instead of 6 to 18.

3. Decentralize tax funding. Push to get the state government, and especially the federal government, out, so that localities have more freedom to set education policy.

4. Even if you advocate charter schools or government vouchers, don't let it distract you. Because so many advocates of school choice in California became involved—both financially and with their time—in the November 2000 proposition to implement vouchers in California, they forgot about point 1. They didn't spend that time and money fighting a sneaky proposition that lowered the threshold for passage of school bond issues to 55 percent from the previous 66.7 percent. As a result, the sneaky proposition won, and California's taxes for schools will probably soon rise.

5. Push your state government to relax its rules on home-schooling. Some of the biggest success stories in recent years in precollege education have been in home-schooling, as we learn every year when we see home-schoolers disproportionately represented in the national spelling bee.

And just as those who advocated abolishing slavery didn't have to wait until governments did so, but instead could free their own slaves, you too can free some child slaves.

1. Remove your child from the clutches of government. Send him or her to a private school, either a pricey one or one of the religious schools where tuition typically ranges between $2,000 and $4,000. Or consider home-schooling your child.

2. If you home-school, combine with other home-schoolers to take advantage of division of labor. You might teach six children math while another parent teaches them English. In some states, it's illegal to teach other parents' children, which should make you wonder about the motives of the government-schoolers who support that law. If it is illegal in your state, challenge the law—see number 5 above. And while you're challenging the law, it can be a good idea to ignore the law.

While doing so, you'll be teaching your children an eloquent lesson in civil disobedience. We hear so much about Rosa Parks, an ordinary woman in Montgomery, Alabama, who had the courage to break the local law requiring segregation. We need, at least occasionally, to have as much courage as she had.

3. If you don't have kids, but want to educate people, put out your shingle as a tutor, free-of-charge.

4. If you don't want to spend your own time, but want kids to get education, donate to another family so that they can send their child to private school.

5. Get your child a computer and that other window on the worldwide web of learning—a library card.

Finally, if you have teenagers or preteens, or if you are a teenager, open yourself to a new possibility. People say that the reason teenagers are so hard to get along with is that that stage "is part of growing up." But, then, why don't teenagers have the same problems when they work at a summer job or a part-time job during the school year? They are exposed to lots of people, often within a wide age range, but they aren't treated cruelly, and they don't treat others cruelly, nearly as frequently. Could their better attitude be the result of three facts: they are free to quit that job; the other people at the job typically want to be there; and there's not as much time for cruelty when you're trying to be productive? Teenagers treating other teenagers cruelly is part of growing up—when compulsory schooling is part of growing up.

ENDNOTES

1. Telephone interview on May 7, 1993.

2. The story is told in "The Valedictorian," *Newsweek,* September 6, 1976, p. 52 and retold in Paul Copperman, *The Literacy Hoax,* New York: Morrow, 1978, p. 105.

3. Bonita Brodt, "Inside Chicago's Schools," as quoted in David Boaz, ed., *Liberating Schools: Education in the Inner City,* Washington, D.C.: Cato Institute, 1991.

4. Charles Johnsen, "Small Reforms, Little Victories," Vol. 1, No. 1, September 1995, *The Education Liberator,* published by Separation of School and State Alliance.

5. "Chicago Schools Rebuff Wounded Hero-Teacher," *St. Louis Post-Dispatch,* October 1, 1994.

6. The data on pay and tuition are from *Digest of Education Statistics, 1999,* U.S. Department of Education, Office of Educational Research and Improvement.

7. "Georgia girl's Tweety Bird chain runs afoul of weapons policy," *CNN.com,* September 28, 2000.

8. For details, see *http://www.nces.ed.gov/pubs/d96/D96T149.html.*

9. In alphabetical order: John Chubb, Williamson Evers, Chester Finn, Jr., Eric Hanushek, E.D. Hirsch, Paul Hill, Caroline Hoxby, Terry Moe, Paul Petersen, Dianne Ravitch, and Herb Wahlberg.

10. Edwin G. West, *Education and the State,* 2nd. ed., London: Institute of Economic Affairs, 1970, p. 127.

11. West, *Education and the State*, p. 128.

12. West, *Education and the State*, p. 129.

13. West, *Education and the State*, p. 130.

14. West, *Education and the State*, p. 136.

15. Quoted from Mill article in *Edinburgh Review,* October 1813 in West, *Education and the State*.

16. West, *Education and the State,* p. 149.

17. West, *Education and the State,* p. 137.

18. John Taylor Gatto, "Our Prussian School System," *Cato Policy Report,* March/April 1993, Volume XV, Number 3.

19. How did I get this? In 1830, British income per person was $498, in 1970 dollars, according to economic historian Nicholas F. R. Crafts, *British Economic Growth During the Industrial Revolution,* 1985. (Quoted in Clark Nardinelli, "Industrial Revolution and the Standard of Living," in David R. Henderson, ed., *The Fortune Encyclopedia of Economics,* New York: Warner Books, 1993, p. 13.) In 1970, the Consumer Price Index, with a base year of 1984, was 38.8. In 2001, it is about 176. Therefore, the 1830 British income per person, in 1999 dollars, is 176/38.8 * $498 = $2,259. Today's per capita income in the United States is $8.2 trillion divided by 280 million, which equals $29,286.

20. John Taylor Gatto, "Our Prussian School System," *Cato Policy Report,* Volume XV, No. 2, March/April 1993.

21. Gatto, "Prussian School System."

22. Estelle James, "Private School Finance and Public Policy in Cross-Cultural Perspective," unpublished paper prepared for U.S. Department of Education Conference on the Economics of Private Schools, May 1991.

23. The story of my "conversion" away from vouchers is told in *http://www.sepschool.org/edlib/v2n6/squirm.html.*

CHAPTER 17

THE ENVIRONMENT: OWN IT AND SAVE IT

I n the early 1940s, a chemical company began to dump toxic chemicals into a site in a sparsely populated area of New York State. The company chose this site after careful investigation had shown that the soil was impermeable clay and that, therefore, the chemicals would not seep into ground water and harm people. The United States Army also dumped toxic wastes in that site during and after World War II, and the local city government dumped refuse in the site.

Then, in 1952, the school board in the city where the toxic waste was buried threatened to use its eminent domain power to take the site from the company. The school board made clear that its goal was to build a school on the site. Rather than fight the action, the company gave in and offered to sell the land to the school board for one dollar. The school board accepted. The company wrote the following closing paragraph in the deed:

> Prior to the delivery of this instrument of conveyance, the grantee herein has been advised by the grantor that the premises above described have been filled, in whole or in part, to the present grade level thereof with **waste products resulting from the manufacturing of chemicals** by the grantor at its plant in the City of ———, New York, and the grantee assumes all risk and liability incident to the use thereof. It is therefore understood and agreed that, as a part of the consideration for this conveyance and as a condition thereof, no claim, suit, action or demand of any nature whatsoever shall ever be made by the grantee, its successors or assigns, for injury to a person or persons, including death resulting therefrom, or loss of or damage to property caused by, in connection with or by reason of the presence of said industrial wastes. It is further agreed as a condition hereof that each subsequent conveyance of the aforesaid lands shall be made subject to the foregoing provisions and conditions. (bold added)

In 1952, liability laws were such that the company had nothing to fear even without this clause. The new owner of the land automatically became liable for any damage done by toxic waste on the land. So the company was not so much trying to protect itself as to warn anyone who was listening that these chemicals were dangerous and should not be disturbed. Unfortunately, no one was listening. Nor were they looking. In March 1952, a company official escorted school board officials to the site and, with them present, made test borings into the protective clay cover to convince the school board officials that chemicals really were there. Yet in August 1953, the school board unanimously voted to remove 4,000 cubic yards of fill from the waste site to complete the grading of another school site. The school board also went ahead and built the school, which opened its doors in February 1955.

Then, in 1957, the school board considered trading chunks of the property to two developers in exchange for some other land and $11,000 in cash. The chemical company that had originally owned the land, hearing about the proposal, sent its attorney to attend the board meeting where the proposal was discussed. Reminding the board that chemicals were buried under the land's surface, the attorney pleaded with them not to let houses be built on the land. This time, finally, the board was listening: It voted 4 to 4, with the result that the resolution to sell the land failed.

Unfortunately, the city government was not listening. During the period that the land sale was contemplated, city workmen were busy constructing a sewer that punctured the walls of the site and its clay cover. They were doing this even though articles in the local paper at the time were regularly warning that the construction was "dangerous" and "injurious." So, while some people were listening, they apparently weren't reading.

Then in 1978, a reporter named Michael Brown began reporting health problems for residents of the area that were apparently connected with the release of the toxic waste. The issue soon got national attention, and President Carter declared the area a national disaster.

The name of the company that had buried the waste and warned the government, if you have not already guessed it, was Hooker Chemical, which was a subsidiary of Occidental Petroleum. The name of the city whose government blithely built a school on top and a sewer below was Niagara Falls. The toxic waste site: Love Canal.[1]

Ask Americans over age 40 what few incidents summarize for them the horrors of pollution, and the odds are that one incident most of them will name is Love Canal. Most of them will probably tell you that Love Canal epitomizes the greedy profit-making companies that despoil the environment for profit, harming innocent people in the process. But the best example they can come up with doesn't make their case at all. The company involved, Hooker Chemical, was very careful about the environment. Love Canal is really an example of a government agency pursuing narrow goals while blithely ignoring the harm it caused the environment. To the extent Love Canal was a problem, it was a problem created by government officials with perverse incentives who violated property rights.

TIME TRAVEL

Imagine that you and I can get in a time machine together and set the dial to 1990, and that we can fly around the world checking on the state of the environment. In the Soviet Union, we see things that probably would make us throw up. We see the Baltic Sea, where the Soviet navy regularly dumps nuclear waste. When the barrels containing nuclear waste float, the Soviets puncture them so the barrels sink.[2] We see Lake Baikal, believed to be the oldest freshwater lake in the world, with twice Lake Superior's volume of water,[3] into which factories and pulp mills have dumped pollution. Untreated sewage has been dumped into the lake's main tributaries. The results: islands of alkaline sewage have been observed floating on Lake Baikal. One of these measured 18 miles long and 3 miles wide.[4] Lake Baikal is not the only water body that the Soviets destroyed. The Aral Sea has shrunk by about half because the Soviets sucked water out of it for irrigation. The remaining half has become increasingly salty and polluted as untreated sewage has flowed freely into it. The Aral Sea's former shoreline is now arid desert. Muynak, a former port city, is now 44 miles from the water's edge.[5] So much oil floats on the legendary Volga river that signs on steamboats forbid passengers from tossing cigarettes overboard, for fear that it will start a fire.[6]

Why this rampant disregard for the environment? Marshall Goldman puts it bluntly: "The attitude that nature is there to be exploited by man is the very essence of the Soviet production ethic."[7]

Imagine that we continue our journey through time and space to other countries of eastern Europe that Communist governments run. In Cracow, we see the Vistula River, Poland's largest. That year, according to the *New York Times,* Cracow's mayor calls the Vistula "nothing but a sewage canal."[8] Under Communist rule, fully half of Poland's cities, including Warsaw, do not even treat their wastes.[9] And one in every three Poles lives in regions that the Polish Academy of Sciences called "areas of ecological disaster."[10] The concentration of sulfur dioxide in Czechoslovakia is eight times higher than in the

United States. In Leipzig, East Germany, the air is so polluted that half of Leipzig's children are treated each year for diseases thought to be associated with air pollution. Here's how *Fortune* writer Allan T. Demaree puts it after a trip to East Germany in late 1990:

> Travel south on the road from Leipzig to Chemnitz and you gradually find yourself under a forbidding cloud that's too high to be fog, too low to hold rain. It emanates from the stacks of an electrical plant burning sulfurous brown coal stripped from the ground surrounding it. Open pits yawn grotesquely as far as the eye can see. In the distance, other plants, other stacks, other plumes of smoke.[11]

Now we travel south and across the Mediterranean to the continent of Africa. We are on this hunt, not to shoot, but to count. Between 1979 and 1989, Central Africa's elephant population has dropped from 497,400 to 274,800, and East Africa's has dropped from 546,650 to 154,720. In Kenya, we count only 16,000 elephants, versus 140,000 when the Kenyan government banned hunting elephants. In Tanzania, there are only 61,000 elephants, whereas there were 250,000 in 1970. In Uganda, the elephant population is down to only 1,600 versus 20,000 in 1970. Funny thing, though: Uganda and Tanzania, like Kenya and like most countries in Central and East Africa, have also banned hunting.

That's the bad news. Does anything make us hopeful about the environment? Actually, yes, and to see the good news, we must travel to five countries in southern Africa: Zimbabwe, Malawi, Namibia, Botswana, and South Africa. Zimbabwe's elephant population has soared from 30,000 in 1979 to about 70,000 today. Botswana's has more than tripled, from 20,000 then to 68,000 now. And the elephant population in Malawi, Namibia, and South Africa is growing at a steady rate of 5 percent per year. Interestingly, governments of those five countries allow villagers nearby to charge for hunting of elephants, which gives the villagers an incentive to reduce poaching.[12]

While in Africa, let's go back to Central Africa and stop at the Sahel semidesert. In the midst of the desert, we observe a lush green pentagon—390 square miles in area—in the midst of a sea of sand. This pentagon first came to the world's attention as a dark patch in a satellite photo taken in 1974. Scientists at the time were astonished, all the more so because the Sahel was in the midst of a prolonged drought. Ground-level investigation of this mystery by American University agronomist Norman MacLeod quickly solved the puzzle. The area, he found, was surrounded by a barbed-wire fence. It was private property. The fence kept out the animals that were grazing the surrounding land to death. The pentagon was subdivided into five portions. Each year the owners moved their animals to a new section, giving each section four years to recover from the previous grazing.[13] The surrounding desert, on the other hand, was and is a "commons." In other words, no one owned it and everyone was free to use it. It was overused because no one had enough incentive to take care of it.

Now let's continue our time travel to England and Scotland. In those countries we notice that many rivers that anglers fish in are particularly clean. This must be the result of stringent regulations, mustn't it? Actually, no. Scotland has no government agency that protects water quality. Zero. Zilch. Nada. It turns out that the right to fish for sport and for commerce is a transferable right and that owners of fishing rights can and do obtain damages and injunctions against those who pollute streams. They rarely have to go to court, it turns out, because the rights have been so well established.[14]

On we travel to the United States. First, we land near Hawk Mountain in eastern Pennsylvania. We notice, not surprisingly, lots of hawks. In the autumn, hawks and other raptors migrate south along the mountain ridges and come by Hawk Mountain. For that reason, it was a popular place for shooting hawks and other birds. In 1934, a woman who was concerned about the slaughter did something about it. Rosalie Edge, born in 1877, was one of the nation's first prominent conservationists. After failing to persuade the Audubon Society to purchase Hawk Mountain and stop the slaughter, she decided to purchase it herself. She leased Hawk Mountain for one year and bought it a year later for $3,500. Since then, Hawk Mountain has become popular with people who want to come and see hawks and other birds, and their admissions fees, plus member dues, allow the Hawk Mountain Sanctuary Association to hire a few full-time employees.[15]

Let's head south to the Rainey Wildlife Sanctuary in Louisiana. This 26,000-acre sanctuary is private property owned by National Audubon Society. The refuge is so sensitive that tourists are not allowed. But natural gas production is. Three oil companies operate gas wells in the sanctuary and pay the Audubon Society hundreds of thousands a year in gas royalties. Has the Audubon Society caved to the oil companies? Not at all. Rather, the Society puts stringent conditions on the methods that the oil companies may use to get the gas so that the environment is protected, and the Society uses the royalties to purchase and maintain more wilderness areas.[16]

WHAT WORKS

Now let's come back in our time machine to today and think about what we've seen. There was a definite pattern. Where government was in charge, the environment was trashed. This is what we observed in the Eastern Europe countries that were under the totalitarian control of Communist governments. It's also what we saw in the parts of Africa where governments did not allow the people they governed to have control over elephants. And it's what happened at Love Canal, where a government agency carrying out its narrow goal of building schools blithely ignored the harmful consequences to the environment.

On the other hand, private property seems to protect the environment pretty well. When people can profit from elephant hunting, they have a strong incentive to make sure that the elephant herds grow rather than shrink. Even in the middle of a semidesert, private property gives owners the incentive to care for their land. It recalls the old Chinese saying: "Lease a man a desert for 100 years, and he will turn it into a garden." Rivers in Scotland are clean because fishermen have well-defined property rights to fish in these rivers, rights that are enforceable in court. The birds at Hawk Mountain and the wildlife at the Rainey Wildlife Sanctuary are safe because people own these pieces of property and can therefore protect them from encroachment by hunters, tourists, and others who might harm them.

Here is how environmentalist Richard L. Stroup, who is also an economics professor at Montana State University, puts it:

> For markets to work in the environmental field, as in any other, rights to each important resource must be clearly defined, easily defended against invasion, and divestible (transferable) by owners on terms agreeable to buyer and seller. Well-functioning markets, in short, require "3-D" property rights.[17]

If people have well-defined rights to their property and can easily defend them, as is true for the Hawk Mountain Sanctuary Association and the anglers' associations in Scotland, then no one is forced to accept any unwanted pollution. Furthermore, when rights to the resource can be sold, the third "D," as is true with fishing rights in Scotland, owners of the rights have an incentive to be good stewards: Their wealth depends directly on how well they take care of the property.

It is not always easy to define property rights. What is striking, though, is how often government legislation and court rulings have prevented the common law system from handling pollution problems even when common law seemed to be working well toward resolving them. Take, for example, the infamous Cuyahoga River, which flows through Cleveland into Lake Erie, and which was so polluted with logs, debris, household waste, and oil that it caught on fire in 1932, 1952, and 1969. In 1999, Stacie Thomas, an economist with the Senate Banking Committee in Washington, D.C. uncovered the history of the laws that led to these disasters.[18]

It turns out that in 1936 a paper manufacturer on a tributary of the Cuyahoga sued the city government of Cleveland to stop it from dumping raw sewage into the tributary. The court granted the city government the right to keep dumping, on the grounds that it had been dumping for 76 years. Then, in 1948, an Ohio court established property rights against pollution, stating "one may not obtain by prescription, or otherwise by any purchase, a right to cast sewage upon the lands of another without his consent."[19] This decision and other similar ones led municipal governments and firms along the Cuyahoga to install pollution control technology. However, in 1951, the state government of Ohio created the Ohio Water Pollution Control Board. The law created a big loophole for polluters by stating that it was unlawful to pollute any Ohio waters "except in such cases where the water pollution control board has issued a valid and unexpired permit."[20] The Water Pollution Control Board then denied permits to pollute if the discharger was on a trout stream classified as "recreational use." But it issued permits to pollute if the polluter intended to pollute an already polluted stream classified as "industrial use." In other words, the government made it legally impossible to prevent polluters from keeping a river polluted. Thus was set up the inevitable: a fire on the "industrial-use" Cuyahoga.

If all of the resources in the world could be privately owned, including air and water, and if the cost of detecting the source and extent of damages on those private assets were suitably low, then a common law system would work to solve all pollution problems. Just as your ownership of your yard gives you the right to prevent me from dumping garbage on your lawn, so also would private property in your air give you the right to prevent someone from dumping soot in your air. That doesn't mean there would be no pollution. What it does mean is that all pollution would be consented to. If you paid me enough, I would let you dump garbage on my lawn. (You probably wouldn't be willing to pay me enough.) If you paid me enough, I would let you make my air slightly dirtier.

It's fairly easy for me to detect someone dumping garbage on my lawn. But how could a house owner in Manchester, New Hampshire, know whether the soot in his air comes from a particular power plant in Columbus, Ohio, rather than from another power plant in Pittsburgh, Pennsylvania? It seems he would have to know that to know whom to sue.

But before dismissing the possibility that the knowledge needed to define and enforce property rights in air and large bodies of water can be obtained cheaply, consider a similar problem that existed until late in the nineteenth century: the problem of defining and enforcing property rights in land in the midwestern plains of the United States.[21] The land area at the time seemed too vast for a system of property rights to work. But in the 1870s came an invention that changed everything: barbed wire.[22] With that one invention, the cost of defining property rights in land plummeted. People were able, at low cost, to keep out intruding animals, and therefore had an incentive to improve their land.

Fred Smith, a free-market environmentalist who heads the Competitive Enterprise Institute, a public-interest lobby in Washington, D.C., points out that we could imagine similar technological breakthroughs making it easier to define and enforce property rights in air and water. Smith writes,

> Technologies now exist that make possible determining, within limits, the quantity and types of air pollution entering a region. Lasimetrics, for example, could map atmospheric chemical concentrations from orbit. In time, that technology might provide a sophisticated means of tracking cross-boundary pollution flows. Also large installations such as power plants could add (or be required to add) chemical or isotopic "labels" to their emissions to facilitate tracking. Such "labeling" has long been routine in explosives manufacture to help trace explosives used in crime or terrorism.[23]

Private ownership could also help prevent the disappearance of rare species, especially the cute ones. The problem with endangered species is that nobody owns them. That's why they're endangered. We don't ever worry about running out of cows. Why not? The question seems ludicrous, but that's simply because we take cows for granted. But if no one were allowed to own a live cow, the only way to own a cow would be to kill it. Then we certainly would run out of cows. Preventing ownership amounts to enforcing by law a tragedy of the commons for whatever species can't be owned. The reason we don't run out of cows is that people are allowed to own them. Owners have an incentive to take care of the cows and to produce more of them. Similarly, private ownership of rare species would give the owners an incentive, much stronger than the incentive anyone has now, to protect them from poachers and to facilitate their reproduction. It's even conceivable that ocean-going species such as whales could be privately owned. Whales now travel on fairly predictable routes. A private organization could implant electronic devices in whales that would communicate to the new owner exactly where the whales are all the time. That would make it difficult for people to poach whales, and would make it easy for the owner to sell rights to see the whales—he would know exactly where the whales are. Moreover, Greenpeace and other groups could still continue to provide their services. But instead of getting in the way of law-abiding whale hunters, Greenpeace activists would simply be helping to enforce private property rights.

Many environmentalists advocate an alternative way of preserving rare species: Have the government declare them endangered and prohibit private development even of private land when such rare species are found on it. This is the standard way things are done in the United States today. There are two problems with such a proposal. First, it is morally wrong. Why should a private landowner who happens to discover some rare species on his land thereby lose his right to develop it? If the government values such a species, then it should compensate the landowner enough to persuade him voluntarily not to develop. The second problem is that such a strategy doesn't work. It's interesting how often the moral and the practical go together. It doesn't work because it creates perverse incentives. If I own land on which I find a species that might be rare, I know that the government may effectively reduce the value of my land to zero. How can I prevent that? By surreptitiously eliminating the species before anyone else finds out about it. Awareness of this incentive has led some environmentalists to talk about the "three S's": shoot, shovel, and shut up.[24] In other words, kill the species, bury it, and don't tell anyone else about it.

How far could we go in the direction of using private property to solve environmental problems? Could we do totally without any government regulatory agencies and rely solely on common law solutions? I don't know. But I do know two things.

First, as the story of the Cuyahoga River illustrates, the common law could certainly replace much current regulation. Second, if we committed to a common law approach, then the common law solutions, and the technology to accompany them, would occur much faster than if we didn't so commit. Barbed wire probably would not have been invented as early as it was if people had not been allowed to fence off their property. Profit and consumer well-being are the mothers of invention.

Moreover, look how badly government solutions have worked. The Environmental Protection Agency began in 1970 by focusing on a few major pollutants of air and water. It has branched out and now tries to control hundreds of pollutants, even those that pose close to infinitesimal risk. Many regulations authored and enforced by the EPA cost tens of millions of dollars per year of life saved. To put this in perspective, economists have found that in their choices about risks on the job, people act as if the whole rest of their life is worth about $5 million.

Economists from across the political spectrum, including me, have traditionally advocated a system of taxes or marketable permits to pollute as a way to solve pollution problems. The idea with the tax is to give polluters an incentive to reduce pollution. They will do so as long as their cost of doing so is less than the tax per unit of pollution. That way, the pollution that is least costly to eliminate is eliminated. So for a given reduction in pollution, the cost of reducing it is minimized. The idea with marketable permits is to set the amount of pollution allowed, issue permits for that amount, allocate them somehow to various polluters, and let them buy and sell. So, for example, a polluter that wants to pollute more than his permits allow can buy permits from someone who is willing to pollute less than he is allowed. That way, polluters have an incentive to cut pollution as long as the cost of doing so is less than the price of a permit. Polluters who can reduce pollution at a low cost can free up some of their permits and sell them. Polluters who face a high cost of reducing pollution can instead buy permits. Therefore, just as with taxes, a system of marketable permits to pollute achieves a given reduction of pollution at the least cost. A fairly simple mathematical proof shows that a system of marketable permits can be created that gives the exact same results as a system of taxes: The same amount of pollution is eliminated and the price of a permit equals the per-unit tax. The difference is that with taxes, the government takes our money, but with permits, polluters, which means all of us, keep our money.

The saving in moving to such a system is not small change. Spending on reducing pollution is currently about 3 percent of GDP, and economists have estimated that a complete shift to a system of permits would achieve the same pollution reduction for a cost of about 2 percent, for an annual savings of about $100 billion. This is a saving of about $400 a year for every man, woman, and child in the United States.

But I no longer advocate such a solution for two reasons, one pragmatic and one more fundamental. The pragmatic problem has been pointed out by Brookings economist Robert Crandall. When economists advocate marketable permits, and politicians oblige by putting a provision for marketable permits in the law, economists, whose solutions are so often rejected, salivate like Pavlov's dogs and become advocates of the law even if the same law also includes extremely wasteful regulations to eliminate not-very-harmful pollutants. Crandall points out that this is what happened with the Clean Air Act of 1990. Crandall writes,

> The new procedure [for issuing permits] is more heinous than anything imagined by the Russian Gosplan. Not only must all major sources of pollution obtain permits (and "major" is not very large at all), but any change in process resulting in a change in the nature or magnitude of this pollution may be undertaken only after obtaining a change in the environmental operating permit. This requirement likely will handicap our pharmaceutical, chemicals, and electronics companies, which must move quickly in response to changes in market conditions.[25]

The law also required an annual cut of 10 million tons of sulphur dioxide emissions to reduce acid rain, even though the federal government's own $570-million study, the National Acid Precipitation Assessment Program, found "no evidence of widespread forest damage from current ambient levels of acidic rain in the United States." Congress, President George W. H. Bush, and the EPA ignored their own study. After all, the half billion dollars wasted on the study was taxpayers' money, not theirs. But even though it didn't make sense to mandate the sulfur dioxide reduction, the law threw a bone to economists: The reduction would be achieved using marketable permits. So an inefficient result would be reached efficiently. Sure enough, economists have been trumpeting this relatively trivial accomplishment to the high heavens. Yippee!

The second, more fundamental, reason I oppose taxes or permits rather than a market solution is that we have no idea of how high to set such a tax or of how many permits to pollute to issue. The only way to get such an idea is to know how much people value reducing pollution. But by not allowing that decision to be made in a free market, and, instead, by requiring that it be made politically, we are preventing the answer from emerging. As free-market environmentalist Fred Smith pointed out, granting pollution permits and allowing them to be traded is similar in spirit to the "market socialism" that various socialist economists advocated in the 1930s and 1940s. Under market socialism, the government would set prices and let producers and consumers adjust to these prices. Market socialism was never tried. It never made sense because the information that leads to actual prices in a free market is known only to the participants and not to government planners. Similarly, the information required to know how much pollution should be allowed is known only to the polluters and to those who are damaged by pollution. It's true that if markets and common law simply cannot work to solve pollution problems, then a system of permits may be the best we can do. But if we insist on marketable permits, we will never find out whether the common law, free markets, and property rights will work.

One compromise, though, that would be easy to make in the short run would be to insist that the EPA and other environmental regulators promulgate only regulations whose benefits exceed their costs. I used to be skeptical of such a requirement because I believed that government bureaucrats could easily inflate estimated benefits and understate estimated costs to make many bad regulations look good. But there is strong evidence against my old view. First, notes Crandall, who supports a cost-benefit test, the only environmental statute that requires such a test is the 1976 Toxic Substances Control Act. Crandall points out that there have been no horror stories of excessive regulation under TSCA. The EPA tried to justify banning all remaining uses of asbestos, but its own data showed that a complete ban would save fewer than 200 cancers in a period of 25 to 40 years. The costs, on the other hand, would have been enormous: A ban on asbestos in automobile brakes would easily have led to a few hundred deaths a year, not to mention the financial costs of complying. A court threw out the EPA's regulations on the grounds that it had not passed a cost-benefit test. So the cost-benefit test stymied the EPA's attempts to regulate asbestos beyond the level other government agencies had chosen. Crandall writes,

> The effect [of the court decision] was so severe that it [EPA] has not moved to advance a new proposal. In fact, as far as I am aware, EPA cannot find anything else to regulate under TSCA that would pass a cost-benefit test.[26]

GLOBAL WARMING

One big environmental concern that has caused people to want more government regulation in recent years is fear of global warming. The fear is that as we burn carbon and create more carbon dioxide, we create a greenhouse effect that traps heat in the earth's atmosphere and gradually warms the earth over the next century. According to this view, the atmosphere is a big global commons. If I hold back in the amount of carbon I use in order to slow or prevent global warming, the benefit I get from my restraint is roughly one six-billionth of the benefit that my restraint creates. In other words, almost the whole of the benefit goes to the other six billion people in the world, virtually all of whom are strangers and, therefore, not people I care about as much as I care about myself. Virtually everyone else is in this position too, and so even if global warming is bad for the world, no one has an adequate incentive to refrain from warming the globe. This is a classic case of a public good, because you can't exclude nonpayers from benefiting from other people's restraint. When you can't exclude nonpayers, you get free riders; almost all economists and almost everyone else advocates a government solution in such situations. In this case, since the problem is global, simple restraint by any one country, even a country that uses as much carbon as the United States does, is not enough. Thus the call by various people for an international treaty to restrict carbon use by all countries. The Kyoto Protocol, negotiated in Kyoto, Japan, would not do that because it would allow poor countries to continue unrestrained use of carbon. This is one of the reasons that the Senate voted 95–0 against any treaty that excluded some countries. The ideal treaty, from the viewpoint of those who want government intervention, is one that probably could not come about politically. Economists have entered the debate by pointing out that the most efficient way to limit carbon use is to have governments issue marketable permits for carbon or to tax the use of carbon.

If greenhouse gases use definitely led to substantial global warming, and if substantial global warming were definitely bad for the world, then the case would be strong for an international treaty to limit greenhouse gases. But those are both big "ifs." On the issue of whether greenhouse gases cause much global warming, there is no consensus among scientists. The most prominent person who pushed the idea that there was such a consensus was former Vice President Al Gore. In 1997 he claimed that 2,500 scientists supported his view that man-made emissions of greenhouse gases were disrupting the Earth's climate. In fact, these scientists helped assemble the IPCC's report on global climate change. The statement in the report that Gore claimed backed up his view was the following: "[T]he balance of evidence suggests that there is a discernible human influence on global climate." Notice how mild this sentence is: It doesn't claim that global warming will be even close to catastrophic. Moreover, this sentence was added at the last minute by the editors of the chapter, *after* the report had been approved by the IPCC. A week after the report appeared, Frederick Seitz, president emeritus of Rockefeller University and chairman of the George C. Marshall Institute, blew the whistle on the editors, pointing out that 15 sections of the crucial chapter had been changed or deleted after the scientists who were responsible for that chapter "had accepted the supposedly final text."[27] Seitz noted that the changes were far from neutral but, instead, removed hints of skepticism about global warming. He cited the following sentences that had been approved by the scientists but removed by the editors.

> None of the studies cited above has shown clear evidence that we can attribute the observed [climate] changes to the specific cause of increases in greenhouse gases.

> No study to date has positively attributed all or part [of the climate change observed to date] to anthropogenic [man-made] causes.

> Any claims of positive detection of significant climate change are likely to remain controversial until uncertainties in the total natural variability of the climate system are reduced.

Seitz was outraged. He wrote,

> In my more than 60 years as a member of the American scientific community, including service as president of both the National Academy of Sciences and the American Physical Society, I have never witnessed a more disturbing corruption of the peer-review process than the events that led to this IPCC report.

That the scientists' views would be so distorted makes sense, given the political pressures on this issue. As environmental scientist Patrick Michaels pointed out, the UN General Assembly had earlier directed the IPCC to provide the basis for a convention on climate change.[28] Many people, when told to find a basis for something, will do so. Some of the extreme proponents of global warming, in fact, have admitted that misleading the public about global warming is all right. In 1988, then-Senator Tim Wirth, who went on to be Undersecretary of State for Global Affairs in the Clinton administration, and one of the Clinton administration's major supporters of the Kyoto Protocol, said,

> What we've got to do in energy conversation is to try to ride the global warming issue. Even if the theory of global warming is wrong, to have approached global warming as if it is real means energy conservation, so we will be doing the right thing anyway in terms of economic policy and environmental policy.[29]

Similarly, Al Gore, in his 1992 book *Earth in the Balance,* wrote,

> After years of debate and attempts to convince skeptics that the time for delay is over, I am resigned to the idea that even though we already know more than enough, we must also thoroughly investigate any significant scientific uncertainty that impedes our ability to come together and face this crisis. The knowledge thus gained will not only deprive the skeptics of some of their excuses for procrastination, it will also help us choose strategies for responding to the crisis, identify the most effective and least costly solutions, and solidify public support for the increasingly comprehensive changes that will be necessary.[30]

This passage reminds me of the old saying, "Let's first give him a fair trial and then hang him." Gore was willing to have further investigation, but only of any uncertainty that got in the way of the measures he wanted to take. Of course, when you undertake a scientific study, you never know what you'll find. But Al Gore knew. He was confident that the results would show the skeptics wrong and rally public support for large doses of government intervention. Note also Gore's language. He didn't really believe in further study to get it right; instead, he was "resigned." With fanatics like Gore and Wirth leading the charge, along with their counterparts at the United Nations, it's no wonder that truthfulness in the debate was strictly a secondary consideration.

Because the whole point of this discussion is whether governments should do anything to slow or reverse global warming, it's interesting also to consider the impact on global warming of implementing the Kyoto Protocol. Tom Wigley, a senior scientist at the U.S. National Center for Atmospheric Research, calculated that if every nation met its obligations under the Kyoto treaty, the amount of warming prevented by 2050 would be only 0.07 degrees C.[31] In other words, the costly cut in fuel consumption to attain the Kyoto goals would in fact make a trivial contribution to preventing global warming.

Moreover, a moderate amount of global warming would probably be good. The evidence now suggests that most warming will happen in cold areas and at night, thus lengthening the growing season. My Hoover colleague, economist Thomas G. Moore, has also found that global warming would produce net benefits for the world. Moore used an accepted population model to predict growth of population and found that warmer periods, such as 5000 and 1000 B.C., had higher than predicted population growth and that cooler periods, such as the mini Ice Age from 1300 to 1800 A.D., had lower than predicted population growths. This makes sense. His conclusion, based on a large number of studies, is that warmer is healthier.[32]

In light of these facts, the best thing to do now is not to regulate people's activities to slow down global warming, but instead to learn more about the issue. Contrary to Gore's quoted statement, the odds are high that there will be more surprises. That's the nature of truth seeking. And the best way to get to the truth is not to censor and attack those who are honestly studying the issue, whatever they find. The danger will be that so much of the research money to study global warming will come from government that research and reporting of the research will be corrupted. That's what happened with the IPCC report and is probably happening in government-funded research institutes around the country. I say this, not having any particulars about corruption in such institutes but, rather, having a solid understanding of government and incentives.

Couldn't it make sense to limit carbon use anyway, just in case global warming will be catastrophic? It could, but it's unlikely to. What if carbon use is offsetting some other factor in nature that would otherwise lead to another mini ice age? We simply don't know enough to exclude that possibility. The so-called "precautionary" argument that we should limit carbon use "just in case" reminds me of Pascal's wager. Blaise Pascal, the famous French mathematician, argued that although he didn't have enough evidence for believing in God, believing in God was a safe bet anyway because if he believed in God and there wasn't a God, he was no worse off, whereas if he believed in God and there is a God, he would go to Heaven and be better off. The problem with Pascal's wager is that since he had no information about God, he had no way of knowing whether God was malevolent or benevolent. What if God were malevolent and punished those who believe in him. Then there is a downside to believing in him. Similarly, limiting carbon use could make the planet too cold. Moreover, even worse than in Pascal's wager, steps taken to limit carbon use would be very costly, with fuel prices being substantially higher than they are now. So it's not a "free" belief, as in the case of Pascal's wager.

TWO KINDS OF ENVIRONMENTALISM

Early in her government-school education, my daughter Karen was told how great nature is. On its own, that view is harmless, but it can also leave out humans. So the next time we drove to our cottage in Canada and she commented on all the nature she was seeing, I pointed to an Ontario Hydro employee climbing a pole and said to 6-year-old Karen, "He's part of nature too." My point was that we can't forget that we are part of nature and that we are the most important part of nature.

We want a clean and safe environment. We want nice, furry animals to thrive. We want clean air and water. We want large beautiful parks with pristine mountain views. But the key word in all of those sentences is "we." We want those things for *us*. Unfortunately, much of environmentalism mutates into a second form, the desire to save the environment independent of what it will do for people. The ultimate mutation is a desire to save the environment even if doing so kills people. Many environmentalists value nature per se, even if it harms humans. And these environmentalists aren't always just hermits who mail bombs once in a while. They often get into important government jobs and legally inflict their harm. The U.S. government, for example, made an official policy of populating government land with wolves. But wolves attack another parts of nature, namely cattle, sheep, and dogs, and so are threatening ranchers.

So we really have two forms of environmentalism: environmentalism for people's sake and environmentalism for the environment's sake. The first is pro-human and the second is fundamentally anti-human. It's no coincidence that the Unabomber felt justified in killing innocent people in pursuit of his goals. He put into action thoughts that have been in the mainstream of environmentalism for some time now. Environmentalist David M. Graber, for example, a research biologist with the National Park Service, wrote the following in the *Los Angeles Times*:

> ...We are not interested in the utility of a particular species or free-flowing river, or ecosystem, to mankind. They have intrinsic value, more value—to me—than another human body, or a billion of them.

> Human happiness, and certainly human fecundity, are not as important as a wild and healthy planet. I know social scientists who remind me that people are part of nature, but it isn't true. Somewhere along the line—at about a billion years ago, maybe half that—we quit the contract and became a cancer. We have become a plague upon ourselves and upon the Earth.

> It is cosmically unlikely that the developed world will choose to end its orgy of fossil-energy consumption, and the Third World its suicidal consumption of landscape. Until such time as Homo sapiens should decide to rejoin nature, some of us can only hope for the right virus to come along.[33]

Think about that. For most of us, the appeal of environmentalism has been that environmentalists worried, rightly, about pollution that made our air and water unsafe for humans. But why care about pollution killing humans or making them less healthy if, like Graber, you want all humans to die? Or consider the recent controversy over the amount of arsenic in the water supply. Much of the arsenic in the water supply occurs naturally. But it is we humans who want it removed. If Graber wants a virus to kill us all, then how could he object to naturally occurring arsenic?

The fact is that we are part of nature and that we have mightily improved on what nature gave us. The reason Graber can write his poisonous thoughts, that most of us can live past the age of 70, and that we can visit Yellowstone Park even if we live 2,000 miles away is that millions of humans through history have been unwilling to settle for nature's stingy benefits. They thought they could do better, and they were right.

Endnotes

1. For a complete and utterly fascinating telling of this story, see the article, "Love Canal: The Truth Seeps Out," *Reason,* February 1981, by Eric Zuesse, the investigative reporter who uncovered it.

2. Paul Hofheinz, "The New Soviet Threat: Pollution," *Fortune,* July 27, 1992, pp. 110–114.

3 Marshall Goldman, *The Spoils of Progress: Environmental Pollution in the Soviet Union,* Cambridge, MIT Press, 1972, p. 179.

4. Marshall Goldman, *The Spoils of Progress: Environmental Pollution in the Soviet Union,* Cambridge, MIT Press, 1972, pp. 200–201.

5. Hofheinz, "New Soviet Threat," p. 112.

6. Goldman, *Spoils of Progress,* p. 231.

7. Goldman, *Spoils of Progress,* p. 66.

8. Marlise Simons, "A Green Party Mayor Takes On Industrial Filth of Old Cracow," *New York Times,* March 25, 1990, p. 18.

9. Thomas DiLorenzo, "Does Capitalism Cause Pollution?" Center for the Study of American Business, Washington University, St. Louis, Contemporary Issues Series 38, August 1990.

10. Marlise Simons, "Rising Iron Curtain Exposes Haunting Veil of Polluted Air," *New York Times,* April 8, 1990, p. 1.

11. Allan T. Demaree, "The New Germany's Glowing Future," *Fortune,* December 3, 1990, p. 148.

12. The data in this paragraph are from Randy T. Simmons and Urs P. Kreuter, "Herd Mentality: Banning Ivory Sales is No Way to Save the Elephant," *Policy Review,* Fall 1989, pp. 46–49, and from "Riding the 'Ban' Wagon: Unsafe for Any Species," *CEI Update,* June 1991, No. 6.

13. This story is told in Garrett Hardin, *Filters Against Folly,* New York: Viking Books, 1985, p. 89.

14. See Richard Stroup, "Environmentalism, Free Market," in David R. Henderson, ed., *The Fortune Encyclopedia of Economics,* New York: Warner Books, 1993, p. 443.

15. These facts are from Council on Environmental Quality, *Environmental Quality,* 15th Annual Report, 1984, Chapter 9, "Special Report: The Public Benefits of Private Conservation."

16. These facts are taken from Robert J. Smith, "Conservation Capitalism," *Libertarian Review,* October 1979, p. 21, and from John Baden and Richard L. Stroup, "Saving the Wilderness," *Reason,* July 1981, p. 33.

17. Quoted from, Richard Stroup, "Environmentalism, Free Market," p. 442.

18. Stacie Thomas, "Cuyahoga Revisited," *PERC Reports,* June 1999.

19. *Vian v. Sheffield* (June 14, 1948), 85 Ohio App. 191, 88 N.E. 2d 410, cited in Stacie Thomas, "Cuyahoga Revisited," *PERC Reports,* June 1999.

20. The Water Pollution Control Act of Ohio, Sec. 1261-1e of the Act, Violations of Act Defined.

21. I owe this insight to Fred L. Smith, Jr., "Markets and the Environment: A Critical Reappraisal," *Contemporary Economic Policy,* Vol. XIII, January 1995, pp. 62–73.

22. See Terry L. Anderson and P. J. Hill, "The Evolution of Property Rights: A Study of the American West," *Journal of Law and Economics,* Vol. XVIII, No. 1, April 1975, p. 172.

23. Smith, p. 72.

24. Robert H. Nelson, "Shoot, shovel and shut up," *Forbes,* December 4, 1995, p. 82.

25. Robert W. Crandall, "Is There Progress in Environmental Policy?" *Contemporary Economic Policy,* Vol. XIII, January 1995, p. 82.

26. Crandall, p. 83.

27. Frederick Seitz, "A Major Deception on 'Global Warming,'" *Wall Street Journal,* June 12, 1996.

28. Michaels cites Daniel Bodansky, "Prologue to the Climate Change Convention," in *Negotiating Climate Change: The Inside Story of the Rio Convention,* ed. Irving Mintzer and J. A. Leonard, Cambridge: Cambridge University Press, 1994, p. 53.

29. Rochelle Stanfield, "Less Burning, No Tears," *National Journal,* August 13, 1988, pp. 2095-2096.

30. Excerpt from EARTH IN THE BALANCE by Al Gore. Copyright © 1992 by Senator Al Gore. Reprinted by permission of Houghton Mifflin Company. All rights reserved.

31. Thomas Wigley, "The Kyoto Protocol: CO_2, CH_4, and Climate Implications," *Geophysical Research Letter* 25, 1998, pp. 2285–2288.

32. Thomas Gale Moore, *Climate of Fear,* Washington, D.C.: Cato Institute, 1998.

33. *Los Angeles Times Book Review,* Sunday, October 22, 1989, p. 9.

18

FREEDOM
IN OUR TIME

The philosophy that can't help you do things,
does nothing.

—ARISTOTLE

I'm writing this chapter on the assumption that you agree with some or most of the ideas I've presented so far and that you want to do something about it. The rest of this chapter shares what is being done and what you can do, whether you want to make a large commitment of time or a small one, and whether you want to give a lot of financial support or a little.

Friedrich Hayek once wrote that it was the socialists' courage to be utopian that captured the imagination of the intellectuals. These intellectuals then transmitted these socialist ideas to the culture generally, causing socialist policies to be implemented in Europe and, to a lesser extent, in the United States and Canada during the first 70 or so years of the twentieth century. When I met Hayek a few months after he had won his Nobel prize, it was at a week-long conference of young pro-free-market economists and economic students. Hayek was delighted that there were so many of us and that we would be in the academy for the next few decades, educating thousands of students about the benefits of freedom. Because young believers in freedom don't always get moral and financial support on their various campuses, an organization exists to help that happen. The Institute of Humane Studies, based at George Mason University in Fairfax, Virginia, helps educate and financially support many students who will be the future scholars of liberty. It also has branched out to help those believers in freedom who want to build careers in journalism and in film.

Getting our voices heard in academia is something that believers in freedom have always been pretty good at. We have not been as good at activism.[1] But we're getting better. One bright spot is the Institute for Justice *(www.ij.org)*, which sues government when it violates people's property rights or their right to work. The government is keeping it busy. In the last few years, IJ successfully protected the property of Vera Coking, an elderly widow from Atlantic City, whose property was about to be grabbed by a government agency and handed over to Donald Trump so he could build a parking lot. It also successfully defended the right of Dr. JoAnne Cornwell, a "locktician" from San Diego, to earn her living doing African hairbraiding. The state government had required African hairstylists to spend nine months and at least $5,000 at state-approved cosmetology schools before they could practice their trade, even though none of these classes taught how to braid hair. Now that IJ has sued and won, African hairstylists are free to practice in California.

This suggests two options if you want to sue the government or to support such lawsuits. One is to donate funds to the Institute for Justice and other pro-freedom groups, of which there are many. The other is to take a stand when the government violates your rights and find an organization that will help with your suit. One person who did so recently was Joell Palmer, a 21-year-old waiter at an Outback Steak House in Indianapolis, who also ran as a Libertarian Party candidate for the Indiana House of Representatives. Palmer, who was stopped at an Indiana roadblock because his 1979 black Pontiac Trans Am "fit the profile," refused to let the police inspect his car for drugs, but they inspected it anyway. After they failed to find drugs, Palmer didn't just let it go. He contacted an attorney from the Indiana Civil Liberties Union and filed a class action suit against the city of Indianapolis. The suit made it all the way to the Supreme Court, where he won, on a 6–3 decision. The court found that random roadblocks for drugs are unconstitutional. Palmer's words can be an inspiration for us all:

> I am standing up to something that I know is wrong. I am fighting for everyone's rights—showing there actually are people who don't let big government bully the people around.[2]

Perhaps getting involved in suits is too active for you. Then choose the level of activism that works. One way is to have local demonstrations about issues. Another way is to write letters to the editor of your local newspaper. It's not as if you'll run out of material. Governments at various levels in the United States infringe on our freedom in so many ways that we could protest a new issue every day for a lifetime. Taxes as a percent of income are at close to a peacetime high. A local government in Fairfax, Virginia, recently sent John Thoburn to jail for refusing to plant trees on his property. The federal government prevents people from using medical marijuana even though the U.S. Constitution gives the federal government no authority to do so and even though voters in many states have actually voted by large margins to permit medical marijuana. The government's successful prosecution of one of its victims, Peter McWilliams, caused McWilliams to quit using marijuana that he badly needed so that he would not throw up when taking his anti-cancer medicines. The result was that McWilliams recently drowned in his own vomit. Governments at all levels grab people's assets—money, cars, and homes—when it suspects them, on scant or no evidence, of being drug dealers or of committing other crimes, and then often refuses to give their assets back even after declining to press charges. The government in California actually advertises socialized medicine for children—they call it "Healthy Children"—to try to get people to sign up for what could be the first step to a lifetime of dependency. I could go on and on, but it would be more effective if you did so.

Of course, one way to help freedom that requires almost none of your time is to give money to pro-freedom causes. Many organizations can use it well to spread the word on freedom. Think tanks like the Cato Institute and the Competitive Enterprise Institute, both in Washington, D.C., are effective advocates. Forfeiture Endangers American Rights (FEAR), also in Washington, is working to end asset forfeiture, a policy under which the government can take people's assets simply on suspicion that they have broken the drug laws. There are many more good pro-freedom organizations. Also, you might want to rethink, as I have done, how you want to help some of your favorite charitable causes. My mother died of cancer and my wife had cancer. An obvious way to help find a cure for cancer is to send money to the American Cancer Society, and I do that. A less obvious, but possibly more effective, way to hasten a cure for cancer and for other diseases is to give money to organizations that are trying to stop the FDA from denying us life-saving drugs. When my father asked, years ago, if he could give $300 in my name and my late mother's name to a nursing home, I persuaded him instead to send the check to an organization that was fighting off the FDA's attempt to regulate vitamins. I sometimes send money to help feed starving children in Africa. Now, having learned the lesson from Chapter 11, I want to send money to free-market think tanks in Africa that are trying to end price controls on agricultural crops so that more food will be grown, and that are trying to get property rights enforced so that people can get out of poverty.

Moreover, we believers in freedom need more than protests. We need songs, posters, slogans, and poems. What about the Ballad of Elian Gonzalez done to the tune of "America the Beautiful" or "Blowin' in the Wind"? One effective poster that the ACLU has created to oppose the U.S. government's policy of seizing people's property simply on suspicion that they are drug dealers shows the traditional Uncle Sam dressed in red, white, and blue pointing his finger and saying, "I want your money, jewelry, car, boat and house."

And don't forget civil disobedience. One way to end oppressive laws is to break them and to support others who do so. Some of the most effective pro-freedom actions were started by people who were fed up with oppressive laws, from American colonists upset about stamp taxes to Rosa Parks, who was upset about the law that forced her to give up her seat to a white person. If you break laws, be careful, because the consequences can be serious. Therefore, I don't recommend that you break any specific law. I do recommend that you not dismiss the idea.

Finally, there's one bit of activism that all of us can do, that would not take any extra time or any money, and that might be the most effective pro-freedom action we can take. We can speak up in conversations with friends, family, coworkers, and other people with whom we have conversations, even when we fear that it will make us unpopular. Milton Friedman, looking back at his life, realized that although many people think it takes a lot of courage to take an unpopular position, he found that doing so seldom led to bad consequences.[3] When someone suggests that drug companies are evil for trying to make money, ask her if she would rather the drug companies make no money and that she or her children die unnecessarily. When someone says high-income people should be taxed heavily because they have more, ask him for his wallet. When a heterosexual says that gay people should not be allowed to marry, ask him if gay people's objections should be enough to stop *him* from getting married. Of course, challenging people is not always the best way to change minds. Another way is to ask them questions. My friend and colleague, Frank Barrett, found in an experiment in his class that the people who were best able to change other people's minds were not the ones who argued but the ones who asked questions about the other's viewpoint.

I can't say in a short space all the ways that we can work to roll back the huge and destructive power that governments have over our lives. In fact, I don't know all the ways. No one does. No one can, because each person has specific knowledge of his or her own context, knowledge that can be used to limit and roll back government power. So there are probably as many ways to work to increase freedom as there are people. I recommend that you choose whatever methods of activism fit your circumstances. Although I don't know your particular strengths, I know that you have them.

Whatever methods we choose, we believers in freedom need to support each other, to support those who are victims of government oppression, and to support everyone, even those who don't consistently support freedom, for their pro-freedom acts. So, for example, if you see a letter to the editor of the local newspaper that is effectively pro-freedom, contact the letter writer and congratulate her for putting time and attention on an important issue; you might even make a new friend. If the federal government is preventing someone in your community from using medical marijuana to limit the nausea from chemotherapy, give that person moral support in his battle against both cancer and the government. If you run into a congressman who has voted pro-freedom on some issue, congratulate him. A few years ago, I spoke at an event at which one of the other speakers was Charles Stenholm, a Democratic congressman from Texas. I remembered that almost 20 years earlier, his crossover vote had been important in getting Ronald Reagan's package of budget cuts and tax cuts approved by Congress. So I thanked him. He looked very surprised, probably because congressmen aren't used to being thanked for votes from 20 years ago, but also probably because they aren't used to being thanked at all. I mentioned earlier that freedom lets people build communities. I have also learned from experience that activism for freedom builds community. Many of the people whom you touch or who touch you in the fight for freedom will be lifelong friends.

But make no mistake about it. At times, it will be a fight. What activist Frederick Douglass said in the middle of the nineteenth century about the United States' most important libertarian cause, the fight to end slavery, applies just as much today. He said,

If there is no struggle there is no progress. Those who profess to favor freedom, and yet depreciate agitation, are men who want crops without plowing up the ground, they want rain without thunder and lightning. They want the ocean without the awful roar of its many waters.

This struggle may be a moral one, or it may be a physical one, and it may be both moral and physical, but it must be a struggle. Power concedes nothing without a demand. It never did and it never will. Find out just what any people will quietly submit to and you have found out the exact measure of injustice and wrong which will be imposed upon them, and these will continue till they are resisted with either words or blows, or with both. The limits of tyrants are prescribed by the endurance of those whom they oppress.[4]

So let's stop settling. Let's speak out when our freedom is violated and, even better, let's do the same when the freedom of others is violated. It's not too late to seek a freer world.

ENDNOTES

1. For my story of my own first experience at activism, which was tremendously effective, see *www.davidrhenderson.com,* and go to the section, "Fighting the draft."

2. "Indiana LP member gets Supreme Court Hearing," *LP News Online,* September 2000, *www.lp.org/lpnews/0009/palmer.html.*

3. Milton and Rose D. Friedman, *Two Lucky People,* Chicago: University of Chicago Press, 1999, p. 362.

4. Frederick Douglass, "The Significance of Emancipation in the West Indies," Speech, Canandaigua, New York, August 3, 1857, in *The Frederick Douglass Papers.* Series One: Speeches, Debates, and Interviews. Volume 3: 1855-63. Edited by John W. Blassingame. New Haven. Yale University Press, p. 204.

INDEX

Peikoff, Leonard, 6
Penn, William, 61
Perkins, Frances, 80
Permits, marketable
    to reduce pollution, 332-34
Peterson, Peter, 249, 250
Pierce, Robert J., 68
Plourde, Charles, 27-29
Polanyi, Michael, 34
Pollution
    incentives to reduce, 332-33
    spending to reduce, 333
Ponzi, Charles, 234
Ponzi scheme, 234-35, 238
Popkin, Joel, 191-92
Popper, Karl, 34
Postrel, Virginia, 144, 271
Pregnancy Discrimination Act (1978), 286
Price controls
    of Carter administration, 16
    of Nixon administration, 16, 189-94
    in Soviet Union, 36-37
    during World War II, 258
Prime, Michael, 6
Profit motive
    of private-sector businesses, 175
Property rights
    economic effects of, 64
    government disrespect for, 66-68
    incentives generated by, 70-71
    people's understanding about, 62
    power of, 69-70
    protect people, 62-63, 66
    role in resolution of other issues, 71-72
    tragedy of the commons, 68-69, 167-68, 203
    when not well defined, 64-66
Puffert, Douglas, 239

Racism. See Discrimination, racial
Rand, Ayn, 3, 6
Ravitch, Diane, 308
Read, Leonard, 14, 222

Reagan, Ronald, 35-36, 80, 204, 205
Reagan administration, 205
Regulation
    to control global warming, 335
    employer-provided health insurance
        as result of, 258
    by Food and Drug Administration,
        206-7, 276-80
    of government-run education voucher
        system, 315
    of insurance pricing at state level,
        287
    of subsidized private schools, 315
    against working at home, 79-82
    See also Deregulation
Reich, Robert, 85-87
Resentment
    factors influencing diminished, 151-52
    against people with wealth, 149-51
Riegle, Donald, 67
Robbins, Lionel, 34
Roberts, Russell, 185
Roosevelt, Franklin D. (FDR), 48, 80,
    218, 220-21, 236-37, 246
Rose, Alex, 83
Rosenfeld, Robert, 81-82
Rothbard, Murray, 14, 16, 72

Sachs, Jeffrey, 249
Samuelson, Paul A., 20-21, 237-38
Samwick, Andrew, 239, 245
Schabowsli, Gunter, 38
Schenck v. United States, 72
Schieber, Sylvester, 249
Schindler, Oskar, 120-21, 171-73
School choice, self- and tax-financed,
    314
Schools, private
    differences from public schools, 302-3
    government-subsidized, 315
    sending children to, 317
Schools, public
    after-school sports programs of, 304-5
    differences from private schools, 302-3
    as enforced monopoly, 297-98